Regulating the Sea

This book is the first ever written on English marine conservation regulation from a socio-legal perspective. The monograph presents an in-depth analysis of key aspects of Marine Protected Areas regulation in England, offering the reader access to an under-investigated field. Such regulatory mapping is complemented by an interdisciplinary treatment of the subject exploring the relationship between people and marine parks through central themes in environmental social sciences and regulatory theory, namely space, rationalisation, democracy and adaptation. Thus, the book is of interest to environmental lawyers and regulatory scholars but also to human geographers, environmental sociologists and political scientists. As the book provides critical reflections on current legal and regulatory structures, it contains valuable insights for policymakers and regulators. The book has a strong methodological basis drawing on in-depth desk-based research, complemented by primary qualitative research, conducted over a number of years.

Margherita Pieraccini is Professor of Law at the University of Bristol. She has been researching in the field of environmental law and socio-legal studies for over ten years, focussing on protected areas and commons in the UK and Italy. Her work crosses the boundaries between law and environmental social sciences.

Law in Context

Since 1970, the Law in Context series has been at the forefront of a movement to broaden the study of law. The series is a vehicle for the publication of innovative monographs and texts that treat law and legal phenomena critically in their cultural, social, political, technological, environmental and economic contexts. A contextual approach involves treating legal subjects broadly, using materials from other humanities and social sciences, and from any other discipline that helps to explain the operation in practice of the particular legal field or legal phenomena under investigation. It is intended that this orientation is at once more stimulating and more revealing than the bare exposition of legal rules. The series includes original research monographs, coursebooks and textbooks that foreground contextual approaches and methods. The series includes and welcomes books on the study of law in all its contexts, including domestic legal systems, European and international law, transnational and global legal processes, and comparative law.

Books in the Series

Acosta: *The National versus the Foreigner in South America: 200 Years of Migration and Citizenship Law*
Ali: *Modern Challenges to Islamic Law*
Alyagon Darr: *Plausible Crime Stories: The Legal History of Sexual Offences in Mandate Palestine*
Anderson, Schum & Twining: *Analysis of Evidence, 2nd Edition*
Ashworth: *Sentencing and Criminal Justice, 6th Edition*
Barton & Douglas: *Law and Parenthood*
Baxi, McCrudden & Paliwala: *Law's Ethical, Global and Theoretical Contexts: Essays in Honour of William Twining*
Beecher-Monas: *Evaluating Scientific Evidence: An Interdisciplinary Framework for Intellectual Due Process*

Bell: *French Legal Cultures*
Bercusson: *European Labour Law, 2nd Edition*
Birkinshaw: *European Public Law*
Birkinshaw: *Freedom of Information: The Law, the Practice and the Ideal, 4th Edition*
Blick: *Electrified Democracy: The Internet and the United Kingdom Parliament in History*
Broderick & Ferri: *International and European Disability Law and Policy: Text, Cases and Materials*
Brownsword & Goodwin: *Law and the Technologies of the Twenty-First Century: Text and Materials*
Cane & Goudkamp: *Atiyah's Accidents, Compensation and the Law, 9th Edition*
Clarke: *Principles of Property Law*
Clarke & Kohler: *Property Law: Commentary and Materials*
Collins: *The Law of Contract, 4th Edition*
Collins, Ewing & McColgan: *Labour Law, 2nd Edition*
Cowan: *Housing Law and Policy*
Cranston: *Making Commercial Law Through Practice 1830–1970*
Cranston: *Legal Foundations of the Welfare State*
Darian-Smith: *Laws and Societies in Global Contexts: Contemporary Approaches*
Dauvergne: *Making People Illegal: What Globalisation Means for Immigration and Law*
David: *Kinship, Law and Politics: An Anatomy of Belonging*
Davies: *Perspectives on Labour Law, 2nd Edition*
Dembour: *Who Believes in Human Rights?: Reflections on the European Convention*
de Sousa Santos: *Toward a New Legal Common Sense: Law, Globalization, and Emancipation*
Diduck: *Law's Families*
Dowdle: *Transnational Law: A Framework for Analysis*
Dupret: *Positive Law from the Muslim World: Jurisprudence, History, Practices*
Emon: *Jurisdictional Exceptionalisms: Islamic Law, International Law, and Parental Child Abduction*
Estella: *Legal Foundations of EU Economic Governance*
Fortin: *Children's Rights and the Developing Law, 3rd Edition*
Garnsey: *The Justice of Visual Art: Creative State-Building in Times of Political Transition*
Garton, Probert & Bean: *Moffat's Trusts Law: Text and Materials, 7th Edition*
Ghai & Woodman: *Practising Self-Government: A Comparative Study of Autonomous Regions*
Glover-Thomas: *Reconstructing Mental Health Law and Policy*
Gobert & Punch: *Rethinking Corporate Crime*
Goldman: *Globalisation and the Western Legal Tradition: Recurring Patterns of Law and Authority*
Haack: *Evidence Matters: Science, Proof, and Truth in the Law*
Harlow & Rawlings: *Law and Administration, 4th Edition*
Harris: *An Introduction to Law, 8th Edition*
Harris, Campbell & Halson: *Remedies in Contract and Tort, 2nd Edition*
Harvey: *Seeking Asylum in the UK: Problems and Prospects*
Herring: *Law and the Relational Self*
Hervey & McHale: *European Union Health Law: Themes and Implications*
Hervey & McHale: *Health Law and the European Union*

Holder & Lee: *Environmental Protection, Law and Policy: Text and Materials, 2nd Edition*
Jackson & Summers: *The Internationalisation of Criminal Evidence: Beyond the Common Law and Civil Law Traditions*
Kostakopoulou: *The Future Governance of Citizenship*
Kreiczer-Levy: *Destabilized Property: Property Law in the Sharing Economy*
Kubal: *Immigration and Refugee Law in Russia: Socio-Legal Perspectives*
Lewis: *Choice and the Legal Order: Rising above Politics*
Likosky: *Law, Infrastructure and Human Rights*
Likosky: *Transnational Legal Processes: Globalisation and Power Disparities*
Lixinski: *Legalized Identities: Cultural Heritage Law and the Shaping of Transitional Justice*
Loughnan: *Self, Others and the State: Relations of Criminal Responsibility*
Lunney: *A History of Australian Tort Law 1901–1945: England's Obedient Servant?*
Maughan & Webb: *Lawyering Skills and the Legal Process, 2nd Edition*
McGaughey: *Principles of Enterprise Law*
McGlynn: *Families and the European Union: Law, Politics and Pluralism*
Mertens: *A Philosophical Introduction to Human Rights*
Moffat: *Trusts Law: Text and Materials*
Monti: *EC Competition Law*
Morgan: *Contract Law Minimalism: A Formalist Restatement of Commercial Contract Law*
Morgan & Yeung: *An Introduction to Law and Regulation: Text and Materials*
Nash: *British Islam and English Law: A Classical Pluralist Perspective*
Ng, *Political Censorship in British Hong Kong: Freedom of Expression and the Law (1842–1997)*
Nicola & Davies: *EU Law Stories: Contextual and Critical Histories of European Jurisprudence*
Norrie: *Crime, Reason and History: A Critical Introduction to Criminal Law, 3rd Edition*
O'Dair: *Legal Ethics: Text and Materials*
Oliver: *Common Values and the Public–Private Divide*
Oliver & Drewry: *The Law and Parliament*
Palmer & Roberts: *Dispute Processes: ADR and the Primary Forms of Decision-Making, 1st Edition*
Palmer & Roberts: *Dispute Processes: ADR and the Primary Forms of Decision-Making, 3rd Edition*
Picciotto: *International Business Taxation*
Pieraccini: *Regulating the Sea: A Socio-Legal Analysis of English Marine Protected Areas*
Probert: *The Changing Legal Regulation of Cohabitation, 1600–2010: From Fornicators to Family, 1600–2010*
Radi: *Rules and Practices of International Investment Law and Arbitration*
Reed: *Internet Law: Text and Materials*
Richardson: *Law, Process and Custody*
Roberts & Palmer: *Dispute Processes: ADR and the Primary Forms of Decision-Making, 2nd Edition*
Rowbottom: *Democracy Distorted: Wealth, Influence and Democratic Politics*
Sauter: *Public Services in EU Law*
Scott & Black: *Cranston's Consumers and the Law*

Seneviratne: *Ombudsmen: Public Services and Administrative Justice*
Seppänen: *Ideological Conflict and the Rule of Law in Contemporary China: Useful Paradoxes*
Siems: *Comparative Law, 3rd Edition*
Stapleton: *Product Liability*
Stewart: *Gender, Law and Justice in a Global Market*
Tamanaha: *Law as a Means to an End: Threat to the Rule of Law*
Tuori: *Properties of Law: Modern Law and After*
Turpin & Tomkins: *British Government and the Constitution: Text and Materials, 7th Edition*
Twining: *General Jurisprudence: Understanding Law from a Global Perspective*
Twining: *Globalisation and Legal Theory*
Twining: *Human Rights, Southern Voices: Francis Deng, Abdullahi An-Na'im, Yash Ghai and Upendra Baxi*
Twining: *Jurist in Context: A Memoir*
Twining: *Karl Llewellyn and the Realist Movement, 2nd Edition*
Twining: *Rethinking Evidence: Exploratory Essays, 2nd Edition*
Twining & Miers: *How to Do Things with Rules, 5th Edition*
Wan: *Film and Constitutional Controversy: Visualizing Hong Kong Identity in the Age of 'One Country, Two Systems'*
Ward: *A Critical Introduction to European Law, 3rd Edition*
Ward: *Law, Text, Terror*
Ward: *Shakespeare and Legal Imagination*
Wells & Quick: *Lacey, Wells and Quick: Reconstructing Criminal Law: Text and Materials, 4th Edition*
Young: *Turpin and Tomkins' British Government and the Constitution: Text and Materials , 8th Edition*
Zander: *Cases and Materials on the English Legal System, 10th Edition*
Zander: *The Law-Making Process, 6th Edition*

International Journal of Law in Context: A Global Forum for Interdisciplinary Legal Studies

The *International Journal of Law in Context* is the companion journal to the Law in Context book series and provides a forum for interdisciplinary legal studies and offers intellectual space for ground-breaking critical research. It publishes contextual work about law and its relationship with other disciplines including but not limited to science, literature, humanities, philosophy, sociology, psychology, ethics, history and geography. More information about the journal and how to submit an article can be found at http://journals.cambridge.org/ijc

Regulating the Sea

A Socio-Legal Analysis of English Marine Protected Areas

MARGHERITA PIERACCINI
University of Bristol

CAMBRIDGE
UNIVERSITY PRESS

CAMBRIDGE
UNIVERSITY PRESS

Shaftesbury Road, Cambridge CB2 8EA, United Kingdom

One Liberty Plaza, 20th Floor, New York, NY 10006, USA

477 Williamstown Road, Port Melbourne, VIC 3207, Australia

314–321, 3rd Floor, Plot 3, Splendor Forum, Jasola District Centre, New Delhi – 110025, India

103 Penang Road, #05–06/07, Visioncrest Commercial, Singapore 238467

Cambridge University Press is part of Cambridge University Press & Assessment,
a department of the University of Cambridge.

We share the University's mission to contribute to society through the pursuit of
education, learning and research at the highest international levels of excellence.

www.cambridge.org
Information on this title: www.cambridge.org/9781108823883

DOI: 10.1017/9781108914833

First published 2022
First paperback edition 2026

A catalogue record for this publication is available from the British Library

Library of Congress Cataloging-in-Publication data
Names: Pieraccini, Margherita, author.
Title: Regulating the sea : a socio-legal analysis of English marine
protected areas / Margherita Pieraccini, University of Bristol.
Description: Cambridge, United Kingdom ; New York, NY : Cambridge
University Press, 2022. | Series: Law in context | Includes
bibliographical references and index.
Identifiers: LCCN 2022026116 | ISBN 9781108843119 (hardback) |
ISBN 9781108914833 (ebook)
Subjects: LCSH: Marine resources conservation – Law and
legislation – England. | Fishery law and legislation – England. | Law of
the sea – Great Britain. | BISAC: LAW / Environmental
Classification: LCC KD1035 .P54 2022 | DDC
346.4204/695616–dc23/eng/20220831
LC record available at https://lccn.loc.gov/2022026116

ISBN 978-1-108-84311-9 Hardback
ISBN 978-1-108-82388-3 Paperback

Contents

Preface and Acknowledgements

The seeds of this book were planted a long time ago, when I embarked on an Economic and Social Research Council (ESRC)-funded project (ES/K001043/1) from 2012 to 2015 to study the development of the UK marine protected areas (MPAs) network following the entry into force of the Marine and Coastal Access Act 2009. The research consisted in doctrinal analysis and in-depth primary qualitative research in selected case study areas across the UK. Some of the voices of the research participants, which were interviewed during that project, are reported in this book, especially in Chapter 5. Others, although not explicitly present here, have still been immensely valuable in helping me understanding what the real issues are, giving me a grounded perspective on the topic.

It was during the ESRC-funded project that I developed an interest in regulatory impact assessments too when exploring what went well and what went wrong in the designation of the first tranche of Marine Conservation Zones (MCZs). Hence, some of the background research for Chapter 3 can be traced back to that project, although the designation of new tranches in 2016 and 2019 demanded new research in regulatory impact assessments to provide an up-to-date picture. Whilst conducting the study and asking research participants about the designation of the new MCZs, I noticed that local regulators (the Inshore Fisheries Conservation Authorities) were preoccupied also with something else, that is, the management of fisheries within European Marine Sites, adopting a risk-based approach. This topic was beyond the scope of the ESRC project, so I investigated it in the following years, and the findings are presented in Chapter 4.

At the same time, marine conservation was experiencing political and ecological changes. Politically, the Brexit referendum in 2016, leading (slowly) to the UK departure from the European Union in 2020, was a cause of uncertainty for marine conservation law and regulation. Ecologically, climate change having impacts on marine ecosystems could not be left out of an analysis of marine conservation. It became interesting to explore the extent to which regulation was adapting to these ecological and political changes, as discussed in Chapters 7 and 8. Finally, in line with a long-standing interest of mine in environmental democracy, I decided to investigate key institutions contributing to it, as visible in Chapter 6.

Next to this regulatory analysis on English MPAs and a legal map presented in Chapter 2, the book attempts also to deliver a critical assessment of the relationship between people and parks by drawing on the concepts of commons and commoning, which are introduced in Chapter 1 and then return throughout the book. This conceptual contribution and the theoretical bridges the book forges between legal and regulatory studies, on the one hand, and environmental social sciences, on the other, is what I hope will continue to be valuable to scholars now and in the future as, realistically, some of the laws discussed are likely to change rapidly. The law is stated as at 31 December 2021.

I would like to express my sincere gratitude to various people who have contributed in different ways to this study. Thanks go to all research participants who agreed to take part in semi-structured interviews with me both during the ESRC-funded project and more recently in May 2021, and thanks to the ESRC for funding the initial project and Dr Emma Cardwell for her research assistance for part of the ESRC project.

Many thanks to Professor Tony Prosser, who has provided feedback on all the chapters of this book, to Professors Tonia Novitz and Anna Grear for having provided feedback on Chapter 1 and Professors Maria Lee, Phil Syrips and Giuseppe Martinico for their feedback and thoughts on Chapter 8. Thanks also to Mr Jack Brett, who provided research assistance for Chapters 3 and 4. Many thanks also to Professor Bronwen Morgan with whom I discussed the book proposal and to the Cambridge University Press team for their support during the writing of the book. Finally, I would like to thank Stefano, who has been an important person to share ideas with, especially regarding the ecological aspects of the book, who has helped with presentational aspects of the book such as Index formatting and who has been a supportive, caring and encouraging companion. This book is dedicated to Stefano and to the little Elio, who I hope will appreciate the sea as much as his parents do when he grows up.

Table of Cases

Domestic

Southern Water Authority v Nature Conservancy Council [1992] 1 WLR 775
Hart DC v Secretary of State for Communities & Local Government & Ors [2008] EWHC 1204 (Admin)
Champion v North Norfolk District Council [2015] UKSC 52
Gladman Developments Limited v Secretary of State for Housing, Communities and Local Government and Medway Council [2019] EWHC 2001 (Admin)
R (Client Earth and MCS) v Secretary of State for Environment Food and Rural Affairs [2019] EWHC 2682 (Admin)
Lipton v BA City Flyer [2021] EWCA Civ 454
Pearce v Secretary of State for Business Energy and Industrial Strategy [2021] EWHC 326 (Admin)
TuneIn Inc v Warner Music UK Limited and Sony Music Entertainment UK Limited [2021] EWCA Civ 441

EU

Case C-355/90 *Commission v Spain* [1993] ECR I-4221
Case C-44/95 *R v Secretary of State for the Environment, ex parte Royal Society for the Protection of Birds* [1996] ECR I-03805
Case C-371/98 *R v Secretary of State for the Environment, Transport and the Regions, ex parte First Corporate Shipping Ltd* [2000] ECR I-09235
Case C-127/02 *Landelijke Vereniging tot Behoud van de Waddenzee, Nederlandse Vereniging tot Bescherming van Vogels v Staatssecretaris Van Landbouw, Natuurbeheer en Visserij (Waddenzee)* [2004] ECR I-07405
Case C-239/04 *Commission v Portugal* [2006] ECR I-10183
Case C-6/04 *Commission v UK* [2005] ECR I-9017
Case C-2/10 *Azienda Agro-Zootecnica Franchini sarl and Eolica di Altamura Srl v Regione Puglia* [2011] ECR I-6561
Case C-258/11 *Peter Sweetman and Others v An Bord Pleanála* ECLI:EU:C:2013:220

International

Table of Legislation

Domestic

Protection of Wrecks Act 1973
Wildlife and Countryside Act 1981
Sea Fisheries Regulation Act 1988
Sea Fisheries (Wildlife Conservation) Act 1992
The Conservation (Natural Habitats, &c.) Regulations 1994 (SI 1994/2716)
Environment Act 1995
Sea Fisheries Regulation Act 1996
Countryside and Rights of Way Act 2000
Regulation (EC) No. 261/2004 of the European Parliament and of the Council of 11 February 2004 establishing common rules on compensation and assistance to passengers in the event of denied boarding and of cancellation or long delay of flights, and repealing Regulation (EEC) No. 295/91 (SI 2004/261)
Legislative and Regulatory Reform Act 2006
Natural Environment and Rural Communities Act 2006
The Offshore Marine Conservation (Natural Habitats, &c.) Regulations 2007 (SI 2007/1842)
Marine and Coastal Access Act 2009
The Conservation of Habitats and Species Regulations 2010 (SI 2010/490)
Marine Strategy Regulations 2010 (SI 2010/1627)
Sea Fishing (Penalty Notices) (England) Order 2011 (SI 2011/758)
The Conservation of Habitats and Species Regulations 2017 (SI 2017/1012) (Habitats Regulations)
The Conservation of Offshore Marine Habitats and Species Regulations 2017 (SI 2017/1013) (Offshore Habitats Regulations)
Marine Environment (Amendment) (EU Exit) Regulations 2018 (SI 2018/1399)
The Air Passenger Rights and Air Travel Organisers' Licencing (Amendment) (EU Exit) Regulations 2019 (SI 2019/278)
The Conservation of Habitats and Species (Amendment) (EU Exit) Regulations 2019 (SI 2019/579)

Freedom of Establishment and Free Movement of Services (EU Exit) Regulations 2019 (SI 2019/1401)
European Union (Withdrawal) Act 2018 (Relevant Court) (Retained EU Case Law) Regulations 2020 (SI 2020/1525)
Fisheries Act 2020
European Union (Withdrawal Agreement) Act 2021
Environment Act 2021

EU

Council Directive 92/43/EEC of 21 May 1992 on the conservation of natural habitats and of wild fauna and flora, OJ 1992 No. L 206/7 (the Habitats Directive)
Council Directive 2008/56/EC of the European Parliament and of the Council of 17 June 2008 establishing a framework for community action in the field of marine environmental policy, OJ L 2008 No. 164/19 (Marine Strategy Framework Directive)
Directive 2008/98/EC of the European Parliament and of the Council of 19 November 2008 on waste and repealing certain Directives, OJ 2008 No. L 312/3
Directive 2009/147/EC of the European Parliament and of the Council of 30 November 2009 on the conservation of wild birds, OJ 2009 No. L20/7 (Birds Directive)
Commission Implementing Regulation (EU) No. 404/2011 of 8 April 2011 laying down detailed rules for the implementation of Council Regulation (EC) No. 1224/2009 establishing a Community control system for ensuring compliance with the rules of the Common Fisheries Policy OJ 2011 No. L112/1
Consolidated version of the Treaty of the Functioning of the European Union, OJ 2012 C 326/47
Regulation (EU) No. 1380/2013 of the European Parliament and of the Council of 11 December 2013 on the Common Fisheries Policy amending Council Regulations (EC) No. 1954/2003 and (EC) No. 1224/2009 and repealing Council Regulations (EC) No. 2371/2002 and (EC) No. 639/2004 and Council Decision 2004/585/EC OJ 2013 No. L 354/22

International

International Convention for the High Sea Fisheries of the North Pacific Ocean (Tokyo) 9 May 1952, in force 12 June 1953, 205 UNTS 65 (North Pacific Fisheries Convention)
Antarctic Treaty (Washington) 1 December 1959, in force 23 June 1961, 402 UNTS 71 (Antarctic Treaty)

Ramsar Convention on Wetlands of International Importance Especially as Waterfowl Habitat (Ramsar) 2 February 1971, in force 21 December 1975, 996 UNTS 245 (Ramsar Convention)

Convention on the Conservation of Migratory Species of Wild Animals (Bonn) 23 June 1979, in force 1 November 1983, 19 ILM 15 (1980) (Bonn Convention)

United Nations Convention on the Law of the Sea (Montego Bay) 10 December 1982, in force 16 November 1994, 21 ILM 1261 (1982) (UNCLOS)

United Nations Framework Convention on Climate Change (New York) 9 May 1992, in force 24 March 1994, 1771 UNTS 107 (Climate Change Convention)

Convention on Biological Diversity (Rio de Janeiro) 5 June 1992, in force 29 December 1993, 31 ILM 822 (1992) (Biodiversity Convention)

Convention for the Protection of the Marine Environment of the North-East Atlantic (Paris) 22 September 1992, in force 25 March 1998, 32 ILM 1068 (1993) (OSPAR Convention)

Convention on Access to Information, Public Participation and Decision-Making and Access to Justice in Environmental Matters (Aarhus) 25 June 1998, in force 30 October 2001, 38 ILM 517 (1999) (Aarhus Convention)

Paris Agreement (Paris) 22 April 2016, in force 4 November 2016, C.N.92.2016. Treaties-XXVII.7.d (Paris Agreement)

Abbreviations

Aarhus Convention	Convention on Access to Information, Public Participation and Decision-Making and Access to Justice in Environmental Matters (full citation in the Table of Legislation)
BEIS	Department for Business, Energy and Industrial Strategy
Biodiversity Convention	The Convention on Biological Diversity (full citation in the Table of Legislation)
Birds Directive	Directive 2009/147/EC of the European Parliament and of the Council of 30 November 2009 on the conservation of wild birds (full citation in the Table of Legislation)
CJEU	Court of Justice of the European Union
Climate Change Convention	United Nations Framework Convention on Climate Change (full citation in the Table of Legislation)
COP	Conference of the Parties
CPR	Common-Pool Resource
DEFRA	Department of Environment Food and Rural Affairs
EU	European Union
EU Exit Habitats Regulations	The Conservation of Habitats and Species (Amendment) (EU Exit) Regulations 2019 (full citation in the Table of Legislation)
EUWA	European Union Withdrawal Act
EUWA (Relevant Court) Regulations	European Union (Withdrawal) Act 2018 (Relevant Court) (Retained EU Case Law) Regulations 2020 (full citation in the Table of Legislation)
Habitats Directive	Council Directive 92/43/EEC of 21 May 1992 on the conservation of natural habitats and of wild fauna and flora (full citation in the Table of Legislation)
Habitats Regulations	Conservation of Habitats and Species Regulations 2017 (full citation in the Table of Legislation)
HPMA	Highly Protected Marine Area
HRA	Habitat Regulation Assessment
IA	Impact Assessment
IFCA	Inshore Fisheries Conservation Authority

IPPC	Intergovernmental Panel on Climate Change
IROPI	Imperative Reasons of Overriding Public Interest
IUCN	International Union for the Conservation of Nature
JNCC	Joint Nature Conservation Committee
MCAA	Marine and Coastal Access Act
MCZ	Marine Conservation Zone
MMO	Marine Management Organisation
MPA	Marine Protected Area
MSFD	Marine Strategy Framework Directive (full citation in the Table of Legislation)
NERC Act	Natural Environment and Rural Communities Act
OECD	Organisation for Economic Co-operation and Development
OEP	Office for Environmental Protection
Offshore Habitats Regulations	Conservation of Offshore Marine Habitats and Species Regulations 2017 (full citation in the Table of Legislation)
OSPAR Convention	Convention for the Protection of the Marine Environment of the North-East Atlantic (full citation in the Table of Legislation)
Ramsar Convention	Ramsar Convention on Wetlands of International Importance Especially as Waterfowl Habitat (full citation in the Table of Legislation)
RPC	Regulatory Policy Committee
SAC	Special Areas of Conservation
SFC	Sea Fisheries Committee
SNCBs	Statutory Nature Conservation Bodies
SPA	Special Protection Area
SSSI	Site of Special Scientific Interest
TFEU	Treaty on the Functioning of the European Union
UK	United Kingdom
UNCLOS	United Nations Convention on the Law of the Sea (full citation in the Table of Legislation)

Introduction

Context

Following a long gestation, in 2009, a new Act entered the English legislative seascape – the Marine and Coastal Access Act (MCAA). The MCAA provides a comprehensive regulatory framework for all things marine,[1] including marine conservation in Part 5. The Act brings in many new institutional and regulatory tools for the conservation of the marine environment, constituting a notable addition to the pre-existing marine conservation framework, primarily reliant on EU conservation law. Until the MCAA, the predominant marine protected areas (MPAs) in English waters were Special Areas of Conservation (SACs) and Special Protection Areas (SPAs), known as European Marine Sites, designated respectively under the Habitats and Birds Directives.[2] In terms of domestically driven marine designations, the Wildlife and Countryside Act 1981 provided for the designation of Marine Nature Reserves.[3] However, Marine Nature Reserves could stretch only to three nautical miles, and their accompanying byelaws had a very limited scope. Only one Marine Nature Reserve was designated in England.[4]

This introduction begins with a brief discussion of the salient innovations that are found in Part V of the MCAA that trigger the wider questions at the core of this book, emphasising how English marine conservation law provides an interesting example to explore complex and foundational issues in environmental law and environmental social sciences.

The MCAA provides for the establishment of a new type of nationally important MPA, the Marine Conservation Zone (MCZ).[5] MCZs, together with

[1] For an overview of the MCAA, see T. Appleby and P. J. S. Jones, 'The Marine and Coastal Access Act – A Hornets' Nest?' (2012) 36 *Marine Policy* 73–77.

[2] Council Directive 92/43/EEC of 21 May 1992 on the conservation of natural habitats and of wild fauna and flora, OJ L 206/7 (the Habitats Directive) and Directive 2009/147/EC of the European Parliament and of the Council of 30 November 2009 on the conservation of wild birds, OJ L20/7 (Birds Directive).

[3] Sections 36 and 37 of the Wildlife and Countryside Act 1981.

[4] The first and only English Marine Nature Reserve was Lundy Island.

[5] Section 116 of the MCAA.

European Marine Sites, Ramsar sites[6] and the marine components of Sites of Special Scientific Interest (SSSIs),[7] form an MPA network under Section 123 of the MCAA. The network approach, championed by the MCAA, is in line with international calls to build ecologically coherent networks of MPAs.[8] On the one hand, this reflects the impact of international policy targets on domestic law, hence pointing to the interaction of multiple scales in marine governance. On the other hand, it reflects the scientific acknowledgement that networks, rather than isolated sites, are better instruments to conserve biodiversity in an environment subject to global environmental change and consequently ecological variation and adaptation. In a fluid marine environment and a time of global environmental change, it is difficult to imagine conservation law creating fixed boundaries and it is reductive to discuss conservation initiatives as detached from those larger issues, affecting regulatory solutions and requiring adaptation strategies. Adaptive governance for conservation law in the context of climate change will be discussed in Chapter 7 of this book.

Another section of Part V of the MCAA is also of primary interest because of its innovative nature. This is Section 117(7) that allows the appropriate authority to have regard to socio-economic consequences in designating MCZs. Although the section does not express a mandatory requirement, it is ground-breaking because it contemplates the possibility to consider more-than scientific reasons for establishing an MPA. Until the MCAA, English conservation law,[9] including the Habitats Regulations[10] transposing EU Habitats and Birds Directives into domestic law, had restricted the grounds of designation of protected areas to scientific reasons only. The scientific purity of designation has been reiterated by domestic and EU courts on multiple occasions.[11] Thus, Section 117(7) breaks with a tradition and a legal culture that has separated scientific reasons from social

[6] Ramsar Convention on Wetlands of International Importance Especially as Waterfowl Habitat (Ramsar) 2 February 1971, in force 21 December 1975, 996 UNTS 245 (Ramsar Convention).

[7] Sites of Special Scientific Interests are designated under Section 28 of the Wildlife and Countryside Act 1981.

[8] See for example Decision VII/5 of Conference of the Parties (COP) 7 of the Convention on Biological Diversity, UNEP/CBD/COP/7/5 calling for the establishment of a representative network of MPAs by 2012. This decision was acknowledged by the Johannesburg Plan of implementation of the World Summit on Sustainable Development. Also, the Convention on Biological Diversity's Aichi Target 11 requires ten per cent of marine areas to be conserved by 2020 through ecologically representative and well-connected systems of protected areas.

[9] Section 28(1) of the Wildlife and Countryside Act 1981, as amended, for Sites of Special Scientific Interest.

[10] The Conservation of Habitats and Species Regulations 2017 (SI 2017/1012) (Habitats Regulations) and The Conservation of Offshore Marine Habitats and Species Regulations 2017 (SI 2017/1013) (Offshore Habitats Regulations).

[11] For example, Case C-44/95 *R v Secretary of State for the Environment, ex parte Royal Society for the Protection of Birds* [1996] ECR I-03805; Case C-371/98 *R v Secretary of State for the Environment, Transport and the Regions, ex parte First Corporate Shipping Ltd* [2001] ECR I-9235 (*ex parte First Corporate Shipping*).

considerations in designating protected areas. By contemplating the possibility to take into account socio-economic consequences, Section 117(7) potentially provides a more inclusive way to think about conservation, acknowledging that conservation interventions do not happen in a social vacuum but may impact on societies and economies and that such interests may be considered from the start, rather than only at later stages when management measures are developed, as it is the case under EU conservation law. In England, this provision has been implemented by setting up a participatory process in which four regional projects, involving a range of interest groups, carried out initial site selection of MCZs and gathered local knowledge and views on both ecological and socio-economic issues affected by potential designation. Such process and its pitfalls will be the subject of discussion in Chapter 5 of this book.

The explicit inclusion of socio-economic interests in Section 117(7) of the MCAA and its implementation based on a participatory rhetoric reconnects with a long-standing interest of mine in the relationship, put simply, between people and parks. Exploring such relationship and how it is played out in law enables one to analyse an underlying, wider relationship – the one between society and nature – that has been a central preoccupation of environmental social scientists for a long time. Many studies have questioned the dichotomy between society and nature on philosophical, political and ethnographic grounds.[12]

In the field of conservation, anthropologists, geographers and political ecologists have carried out detailed studies of site-based conservation often condemning protected areas for undermining social interests and advancing a technocratic environmental regime, championed on the basis of rationality, objectivity and science. The literature on fortress conservation has been especially vociferous in uncovering forms of social and economic dispossessions in the name of an (invented) pristine nature, scientifically determined.[13] However, critiques have not stopped at fortress conservation as they have also deconstructed policy discourses and legal practices of community-based conservation projects. Community-based conservation initiatives have been accused of proposing essentialised understanding of community as a homogenous, organic social unit, tied to a specific locality. Far from being fixed coordinates in the geography of conservation, communities and localities are instead created and recreated by complex social–ecological processes, with environmental law

[12] For example P. Descola, *Beyond Nature and Culture* (University of Chicago Press, 2013, translated by J. Lloyd); T. Ingold and G. Palsson (eds.), *Biosocial Becomings: Integrating Social and Biological Anthropology* (Cambridge University Press, 2013); J. W. Moore (ed.), *Anthropocene or Capitalocene?: Nature, History and the Crisis of Capitalism* (Kairos, 2016); B. Latour, *Politics of Nature: How to Bring the Sciences into Democracy* (Harvard University Press, 2004, translated by C. Porter).

[13] See for example, D. Brockington, *Fortress Conservation: The Preservation of the Mkomazi Game Reserve, Tanzania* (African Issues, 2002); R. P. Neumann, *Imposing Wilderness: Struggles over Livelihood and Nature Preservation in Africa* (University of California Press, 1998); N. L. Peluso, 'Coercing Conservation: The Politics of State Resource Control' (1993) 3 *Global Environmental Change* 199–217.

occupying a powerful, but not exclusive, role in such processes. Scholars, especially working in the global South, have argued that community-based natural resource management is part of a transnational discourse shared by top-down development agencies whereby to govern is not to dominate by direct command but to act on the actions of others by producing particular types of environmental subjects and it falls short of expectations.[14] This is not dissimilar to what in the global North has been called the post-regulatory state[15] and linked to the discourse on de-centring of regulation.[16] In the field of community-based conservation and participatory conservation projects, the state does not disappear, but it becomes one element in multiple circuits of power, including statutory nature conservation agencies, non-governmental organisations, local communities and independent scientific experts. The roles of these different institutions in English conservation law will be discussed in Chapters 2, 6 and 8 of this book.

These observations are helpful to start sketching a complex picture of conservation and to show that not all conservation interventions require the preservation of a pure nature and the exclusive use of direct regulation, culminating, in extreme cases, in coercive evictions. Indeed, many conservation initiatives, like the English marine one under the MCAA, involve the setting of conditions for participation and the structuring of a field of possible actions to cultivate new patterns of responsibility, create new environmental subjectivities and steer the behaviour of actors along particular courses to achieved predetermined, often global, environmental goals.[17] There is also an important epistemological opening at play in such participatory initiatives: local and traditional knowledge is not excluded but integrated in the decision-making. However, the way in which this knowledge is conceptualised often requires, to use Scott terminology, 'a narrowing of vision'[18] and may contribute to freeze identities along predetermined stakes.[19] This is most visible in the discussion

[14] See for example, M. Leach, R. Mearnes and I. Scones, 'Environmental Entitlements: Dynamics and Institutions in Community-Based Natural Resource Management' (1999) 27 *World Development* 225–247; T. M. Li, 'Engaging Simplifications: Community-Based Resource Management, Market Processes and State Agendas in Upland Southeast Asia' (2002) 30 *World Development* 265–283; W. Dressler et al., 'From Hope to Crisis and Back Again? A Critical History of the Global CBNRM Narrative' (2010) 37 *Environmental Conservation* 5–15.

[15] C. Scott, 'Regulation in the Age of Governance: The Rise of the Post Regulatory State', in J. Jordana and D. Levi-Faure (eds.), *The Politics of Regulation: Institutions and Regulatory Reforms for the Age of Governance* (Edward Elgar, 2004), pp. 145–174.

[16] J. Black, 'Decentring Regulation: Understanding the Role of Regulation and Self-Regulation in a "Post-Regulatory" World' (2001) 54 *Current Legal Problems* 103–146.

[17] A. Agrawal, *Environmentality: Technologies of Government and the Making of Subjects* (Duke University Press, 2005).

[18] J. Scott, *Seeing Like a State: How Certain Schemes to Improve the Human Condition Have Failed* (Yale University Press, 1998).

[19] M. Pieraccini, 'Re-thinking Participation in Environmental Decision-Making: Epistemologies of Marine Conservation in South-East England' (2015) 27 *Journal of Environmental Law* 45–67.

of MCZs designation, undertaken in Chapter 5 of this book. Besides, public participation is wider than local resource users, and Chapter 6 shows this by concentrating on two institutions to consider the extent to which they help to democratise marine conservation law. The first institution is a statutory one, introduced under Part 6 of the MCAA, the Inshore Fisheries Conservation Authority (IFCA) and the latter is a very well-known actor in the environmental field, the environmental non-governmental organisation (NGO).

Thus, the relationship between people and parks has not simply to do with people in or people out, nature with or without society, but it requires a careful analysis of the ways in which the socio-economic interests are portrayed and included in conservation interventions, the scales that are at play and the production of knowledge(s) accompanying these processes. These issues will be discussed in relation to regulatory impact assessments (IAs) as well as the management of fisheries in MPAs, respectively, considered in Chapters 3 and 4 of this book. Does a division between society and nature persist when socio-economic interests are included in MPAs governance from the start, but they are articulated as separate interests from the environmental ones and their representation is confined to specific local actors/users? Does the law contribute to the establishment of institutional solutions that can help overcoming such dichotomous understanding or does it reinforce it? How are these issues played out at larger scales when conservation initiatives move beyond single site designation and attempt to capture large ecological networks? And finally, how static are these constructions and to what extent social, political and ecological processes destabilise them or contribute to their reproduction?

This book provides answers to these broad questions from the perspective of English marine conservation law and regulation, explored in its social–ecological context. Focusing on English, not even United Kingdom (UK), conservation law and regulation may seem parochial, but it is actually a way to provide a grounded and detailed legal and regulatory analysis, less achievable with a more macro-focus. It is also because the environment is a devolved matter in the UK, and therefore, devolved administrations have their own conservation laws and regulations in place. Having said this, an examination of English law cannot be done in isolation given that its development has been strongly tied with EU conservation law and key international treaties on biodiversity and the sustainable use of the marine environment.[20] An examination of English law reveals the interactions of multiple governance scales and their impact on the domestic approach, as discussed in Chapter 2. With the UK having recently left the

[20] For example, Convention on Biological Diversity (Rio de Janeiro) 5 June 1992, in force 29 December 1993, 31 ILM 822 (1992) (Biodiversity Convention); United Nations Convention on the Law of the Sea (Montego Bay) 10 December 1982, in force 16 November 1994, 21 ILM 1261 (1982) (UNCLOS); Convention for the Protection of the Marine Environment of the North-East Atlantic (Paris) 22 September 1992, in force 25 March 1998, 32 ILM 1068 (1993) (OSPAR Convention).

European Union, the regulatory analysis is even more interesting due to the climate of regulatory uncertainty that such departure has created and the steps the government has taken and is taking in relation to the role of EU law. These issues are to be discussed in Chapter 8, which is dedicated to the effects of the UK exit from the European Union on marine conservation law. As it will be explained in Chapter 2, which provides an overview of the legal framework, the Court of Justice of the European Union (CJEU) has been pivotal in enforcing nature conservation law and supporting a strong precautionary approach to the management of European Marine Sites. The strong precautionary approach of the CJEU has influenced the English approach to fisheries in European Marine Sites leading to a revised approach to ensure that all existing and potential commercial fishing operations are managed in line with article 6 of the Habitats Directive. Such a revised approach to fisheries management follows a risk-based approach and requires a great mapping effort by the regulators of all the fisheries activities, which is explored in depth in Chapter 4 of this book. Thus, England provides a really stimulating case to study MPAs law and regulation in a context of not only environmental change but also regulatory change.

Methodology

Methodologically speaking, the book draws on desk-based research (doctrinal and documentary analysis), complemented by insights from empirical research. Primary sources, studied and analysed during the desk-based research, include marine conservation law, relevant marine and environmental policy documents as well as regulatory tools, such as IAs and byelaws related to MPAs.

The empirical research consisted in semi-structured interviews[21] conducted over a number of years with actors involved in and/or affected by the decision-making processes over European Marine Sites and MCZs. Some of these interviews were conducted as part of a large Economic and Social Research Council (ESRC)-funded project on MPAs governance, which I carried out from 2012 to 2015.[22] During that project, face-to-face semi-structured interviews with marine representatives in three selected case study areas[23] in the UK were held, focusing primarily on issues related to the establishment of MCZs, which was

[21] Semi-structured interviews can be defined as interviews in which the interviewer has an interview guide that is prepared in advance with a series of open-ended questions that can be varied depending on the replies and additional questions can be added. This format is preferable to a structured interview format as it provides flexibility rendering the interview an iterative and reflexive place for the development of thoughts and perspectives for both the interviewer and the research participant. At the same time, semi-structured interviews provide a level of structure that enables the researcher to focus on specific themes of interest (cf. unstructured interviews). For a definition of semi-structured interviews, see A. Bryman, *Social Research Methods*, 4th ed. (Oxford University Press, 2012), p. 419.

[22] ES/K001043/1.

[23] Isles of Scilly, South-East England (Dover to Folkstone) and North-West Scotland (Arran and Barra).

underway as well as European Marine Sites. The cases were selected due to their geographical diversity, type and number of MPAs and conservation histories and approaches. There was an appropriate number of case studies to enable comparative observations without compromising on methodological and analytical depth. Research participants ranged from local sea-users, such as fishers, to regulators, statutory nature conservation bodies and environmental NGOs, following a snowball sampling technique.[24] This meant that I made initial contact with key representatives of the organisation under study, such as the chairman of a fisherman's organisation, and then such contacts provided contacts of other fishers working in the area. Snowballing sampling technique is useful in instances in which the aim is to access networks of participants, who may be reluctant to engage with the researcher without an introduction from a trusted, known individual. The rich empirical data generated by that project has been discussed in various publications already[25] and here only the views gathered during the interviews with South-East fishers are reported and form the basis of the discussion in Chapter 5, as they are most telling in discussing multiple epistemologies at play in MPAs regulation and MPAs law's role in contributing, or failing to contribute, to commoning and environmental democracy.

To provide an up-to-date picture on the implementation of English MPAs law, five elite semi-structured interviews[26] with national-level representatives of government, statutory nature conservation bodies and environmental NGOs, were conducted in May 2021. As the research participants were the key national representatives for their institution on MPAs regulation, they were selected following a purposive sampling technique.[27] Elite interviews have permitted an exploration of current issues such as MCZs management measures, the revised approach to fisheries in European Marine Sites and the UK exit from the European Union, referred to as Brexit. Such elite interviews were conducted online due to the global pandemic brought about by COVID-19. The choice to focus on national representatives for the elite interviews, rather than local representatives, was due to the scope of this book, which is primarily national.

[24] Bryman, Social Sciences Methods, p. 424.

[25] For example, see, M. Pieraccini and E. Cardwell, 'Towards Deliberative and Pragmatic Co-management: A Comparison between Inshore Fisheries Authorities in England and Scotland' (2016) 25 *Environmental Politics* 1–20; M. Pieraccini and E. Cardwell, 'Divergent Perceptions of New Marine Protected Areas: Comparing Legal Consciousness in Scilly and Barra, UK' (2016) 119 *Ocean & Coastal Management* 21–29.

[26] There is no single definition of what an elite is and therefore of elite interviews. Here, I define elite as highly skilled people holding key professional positions and power at the national level in the field of marine conservation. For a critical take on elite interviews and the issue of power, see K.E. Smith, 'Problematising Power Relations in "Elite" Interviews' (2006) 37 *Geoforum* 643–653. For a methodological introduction into elite interviews, see W. S. Harvey, 'Methodological Approaches for Interviewing Elites' (2010) 4 *Geography Compass* 193–205.

[27] Purposive sampling is the opposite of random sampling as its goal is to sample participants in a strategic way. See Bryman, Social Research Methods, p. 418.

The choice to interview regulatory actors, rather than sea-users, was primarily due to the fact that the objective of these interviews was to investigate regulatory strategies and current practices, rather than sector-specific approaches to and sea-users views on conservation. Besides, owing to the safety measures introduced during the COVID-19 pandemic and the unfeasibility of carrying out fieldwork, online interviews were not deemed to be appropriate for reaching certain sea-users, whose work does not afford them much time to spend in front of a computer. To comply with ethical standards for primary qualitative research, names of all research participants are omitted in the text below and only broad group/institutional categorisations are provided. For instance, references are made to a statutory nature conservation body representative, without specifying which statutory nature conservation body it is, thereby maintaining the anonymity of the research participants. When quotations are reported from more than one research participant within the same group, a numbering system has been adopted. For example, environmental NGO representative n. 1, environmental NGO representative n. 2, etc. Again, for ensuring anonymity of research participants, only the month and year of the interview are reported, as participants may be aware of the day of the interviews of other participants, especially when interviews were conducted in small local settings.

Overall, the qualitative data collected empirically has permitted a more nuanced understanding of the processes at play in MPAs law and regulation as it has captured different actors' reflections on these processes and multiple perspectives on marine conservation, not all of which are fully represented in decision-making processes and/or are visible via desk-based research only.

In summary therefore, this book analyses marine conservation in its social and ecological context, employing a mixed method approach.

Structure of the Book

The book is divided into four main thematic areas, each containing two substantive chapters, as follows. The four broad themes used to cluster the discussion are: spatialisation, rationalisation, democratisation and adaptation. These themes, whether explored singularly or as part of a broader narrative, are familiar ones to environmental social science and law scholars and are pertinent for the discussion on MPAs law and regulation, for MPAs are spatial tools and their regulation is the product of interaction among different scales, regulatory choices regarding their establishment and management are deemed to be based on rational and democratic values and strategies and ecological and political changes require their governance to be adaptive.

Part 1 of the book, entitled *Spatialising Regulation*, provides a critical introduction to MPAs as a place-based tool and presents a map of the regulatory actors and institutions involved in English MPAs governance. Chapter 1 employs the language of the commons and commoning to show that MPAs have complex and multiple roles and characterisations. The language of the commons that first appears in Chapter 1 becomes valuable throughout the book in providing analytical categories to explore the different themes. More specifically, Chapter 1 argues that MPAs can be defined in two main ways. The first consists in conceptualising MPAs as spaces for the management of common-pool resources. In this sense, MPAs can be understood as enclosures or new commons depending on the perspective. The second consists in the conceptualisation of MPAs as spaces for commoning, that is, spaces for democratising environmental governance and for the shared production of social–ecological commons. Chapter 2 explores the extent to which these roles and characterisations are played out in English law, focusing on the key institutions and regulations involved and the multiple governance scales at play. Theoretically, Part 1, and especially Chapter 1, is influenced by works of political ecologists and geographers on conservation and the production of territory.[28]

Part 2 of the book, entitled the *Rationalisation of Regulation*, draws on key works on risk in environmental regulation scholarship[29] as well as Science and Technology Studies,[30] which complement the regulatory analysis by problematising the role of science and its relationship to society. This part engages also with the use of cost-benefit analysis, which forms the basis of much risk-based regulation and well embodies the regulatory attempt at rationalising regulation. In discussing cost-benefit measures, this part provides a critical reading of scholarship promoting cost-benefit analysis as the solution.[31] In providing such analysis, this part connects with the characterisation of MPAs as enclosure discussed in Chapter 1, as MPAs are primarily understood as a neutral tool to conserve a scientifically predetermined nature. The first chapter of this section (Chapter 3) discusses the role of cost-benefit analysis using the example of IAs for MCZs, while the second (Chapter 4) explores risk-based regulation using the example of the revised approach to fisheries to European Marine Sites.

To investigate the theme of the *Democratisation of Regulation*, Part 3 of the book uses selected deliberative democratic theories to critically analyse the opening up of decision-making in the field of MPA regulation in England, reconnecting with the literature on commoning explored in Chapter 1. This part asks which voices are heard and which are silenced in the marine political community due to dominant cultural discourses and institutional practices. It considers institutions and processes of decision-making, focusing on the designation of MCZs in Chapter 5 and on two key actors playing a key role in the democratisation of decision-making in Chapter 6, namely environmental NGOs and IFCAs.

[28] For example, R. Sack, *Human Territoriality: Its Theory and History* (Cambridge University Press, 1986); P. E. Steinberg, *The Social Construction of the Oceans* (Cambridge University Press, 2001); S. Whatmore, *Hybrid Geographies: Natures, Cultures, Spaces* (Sage, 2002).

[29] For example, J. Black and R. Baldwin, 'When Risk-Based Aims Low: Approaches and Challenges' (2012) 6 *Regulation and Governance* 131–148.

[30] For example, B. Wynne, 'Uncertainty and Environmental Learning: Reconceiving Science and Policy in the Preventative Paradigm' (1992) 2 *Global Environmental Change* 111–127.

[31] For example, C. R. Sunstein, *The Cost-Benefit Revolution* (MIT Press, 2018).

The final theme of the book, entitled *Adapting Regulation*, is explored in Part 4. Chapters 7 and 8 provide a critical reading of the current efforts to conserve marine biodiversity in a changing ecological and political climate. Chapter 7 argues, from an adaptive governance perspective, that MPA regulation needs to be dynamic, requiring revisions and experimentation to deal with the complexities and uncertainties of environmental change and discusses the extent to which this is what MPAs law in its current state delivers. This chapter connects with the discussion on the continuous production and reproduction of socio-legal systems and the role of the more-than human in supporting or destabilising the boundaries created, discussed in Chapter 1. Chapter 8 continues with the analysis of adaptation and uncertainty but focuses on political, rather than ecological uncertainty, discussing marine conservation law in the context of Brexit, analysing recent legal developments.

The Conclusion of the book (Chapter 9) is primarily of a reflexivenature, summarising the main points running throughout the book by providing an assessment of English MPAs law and regulation using the conceptual categories introduced in Chapter 1.

In navigating English marine conservation law following a thematic socio-legal analysis, the book builds a bridge between environmental law and environmental social sciences scholarship, reflecting on key debates on nature and society and environmental decision-making and showing the usefulness of the language of the commons for the forging of key analytical categories.

1

The Geography of Regulation

Marine Protected Areas, Commons and Commoning

1.1 Introduction

> Oceans may connect or divide, or may be implicated in more radical strategies for the social organization of space that lie outside the norm of state stewardship that traditionally has guided social intervention in marine space.
>
> – Steinberg (1999)[1]

This chapter begins the discussion on the spatialisation of regulation by drawing links between MPAs and the language of the commons. Before explaining the various reasons why the language of the commons offers an interesting conceptual lens or, more accurately, lenses through which the complex character and role of MPAs can be explored, a few words must be spent by understanding what I mean by spatialising regulation as the way I refer to space in this part of the book is twofold. On the one hand, I refer to space in its basic physical sense as MPAs are deemed to be spatial tools, drawing geographical boundaries with regulatory consequences on the sea. On the other, I refer to space in the more abstract sense of institutional spaces and scales, and this meaning of space is employed when exploring the multiple legal scales discussed in Chapter 2 of this book and when discussing MPAs as institutional spaces for the (un)commoning of marine regulation in this chapter.

There are multiple reasons why the language of the commons is useful in providing the key conceptual categories for analysing MPAs law and regulation. Firstly, the language of the commons is not foreign to biodiversity law. Indeed, under international law, biodiversity protection is conceptualised as the *common* concern of humankind. In this context, MPAs as well as other measures emerge as regulatory tools for protecting this common concern.

Secondly, MPAs, and more generally protected areas, have been portrayed as regulatory tools to counteract environmental tragedies by limiting access to common-pool resources (CPRs), regulating uses and protecting biodiversity.

[1] P. E. Steinberg, 'Lines of Division, Lines of Connection: Stewardship in the World Ocean' (1999) 89 *Geographical Review* 254–264, at 262–263.

It is in this light that the commons literature characterises protected areas as new commons.[2] At the same time, in limiting access to CPRs, MPAs act as enclosures so MPAs can also be characterised as political tools used to control and potentially dispossess resource users in the name of predetermined global environmental values and an abstract humanity not necessarily recognised at more local scales. This positive versus negative reading of MPAs is not simply underpinned by a change of perspective from ecocentrism to anthropocentrism, that is to say from an understanding of MPAs as tools for nature conservation to an understanding of MPAs as tools constraining the activities of sea-users. Seeing MPAs as either new commons or enclosures points to broader and more intricate issues of scale and power. In regard to scale, it is not humans in general but local people in particular who tend to shoulder the burden of protection, and it is not only nature as detached from humans that benefits from these enclosures, but it is also the faceless and seemingly homogenous present and future humanity regarded as the beneficiary of biodiversity conservation, that is, *humankind*. In regard to power, MPAs as new commons are often portrayed as neutral, techno-scientific tools, while the representation of MPAs as negative enclosures defines them as historical-specific political tools and spaces in which the operation of power can be repressive and alienating. However, such territorialising strategies are not only the product of human constructions and projects but are constantly negotiated, reproduced and destabilised by the intertwining of humans and non-humans. If MPAs as regulatory tools could be understood as territorialising strategies attempting to render the sea a governable space, a variety of social–ecological events in multiple timespaces emerge, gather and disperse destabilising MPAs boundaries. Such fluidity shows that the establishment of MPAs is far from the drawing of definite lines on a silent sea surface, but it is subject to many social–ecological reworkings and interactions. This is perhaps most visible when discussing environmental change in Chapter 7.

Besides, and more radically, MPAs are not only tools for the regulation of CPRs but can be conceptualised as institutional sites where either commoning or un-commoning experiments take place. Drawing on the commoning literature,[3] which redirects the attention from commons as a thing to commons as a shared practice and emphasises the productive character of the

[2] E. Berge, 'Protected Areas and Traditional Commons: Values and Institutions' (2006) 60 *Norsk Geografisk Tidsskrift-Norwegian Journal of Geography* 65–76; C. Hess, 'Mapping the New Commons', Paper presented at the 12th Biennial Conference of the International Association for the Study of the Commons, Cheltenham, UK (2008); M. Pieraccini, 'Democratic Legitimacy and New Commons: Examples from English Protected Areas' (2015) 9 *International Journal of the Commons* 552–572.

[3] See, for example, P. Linebaugh, *The Magna Carta Manifesto: Liberties and Commons for All* (University of California Press, 2008); M. De Angelis, 'The Production of Commons and the "Explosion" of the Middle Class' (2010) 42 *Antipode* 954–977; D. Bollier and S. Helfrich (eds.), *Patterns of Commoning* (The Commons Strategies Group, 2015).

commons, MPAs can be assessed in their (in)capacity to facilitate strategies aimed at social cooperation and collective decision-making for the production of shared values, responsibilities and actions. Following the commoning literature, more attention is dedicated to matters of a procedural nature and institutional attempts at building environmental democracy.

This chapter, after introducing how international law uses the commons' language, discusses these two main different characterisations of MPAs – MPAs as regulatory tools managing CPRs and MPAs as institutional sites supporting or hindering commoning practices. The discussion draws on three principal strands of the social science literature: political ecology, seminal in showing how rational and scientific interventions are always political; geographical literature, which has recovered the more than human elements in the analysis; and, finally, the literature on the commons, which spans from the more traditional Ostromian analysis of CPRs[4] to the more recent and often politicised literature on commoning. It is worth noting that the two dichotomies introduced here – of MPAs as negative enclosures versus new commons and of MPAs as commoning versus un-commoning institutional sites – are only the starting point. Through the course of this book, these dichotomies are problematised and it is demonstrated how these different characterisations and roles of MPAs may coexist more or less in friction within English marine conservation law. Investigating the relationships between MPAs and commons is thus an essential preliminary step to enable a critical discussion of how English law conceptualises MPAs and contributes to the formation of MPAs as spaces of opening and/or of closing.

1.2 International Environmental Law's Take on the Commons

Under international law, biodiversity conservation is a common concern of humankind. The principle of common concern refers to global environmental issues requiring global cooperation. The principle has found a comfortable place in treaties, more than in the reasoning of the courts.[5] In the

[4] E. Ostrom, *Governing the Commons. The Evolution of Institutions for Collective Action* (Cambridge University Press, 1990).

[5] See, most notably, the United Nations Framework Convention on Climate Change (New York) 9 May 1992, in force 24 March 1994, 1771 UNTS 107 (Climate Change Convention), whose Preamble states that 'acknowledging that change in the Earth's climate and its adverse effects are a common concern of humankind' and the Paris Agreement (Paris) 22 April 2016, in force 4 November 2016, C.N.92.2016, Treaties-XXVII.7.d (Paris Agreement) again repeating in the introductory text that climate change is a common concern of human kind. Also note early, more embryonic, conceptualisations of the principle for example in the preamble of the Antarctic Treaty (Washington) 1 December 1959, in force 23 June 1961, 402 UNTS 71 (Antarctic Treaty) and the International Convention for the High Sea Fisheries of the North Pacific Ocean (Tokyo) 9 May 1952, in force 12 June 1953, 205 UNTS 65 (North Pacific Fisheries Convention), both using the phrase 'common interest of mankind' in their Preambles and the Convention on the Conservation of Migratory Species of Wild Animals (Bonn) 23 June 1979, in force 1 November 1983, 19 ILM 15 (1980) (Bonn Convention) using the term 'good of mankind' and referring to intergenerational obligations to conserve the resources in the Preamble.

Convention of Biological Diversity 1992, it is found in the Preamble, which affirms that 'conservation of biological diversity is a common concern of humankind'. What is of common concern is the conservation of biodiversity, not the resource per se. The principle places emphasis on collective action to be taken to address a concern that is common to the whole of humanity, not only to the traditional international law actors, that is, sovereign states. Although states are still the central actors of the Biodiversity Convention, which is strongly focused on nationally created strategies and plans,[6] they are facilitators and responsible to humankind in sharing the concern of biodiversity conservation.

The concept of common concern has been subject to substantial academic commentary, ranging from discussions of its meaning as a legal principle to exploration of its relationship with *erga omnes* obligations or its links with other principles of international law.[7] There is no need to reopen these discussions here. For the purpose of this chapter, it is sufficient to define common concern by distinguishing it from the principle of common heritage. If the principle of common heritage refers to the resources that are common and therefore can, at least theoretically, be exploited by anyone, the principle of common concern is more action-driven, imposing shared environmental responsibilities.

The principle of common heritage, focusing on equal resource exploitation, has been useful in situations in which access to shared resources was not likely to be equal due to scientific and technological differences among countries. In the marine context, it was used in Part XI of the United Nations Convention on the Law of the Sea (UNCLOS) declaring the so-called Area – the seabed and ocean floor beyond national jurisdiction and its resources – to be the common heritage of mankind and including provisions facilitating equal access, such as mandatory transfer of technologies to developing countries.[8] Such declaration did not gain the support of developed countries. The introduction of the 1994 Implementation Agreement underpinned by a more liberal, free-market approach was necessary to facilitate the ratification of the Convention by the US and other developed

[6] See Article 6(a) of the Biodiversity Convention, which states that each contracting Party shall 'develop national strategies, plans or programmes for the conservation and sustainable use of biological diversity or adapt for this purpose existing strategies, plans or programmes which shall reflect, inter alia, the measures set out in this Convention relevant to the Contracting Party concerned'.

[7] See F. Soltau, 'Common Concern of Humankind' in K. R. Gray, R. Tarasofsky, and C. Carlane (eds.), *The Oxford Handbook of International Climate Change Law* (Oxford University Press, 2016), pp. 203–212; D. Shelton, 'Common Concern of Humanity' (2009) 39 *Environmental Policy and Law* 83–86; J. Brunnée, 'Common Areas, Common Heritage, and Common Concern' in D. Bodansky, J. Brunnée and E. Hey (eds.), *Oxford Handbook of International Environmental Law* (Oxford University Press, 2008), pp. 550–573; F. Biermann, 'Common Concern of Humankind: The Emergence of a New Concept of Environmental Law' (1996) 34 *Archiv des Volkerrechts* 426–481.

[8] Article 136 of UNCLOS.

countries.[9] If there was such opposition in relation to resources in areas beyond national jurisdiction, it is easy to imagine that the principle of common heritage could not be used for biodiversity, which is often found within national boundaries. Making biodiversity a common heritage of humankind could imply opening up national natural resources to the interests of other states. Thus, the principle of common concern was preferred. Moreover, as mentioned earlier, the principle of common concern does something different to the principle of common heritage as it implies shared global environmental responsibilities.

Following Brunnée,[10] it could be argued that the principle of common concern does not only point to a community of needs but also to a community of values, transcending individual interests and embracing the global environmental interest of humankind. This value-centric perspective was also present in Judge Weeramantry' s separate opinion in the *Gabcikovo/Nagymaros*,[11] in which he stated that international environmental law was entering a new era focusing on the global concerns of humanity a whole, rather than weighting the interests of states against each other.

If such value centrism adds an important normative dimension to the principle, it also opens up a number of complexities associated with the assumption of the existence of a single humanity holding a single, universal environmental value. The assumption of the existence of a predetermined shared global value is problematic not only because it is accompanied by a shallow representation of humanity, devoid of differences and singularities, and possessing a universal value system but also because it does not recognise that the protection of such value may not be shared equally, impacting more heavily on the activities of some people rather than others. Who decides which biodiversity should be valued? Who is responsible for the biodiversity crisis and who is affected? Who is required to shoulder the costs of protection? Those salient questions are hidden in the principle of common concern. Through the example of MPAs, it will be demonstrated how these questions do matter and should be asked.

1.3 MPAs as a Regulatory Tool: New Commons or Enclosures?

As biodiversity protection is a common concern of humankind, hence elevated beyond singular interests and assuming normative connotations, tools acting in support of such common concern are generally portrayed in a positive light in law and some of the commons literature. MPAs are one of the preferred tools to achieve biodiversity protection. The MPA is a spatial tool. As defined by the

[9] Agreement Relating to the Implementation of Part XI of the UNCLOS of 10 December 1982, annexed to the General Assembly Resolution 48/263 of 28 July 1994 (A/RE/48/263). For an academic commentary on the Agreement, see B. H. Oxman, 'The 1994 Agreement and the Convention' (1994) 88 *The American Journal of International Law* 687–696.

[10] Brunnée, 'Common Areas'.

[11] Case concerning the *Gabcikovo-Nagymaros Project (Hungary/Slovakia)* 1997 ICJ Reports 7, at 97.

International Union for the Conservation of Nature (IUCN), an MPA is 'a clearly defined geographical space, recognised, dedicated and managed, through legal or other effective means, to achieve the long-term conservation of nature with associated ecosystem services and cultural values'.[12] MPAs as regulatory tools operate by limiting the over-exploitation of CPRs, that are resource systems sharing two key attributes: '(1) the difficulty of excluding individuals from benefiting from a good and (2) the subtractability of the benefits consumed by one individual from those available to others'.[13] Oceans' physical characteristics are such that they lack clear boundaries and fixed owners/occupiers making it more difficult to exclude users. At the same time, oceans host a vast array of attractive resources (biological and non-biological) that are subtractable and therefore they are often subject to over-exploitation. The difficulty to exclude users, coupled with the oceans' CPRs subtractability, makes oceans' governance subject to collective action problems and may create environmental tragedies. It is not by chance that Hardin included the oceans as one example of commons destined to tragedy in his famous 1968 essay,[14] and it is not surprising that calls for the conservation of marine life abound in international and domestic laws and policy instruments to counteract overuse and global environmental change.

As spatial tools, MPAs enclose specific sections of the oceans by regulating the human activities that take place within them and limiting free-riding behaviour and the over-exploitation of CPRs. MPAs as new commons help to avoid the tragedy of the commons by taking biodiversity loss seriously.[15] As we have seen, the language of the commons pervades biodiversity protection law, especially at the international level.[16] Besides, due to the reduced visibility of social relations in the sea and a lack of structured property rights regime, MPAs' establishment may be perceived as less problematic than that of protected areas on land, where conflicts with specific ownership regimes are likely to occur. Indeed, scientific papers characterising MPAs as a positive spatial measure for the health of marine ecosystems and the sustainable use of marine resources abound.[17] The focus on conservation does not exclude resource use

[12] J. Day et al., *IUCN Guidelines for Applying the IUCN Protected Area Management Categories to Marine Protected Areas*, 2nd edition (IUCN, 2019), p. 14.

[13] E. Ostrom, R. Gardner and J. Walker, *Rules, Games and Common-Pool Resources* (The University of Michigan Press, 1994), p. 6.

[14] G. Hardin, 'The Tragedy of the Commons' (1968) 162 *Science* 1243–1248.

[15] MPAs can also be established for recreational, cultural heritage, military and other purposes. Given that in England MPAs are established to promote the conservation of marine biodiversity, other MPAs are excluded from the present analysis.

[16] R. K. Craig, *Comparative Ocean Governance: Place-Based Protections in an Era of Climate Change* (Edward Elgar, 2012).

[17] See T. Agardy, *Marine Protected Areas and Ocean Conservation* (Academic Press, 1997); B. S. Halpern and R. R. Warner, 'Marine Reserves Have Rapid and Lasting Effects' (2002) 5 *Ecology Letters* 361–366; B. C. O'Leary et al., 'Effective Coverage Targets for Ocean Protection' (2016) 9 *Conservation Letters* 398–404; B. S. Cheng et al., 'Can Marine Reserves Restore Lost Ecosystem Functioning? A Global Synthesis' (2019) 100 *Ecology*.

as the improvement, maintenance and/or recovery of marine biodiversity contribute to sustainable use of resources, such as fisheries. Conservation and sustainable resource use are intimately related. No one would argue against the claim that marine resources offer a number of benefits, from food to energy, to raw materials[18] and that marine biodiversity loss, heavily influenced by anthropogenic factors, is one of the most severe global environmental challenges of the present time. Thus, efforts directed at resisting biological loss should be welcomed.

Such positive understanding of MPAs has been reflected in some of the commons literature, which categorises protected areas within the broad umbrella term of new commons. As defined by Hess, new commons are 'various types of shared resources that have recently evolved or have been recognized as commons. They are commons without pre-existing rules or clear institutional arrangements'.[19] Although the concept of new commons is employed by scholars and activist movements in different ways, according to Hess at the roots of these definitions 'one can read a commitment to future generations, to communities beyond the local sphere, to working for both the local and the global common good'.[20] At the same time, the establishment of MPAs is also an act of territorialisation and, if interpreted in this light, it assumes the negative connotations of enclosure. Following Sack, territorialisation is to be defined as 'an attempt by an individual or group to affect, influence, or control people, phenomena, and relationships, by delimiting and asserting control over a geographical area. This area will be called territory'.[21] In this light, the enclosure of marine space for conservation can be understood as a strategy to control who can access resources and what activities can be carried on within the selected space. The establishment of MPAs is thus an exercise of power and a technique of control. This is the way in which protected areas have often been interpreted in the political ecology literature.[22] Although the quote by Sack above does not refer to the state as the sole author of territorialisation, speaking instead of a generic 'individual or group', much of the literature that narrates histories of protected areas' territorialisation as a type of negative enclosure has focused on the state.

Scholars, especially those concerned with conservation interventions in developing countries, have argued that protected areas write out of history and geography local people. Creating new space for nature is linked to histories

[18] S. Fletcher et al., *Marine Ecosystem Services – Natural England Commissioned Reports, Number 088* (Natural England and other parties, 2012); B. Worm et al., 'Impacts of Biodiversity Loss on Ocean Ecosystem Services' (2006) 314 *Science* 787–790.

[19] Hess, 'Mapping the New Commons'.

[20] Ibid, p. 36. [21] Sack, Human Territoriality, p. 19.

[22] See W. B. Adams, *Against Extinction: The Story of Conservation* (Earthscan, 2004); Brockington, *Fortress Conservation*; Neumann, *Imposing Wilderness*; P. Vandergeest and N. L. Peluso, 'Territorialization and State Power in Thailand' (1995) 24 *Theory and Society* 385–426.

of dispossession and displacement and, simultaneously, to the making of the state identity through the appropriation of nature in the name of the collective public good. An archetypal example of fortress conservation is the Mkomazi National Park in Tanzania, whose declaration as park in 2006 meant the eviction of thousands of pastoralists and livestock for the conservation/creation of a mythologised wild Africa.[23] Fortress conservation is not an effort to restore landscapes to an (idealised) natural state, but it is a creative effort of production of such natural state. If such fortress conservation efforts have never been a feature of English conservation, possibly due to the power afforded to (private) property rights in England,[24] the broader point made by these studies remains valid. This point regards the extent to which conservation initiatives are always political interventions, including something and excluding something else and requiring very specific ideas of which one is the nature to be worth of protection.

The technical aspects of establishing protected areas cannot be separated from the strategic-political and economic aspects.[25] Indeed, political ecology literature has made explicit the link between nature, state and territory, showing the role protected areas have in the practice of statecraft and in the production of the territory to be protected. 'Mapping, bounding, constraining and controlling is what makes a state a state'.[26] One of the most significant academic contributions in this context is *Seeing Like a State*,[27] a wide-ranging study in which Scott demonstrates how the state's rationalisation and standardisation techniques serve to make complex social–ecological systems into something legible, simplified and ultimately controllable. Scott opens up the book with the example of the invention of scientific forestry in the late eighteenth century in Prussia and Saxony to serve the state's economic needs. It was scientific forestry that reduced a chaotic forest to a selected number of trees. Seeing only some trees as the whole forest served the purpose of isolating a single element of interest for the state, that is timber production. The administrative ordering of nature and society, through techniques such as cadastral maps, common units of measurement and other schematised processes of abstraction, makes the state knowledgeable by narrowing the visible and representing (also in the Latin sense of *repraesentare*, i.e. making present) the slice of the world that is

[23] Brockington, Fortress Conservation.

[24] A clear example of the supremacy of property rights can be found in relation to the old regime for the management of SSSIs, the key designation under the Wildlife and Countryside Act 1981. Under the 1983 Financial Guidelines, owners and occupiers were compensated for profit forgone in not damaging an SSSI.

[25] This point has been made in the context of discussions on territory, see S. Elden, 'Land, Terrain, Territory' (2010) 34 *Progress in Human Geography* 799–817.

[26] R. P. Neumann, 'Nature-State-Territory: Toward a Critical Theorization of Conservation Enclosures', in R. Peet and M. Watts (eds.), *Liberation Ecologies*, 2nd edition (Routledge, 2004), pp. 179–199.

[27] J. Scott, Seeing Like a State.

of interest to the authorities for the achievement of specific, preset objectives. In doing so, many other knowledges and local histories become invisible and marginalised. Seeing by disembedding a complex set of relations into abstract units is an exercise of power as not only does it make reality manageable but it produces also what is to be considered reality, erasing other temporally and geographically situated visions.

Boundary-making for conservation purposes is therefore an exercise of power in multiple ways. Firstly, the establishment of a protected area is always an act of inclusion and exclusion and therefore a way to control people and resources. This does not necessarily translate in total exclusionary practices and displacements as in the case of fortress conservation. The IUCN categorisation of MPAs shows the wide spectrum of MPAs ranging from strict protected areas (category Ia) to protected areas for the conservation of ecosystems and habitats together with associated cultural values and traditional natural resource management systems (category VI).[28]

Nevertheless, all MPAs always imply a categorisation and subjectification of what is deemed to be considered natural or in agreement with nature. Even in instances of co-managed protected areas or community-based natural resource management, environmental subjects, human and non-human, are made. I borrow the idea of environmental subjects from Agrawal's work on environmentality,[29] in which he showed how the Kumaonis of Northern India, formerly opposed to the protection of the forest, had been turned into environmental subjects, actively and willingly participating in forest protection management, becoming vehicles for the exercise of power. Agrawal, inspired by Foucaultian scholarship,[30] argues that the production of environmental subjectivities is an instance of what Miller and Rose call 'government at a distance',[31] that is a government not exercising direct control but creating 'locales, entities and persons able to operate a regulated autonomy'.[32] Governing at distance using technologies of inscription and calculation enables governments to enrol those distant from them in the pursuit of conservation efforts, without encroaching directly on their freedom and without the exercise of violence as in the case of evictions. This not only has implications for the regulation of natural resources but also for the creation of identities. Through regulation at distance, governments activate particular people and places, forging alliances to affect outcomes in distance places. As Agrawal demonstrates in the case of

[28] Day, IUCN Guidelines, pp. 9–10. [29] Agrawal, Environmentality.

[30] In the Security, Territory and Population lectures, Foucault demonstrated the development of a range of techniques, such as mapping, ordering and measuring) making territory an object of governance. See M. Foucault, *Security, Territory, Population-Lectures at the College the France 1977–1978*, M. Senellart (ed.) (Palgrave, 2007, transl. by G. Burchell).

[31] N. Rose and P. Miller, 'Political Power beyond the State: Problematics of Government' (1992) 43 *The British Journal of Sociology* 173–205.

[32] Ibid, p. 172.

the Kumaonis, new environmental identities and practices emerge as a product of decentralised forest management.[33]

Such observations are useful in going a step forward in thinking about the relationship between power and conservation. If the writings of political ecologists on fortress conservation focus on the state as the locus of power and focus on its territorial strategies to discuss the practice of statecraft linked to dispossession of local peoples and to a specific representation of nature as a pristine wilderness, the work of Agrawal and others[34] serves to move beyond a sole focus on the state by reconceptualising power in a more dispersed way and including into the analysis not only the making of state identity but also the making of non-state actors. When applied to the context of MPAs, these observations permit to focus on processes of human and non-human environmental subjectification in the establishment and management of MPAs, especially considering that there are not strict marine reserves in England to date, although pilot Highly Protected Marine Areas will be established by the end of 2022[35] and that participatory processes are at the core of marine conservation law. Such dispersed power does not mean that the state and/or supra-national bodies fall outside the analytical space, as they often make the initial choices of what nature is worth of protection and who can become an environmental subject and manager.

Secondly, the establishment of MPAs is a way of knowing/seeing and world-making, influenced by particular cultural beliefs and political strategies. For Scott, it was the state who saw through its techniques of simplification and rationalisation, but in a world where the state is re-located within what Rose and Miller call the 'problematic of government', we can expand this by asking who, other than the state, can see, who can render legible the marine space and who or what in this process is made the subject of conservation.[36] As Delany writes, it is essential both to see *through* territory to question assumptions naturalising particular discourses and also *around* territory to contextualise territorial efforts.[37] Territory is not just a static container but a communicative device as its lines signify.[38] The lines of MPAs do indeed communicate. If read positively, they communicate efforts towards global conservation and sustainability. If read negatively, they communicate exercises in simplification and histories of dispossession and subjectification. The positive and negative

[33] Agrawal, Environmentality.

[34] See, for example, T. M. Li, 'Engaging Simplifications'. Li argues that community-based natural resource management in Upland Southeast Asia is not a way to reduce state interference in local environmental management but a shift in territorialising strategies. Li writes that community-based natural resource management moves away from direct state control to 'control over upland populations by pinning them in place, regularizing their resource use according to state-defined rules and procedures and, through the extension of institutions and bureaucratic processes, enmeshing them more firmly as state clients' (p. 274).

[35] See Chapter 7 for a discussion on Highly Protected Marine Areas.

[36] Rose and Miller, 'Political Power beyond the State'.

[37] D. Delaney, *Territory: A Short Introduction* (Blackwell Publishing, 2005).

[38] Ibid.

reading highlight different aspects: the first is purposive, focusing on the aims and values of a protected area, while the second focuses on what the protected area represents and makes present both symbolically and concretely. In the first reading, the technical remains divorced from the political, in the second it does not. Thus, the lines of the MPAs can signify different things: they can signify an a-politicised natural space or a powerful, historically specific social–ecological space produced by particular visions of the relationship between nature and society.

Significantly, MPAs are not only lines that signify but also lines that matter. The turn to the more-than-human in oceanic studies is essential in pointing to the co-constitution of the material and discursive. MPAs as enclosures matter, as their existence is not only indicative of a legal or cultural project, inscribing meaning into pre-existing matter, but it is also produced and destabilised by the multiple events and social–ecological forces whose gathering and dispersing supports or hinder these territorialisation practices. As Steinberg and Peters argue 'the volume of water moves and so its territory and its location cannot be pinned down. This challenges processes of bordering with a particular intensity not found on land'.[39] In speaking of the power of MPAs as regulatory tools, the co-constitution of the material and discursive production of space should not to be forgotten, especially in an environment that for large parts remains invisible and subject to constant re-configurations due to a variety of ecological processes. Attending to the relationships between the human and non-human world was first popularised by Whatmore's 'more-than-human' concept. In *Hybrid Geographies*, Whatmore introduced the concept of 'more-than-human' geography to disrupt dichotomous ontologies of human/subjects versus non-human/objects and introduce a cartography of networks formed by 'the affective relationships between heterogenous actants, distributing their morphological particularity and mutability though all manner of energetic exchanges within and between them'.[40] More-than-human geography is not just about the inclusion of non-human beings in the analysis and the consideration of the interaction between pre-formed entities, but it draws attention to processes of becoming and the production of entities through their relationship with one another, what Whatmore calls 'difference-in-relation', which is not too dissimilar to what, years earlier, the anthropologist Strathern referred to as 'dividuals' in her ethnography about Melanesian people.[41] As Bresnihan

[39] P. Steinberg and K. Peters (2015), 'Wet Ontologies, Fluid Spaces: Giving Depth through Volume through Oceanic Thinking', (2015) 33 *Environment and Planning D: Society and Space* 247–264.

[40] Whatmore, Hybrid Geographies, p. 160.

[41] M. Strathern, *The Gender of the Gift: Problems with Women and Problems with Society in Melanesia* (University of California Press, 1988). Strathern writes 'Far from being regarded as unique entities, Melanesia persons are as dividually as they are individually conceived. They contain a generalized sociality within. Indeed, persons are frequently constructed as the plural and composite site of the relationships that produced them' (p. 13).

states, 'where more than human commons depart from other interpretations is in recognizing how the starting point is not an individual subject separated from other people and the world around them, but a relational subject who is always already caught up in a world that is intimately shared … based on the materially and socially constituted relations and practices that tie human and non-human together within a particular collective or territory'.[42] These observations are useful when thinking about how to value MPAs, which is discussed in Chapter 3 of this book in the context of regulatory IAs.

In the marine context, it is not only particular human actors and their legal and cultural strategies that make visible certain marine spaces and in so doing contribute to the production of particular ecologies and identities, but it is also what the sea renders visible and possible. The sea is more than a space subject to legal and other social interventions aimed at reaching specific social goals. The sea is more than a resource to be managed and a silent background over which human activity is inscribed, as it is involved in the production and destabilisation of boundaries. Ocean's agency and materiality are key components to be taken into account. A paper by Lambert et al[43] first called for considering the relationship between the materials of the sea – from wind to water to salt to plastics – and the cultures and technologies of the sea. Many scholars have employed the fashionable vocabulary of the assemblage to point to such relationality and emergent co-production in their accounts of ocean geography.[44] Although the word assemblage assumes different connotations in social theory,[45] often the meaning that is employed by geographers of the oceans draws on Deleauze and Guattari' s understanding, whereby the assemblage (in French *agencement*, from the verb *agencer* to arrange) is seen not as the bringing together of two or more already existing physical and cultural entities but as a complex and fluid arrangement, a constructive process open to disruption and re-composition.[46]

For example, Bear uses assemblage theory to discuss scallop dredging in Cardigan Bay, Wales, within a protected area impacting the population of bottle-nose dolphins. Bear argues that the issue of unsustainability of scallop dredging is not a simple mismanagement of natural resources, but it is the result of a co-produced assemblage of events, actions and actants. Dolphins, scallops,

[42] P. Bresnihan, 'The More-than-Human Commons: From Commons to Commoning', in S. Kirwan, L. Dawney and J. Brigstocke (eds.), *Space, Power and the Commons: The Struggle for Alternative Futures* (Routledge, 2016), pp. 93–112, p. 99.

[43] D. Lambert, L. Martins and M. Ogborn, 'Currents, Visions and Voyages: Historical Geographies of the Sea' (2006) 32 *Journal of Historical Geography* 479–493.

[44] Steinberg and Peter, 'Wet Ontologies'; P. E. Steinberg, 'Of Other Seas: Metaphors and Materialities in Maritime Regions', (2013) 10 *Atlantic Studies* 156–169; C. Bear, 'Assembling the Sea: Materiality, Movement and Regulatory Practices in the Cardigan Bay Scallop Fishery' (2012) 20 *Cultural Geographies* 21–41; K. Peters, 'Manipulating Material Hydro-worlds: Rethinking Human and More-than-Human Relationality through Offshore Radio Piracy' (2012) 44 *Environment and Planning A* 1241–1254; J. Bull, 'Encountering Fish, Flows, and Waterscapes through Angling' (2011) 43 *Environment and Planning A* 2267–2284.

[45] G. E. Marcus and E. Saka, 'Assemblage' (2006) 23 *Theory, Culture and Society* 101–106.

[46] G. Deleuze and F. Guattari, *A Thousand Plateaus: Capitalism and Schizofrenia* (University of Minnesota Press, 1987, transl. by B. Massumi).

seabed, local and non-local fishing regulations, technologies gather and disperse in multiple timespaces through practices of territorialisation and deterritorialisation. The territorialising strategies of regulation that attempt to create a controllable space are subverted by deterritorialisation strategies including the highly mobile seabed, sea currents and fisheries regulations elsewhere that are displacing fishers pushing them towards Cardigan Bay. Ongoing processes of gathering and dispersion of multiple events and actants produce the scallop fishery, and such complexity renders difficult the straightforward attribution of environmental liability. Not dissimilarly, Bull[47] discusses the practice of angling as an assemblage of fish, water, technology and text, and Peters discusses offshore radio piracy as an example of the binding of human and non-human bodies, arguing for the coming together of the hydro (sea) and the bio (life),[48] rendering suitable for the marine environment Whatmore's[49] call for bringing together the geo (Earth) with bio (life). In this book, destabilising ecological factors are principally discussed in the context of climate change in Chapter 7.

To summarise, if the understanding of MPAs as new commons focuses on the achievement of predetermined environmental values in the name of an abstract present and future humanity, following scientific expertise, the establishment of MPAs as negative enclosures focuses on issues of power and scale, on what happens when these values representing an abstract humanity and an abstract nature are put against local perceptions and practices of social–ecological relationships, as these spatially fixed solutions put in place to defend a general, distant environmental concern are having significant local impacts. MPAs as negative enclosures therefore focus on powerful territorialising strategies that can, however, be subverted by different assemblages of human and non-humans. Chapter 2 below discusses how these two different conceptualisations play out in English marine conservation law, and Chapter 4, focused on the relationship between fisheries management and MPAs, discusses the extent to which risk-based approaches create new commons. Before such discussions, it is essential to introduce the other way in which can think about MPAs, that is as institutional sites which may support or hinder commoning practices.

1.4 MPAs as Institutional Sites: Commoning or Un-Commoning Regulation?

'A commons is not just about allocating a common pool resource, something that a computer algorithm could arguably achieve. A commons requires active, ongoing participation with others in implementing and maintaining a shared purpose'.[50]

[47] Bull, 'Encountering Fish'. [48] Peters, 'Manipulating Material Hydro-Worlds'.
[49] S. Whatmore, 'Materialist Returns: Practising Cultural Geography in and for a More-than-Human World' (2006) 13 *Cultural Geographies* 600–609.
[50] Bollier and Helfrich, 'Overture', in Bollier and Helfrich (eds.) Patterns of Commoning.

So far, the discussion in this chapter has focused on MPAs as either positive or negative tools regulating the activities of resource users in relation to CPRs. It has been argued that the lines drawn by the MPAs can be read either as rational and technical attempts to manage CPRs following scientific criteria to meet a predetermined common concern or as political attempts at territorialisation that may be subject to subversions.

However, what if we move beyond the conceptualisation of commons as a material resource and think in terms of practices of commoning? Can the regulation of MPAs be read as a commoning or un-commoning attempt? The term commoning, first coined by Linebaugh in the *Magna Carta Manifesto*, refers to practices of sharing that (re) produce the commons. Linebaugh writes 'to speak of the commons as if it were a natural resource is misleading at best and dangerous at worst-the commons is an activity and, if anything, it expresses relationships in society that are inseparable from relations to nature. It might be better to keep the words as a verb, an activity, rather than as a noun, a substantive'.[51] If thinking about MPAs as regulatory tools requires thinking about them as spatial tools for regulating the exploitation of CPRs, understood as natural things pre-existing social relations; MPAs as (un) commoning sites focuses on their institutional (in)capacity to foster historically situated horizontal social relations, democratic practices, and inclusive decision-making processes. Commons in this perspective are not a given but are made and remade through multiple practices, they are consciously produced.

It must be clarified from the outset that this is not to imply that scholarship on CPRs has neglected issues of collective decision-making, and it is only through the academic works on commoning that these come to the fore. Indeed, the third design principle of Ostrom for building institutions for the successful governance of CPRs focuses on strengthening collective-choice arrangements: 'individuals, affected by the resource regime, must be able to participate in making and modifying its rules'.[52] Also, as we have seen in Section 1.2 above, even international law points to shared responsibility and collective action when describing biodiversity conservation as a common concern of humankind. Yet as De Angelis and Harvie have pointed out,[53] Ostrom's primary interest lies in the sustainability of the resource system, with collective decision-making functional for ensuring a sustainable distribution of resources among rational appropriators and protect the resources from overuse, avoiding free-riding behaviour. The same can be said for the principle of common concern: collective action and shared responsibility are instrumental for the achievement of a predetermined global value (biodiversity conservation) for

[51] Linebaugh, The Magna Carta Manifesto, p. 279.

[52] Ostrom, Governing the Commons, p. 442.

[53] M. De Angelis and D. Harvie, 'The Commons', in M. Parker, G. Cheney, V. Fournier and C. Land (eds.), *The Routledge Companion to Alternative Organizations* (Routledge, 2014), pp. 280–294.

present and future generations. There are two ways in which commoning departs from such understanding.

Firstly, with commoning there is a rethinking of the subjects beyond rational, autonomous decision-making selves that are only concerned with utility maximisation. Hence, institutions, such as those governing MPAs, do not merely constraint *homo economicus*' actions for the efficiency of natural resource management, but they also change subjects and the relationship between these situated subjects, potentially promoting shared, collective decision-making. This view is underpinned by a more contextual and relational view of social interactions.[54] Secondly, commoning is not only about distribution or protection of resources but also about social production, involving not just collective allocation but an iterative process through which commons are (re) constituted and, as Federici and Caffentzis argue, new forms of sociality, knowledge production and cultural exchange develop.[55]

The concept of the community becomes key in discussions on commoning. Indeed, a recurrent slogan of commoning scholarship is 'there are no commons without community', with Holder and Flessas writing 'the most obvious is the relationship between commons and community, to the extent that they may even be productive of each other'.[56] But, as many commons scholars and anthropologists have pointed out over the years,[57] an equation between commons and community may be misleading because there may be the risk of simplifications and idealism if the community is portrayed as spatially and socially bounded, small scale and homogenous. The commoning communities move beyond these limits, and they are formed by multi-scalar and multi-temporal interrelations and motivated by principles of cooperation and shared responsibility in an attempt to overcome unequal power relations, rather than defined by a sense of belonging to a specific place and driven by a single, pre-existent shared value. As De Angelis puts it, commoning is '*a field of production of values*, and the precondition for this production is that a wide range of different ethics, different cultures, different life-styles, and as we will see, different power positions within the planetary

[54] This is a critique also raised by anthropologists in relation to CPRs literature. See for example, A. Agrawal, 'Sustainable Use of Common-Pool Resources: Context, Methods and Politics' (2003) 32 *Annual Review of Anthropology* 243–262.

[55] G. Caffentzis and S. Federici, 'Commons Against and Beyond Capitalism' (2014) 49 *Community Development Journal* i92–i105.

[56] J. B. Holder and T. Flessas, 'Emerging Commons' (2008) 17 *Social and Legal Studies* 299–310, p. 306.

[57] See for example S. Federici, *Re-enchanting the World: Feminisms and the Politics of the Commons* (PM Press, 2019); S. Rodotà, 'Postfazione. Beni comuni: Una strategia globale contro lo "human divide"', in M. R. Marella (ed.), *Oltre il pubblico e il privato. Per un diritto dei beni comuni*, (Ombre Corte, 2012), pp. 311–331; L. Fortmann, 'What We Need Is a Community Bambi: the Perils and Possibilities of Powerful Symbols', in J. P. Brosius, A. L. Tsing and C. Zerner (eds.), '*Communities and Conservation: Histories and Politics of Community-Based Natural Resource Management*' (AltaMira Press, 2005), pp. 195–205; Agrawal, 'Sustainable Use of Common-Pool Resources'; Li, 'Engaging Simplifications'.

wage hierarchy participate in the co-production of new systems of values, of producing what is of common value together'.[58] Therefore, commons are not about being but about becoming and about what Nancy called 'being-in-common or being-with'.[59] There is no single ontological basis for the commons; there are no objective characteristics that are shared among the goods that are commons because the commons are understood in this context not as things or resources but the outputs of ongoing social processes, joint action and social cooperation.[60]

For many scholars,[61] commoning processes are bottom-up shared endeavours developing through occupations and struggles against capitalism. Commoning is about transformations and the constitution of new social relations beyond those imposed by capitalist relations. Commoning movements are revolutionary in character. Such representation of commoning as a post-capitalist practice is also present in Hardt and Negri's *Commonwealth*,[62] in which the commons revolve around the production of the social as an autonomous mode of organisation outside capitalist relations. It is through these forms of social-ecological organisations that push against practices based on commodity production and capital accumulation, Hardt and Negri argue, that the commons are (re) produced. In a similar vein, reviewing the emergence of different forms of commons beyond the classical physical entities, Holder and Flessas have argued that commons are political tools against capitalism and signifiers of practices of resistance.[63] And again, De Angelis argues that the struggles of the commons are against an outside social force-capital.[64] An often-cited examples is the Italian protest movement No TAV from the 1990s in which citizens have contested the development of high-speed trains as a symbol of the mismanagement of the commons, the environment and state funds. Another example is the occupations of urban cultural spaces such as the Valle Theatre in Rome where the commoners/occupiers were interested in guaranteeing collective use of the spaces through collective decision-making and the development of their own byelaws and rules of self-determination.[65] As for the relationship between commoning and the law, for Hardt and Negri, as much as for Mattei and others,[66] commoning is irreconcilable with the Western

[58] De Angelis, 'The Production of the Commons', p. 958 (emphasis added)

[59] J. L. Nancy, 'Of Being-in-Common', in Miami Theory Collective (ed.), *Community at Loose Ends* (University of Minnesota Press, 1991, transl. by J. Creech), pp. 1–12.

[60] Bollier and Helfrich, 'Overture', in Bollier and Helfrich (eds.), *Patterns of Commoning*; U. Mattei, *Beni Comuni. Un Manifesto* (Laterza, 2011).

[61] Mattei, Beni Comuni; Bollier and Helfrich, 'Overture', in Bollier and Helfrich (eds.), Patterns of Commoning.

[62] M. Hardt and A. Negri, *Commonwealth* (Harvard University Press, 2009).

[63] Holder and Flessas, 'Emerging Commons'.

[64] De Angelis, 'The Production of the Commons'.

[65] Statuto Fondazione Teatro Valle Bene Comune 2013 at: www.teatrovalleoccupato.it/wp-content/uploads/2013/10/STATUTO-FONDAZIONE-TEATRO-VALLE-BENE-COMUNE.pdf.

[66] Holder and Flessas, 'Emerging Commons', p. 301.

juridical system, it is indeed against it, produced by alternative social-ecological relations and ways of being in common. For these authors, the Western legal system, being complicit in the project of capitalism, cannot accommodate the commons. These authors concur in saying that practices creating the commons are radical interventions aimed at subverting the capital-centric hierarchical Western legal system.

Although these arguments are politically interesting, such negative and uni-lateral portrayal of the law contraposed to commoning as anti-capitalist revolutionary practice is too one-sided and potentially misrepresenting a more complex legal framework. This book does not dismiss at once official environmental law and MPAs in search for radical, alternative practices outside capitalist relations because this would simplify the complex field of environmental law and the multiple and diverse engagements that sea-users have with the law. Indeed, what the book does is taking law seriously, showing how marine conservation law sometimes open up spaces for commoning, pushing for the sharing of decision-making while at other times close them off. This is especially visible in Chapter 5 on processes of decision-making and in Chapter 8 on English marine conservation law following EU Exit, which raises key questions of democratic accountability.

Hence, the more politicised discourse that pervades much of the commoning literature is not at the core of this analysis. Rather, what is taken from the literature on commoning is the emphasis on shared practices, decision-making and active (marine) citizenship, the emphasis on the production of the social through a careful legal analysis. Moreover, drawing on the more-than-human literature discussed in Part 2 regarding the processes of territorialisation and deterritorialisation, it is important to add a more relational social–ecological understanding to the productive understanding of the commons envisaged by the commoning scholars. The processes at play in commoning are not just social ones but involve a complex set of relationships between human and non-human subjects. Speaking in terms of the social–ecological production of the commons serves to capture human and non-human interrelations and denotes the continuous remaking of the commons. A commons is not a natural thing existing a priori over which a society operates but something that is constituted through acting and doing in common of human and non-humans. For example, Gibson et al.,[67] using the example of commoning the air through the successful regulatory response to the hole in the ozone layer, show that commoning communities are an assemblage of political, legal entities, people learning to be affected, strategies and more than human elements too, including chemical compound and reactions, satellites and scientific tools. This has important implications for thinking about environmental democracy as the

[67] K. Gibson, S. Healy and J. Cameroon, 'Commoning as a Postcapitalist Politics', in A. Amin and P. Howell (eds.), *Releasing the Commons: Rethinking the Futures of the Commons* (Routledge, 2006), pp. 192–212.

constituencies represented in decision-making should be representative of the more-than-human too and of the multiple interrelations that are formed in marine assemblages. The task of representing the more-than-human is often left to environmental NGOs, whose role will be discussed in Chapter 6.

To a certain extent, the procedural turn in commoning here discussed accords with conservation scholars' longstanding call for participatory decision-making.[68] However, often these accounts do not propose a very nuanced understanding of participation, not asking who/what should be part of such participatory community and which form participation should take. This means that significant and complex multi-scalar social–ecological relations contributing and affecting conservation decision-making and responses may have been overlooked. In my view, the language of commoning permits a more sophisticated analysis of the communities involved or not involved in marine conservation decision-making, as explored in Chapters 5, 6 and 8 below.

1.5 Conclusion

This chapter has introduced the complexity of MPAs using the language of the commons. The loose conceptual boundaries of the commons' scholarship, which could be criticisable for adding vagueness to an already intricate field, have been used productively in this context to offer two main readings of MPAs – one, following the more orthodox CPRs scholarship and the other following scholarship on commoning.

The first reading posits MPAs as a regulatory tool to manage CPRs. Such spatialising strategies can be seen in a positive light if portrayed as an objective and technical attempt to avoid environmental tragedies and free-riding behaviour, falling within the category of new commons or in a negative light if portrayed as a political attempt at dispossessing local resource users, falling within the category of enclosures. In both cases, the commons are conceived as material resources, pre-existing social and regulatory relations. Besides, introducing more than-human geography insights, it was states that MPAs territorialising practices are far from the drawing of definite lines on a muted sea surface but are subject to and affected by many re-workings and interactions

[68] F. Berkes, 'Evolution of Co-management: Role of Knowledge Generation, Bridging Organizations and Social Learning', (2009) 90 *Journal of Environmental Management* 1692–1702; G. Borrini-Feyerabend et al., *Sharing Power. Learning-by-Doing in Co-management of Natural Resources throughout the World* (IIED and IUCN/CEESP, and Cenesta, 2004); J. Pretty and H. Ward, 'Social Capital and the Environment' (2001) 29 *World Development* 209–227; S. Jentoft, B. J. McCay and D. C. Wilson, 'Social Theory and Fisheries Co-management' (1998) 22 *Marine Policy* 423–436; L. Carlsson and F. Berkes, 'Co-management: Concepts and Methodological Implications' (2005) 75 *Journal of Environmental Management* 65–76; E. Pinkerton (ed.), *Co-operative Management of Local Fisheries* (University of British Columbia Press, 1989); B. J. McCay and J. M. Acheson (eds.), *The Question of the Commons: The Culture and Ecology of Communal Resources* (University of Arizona Press, 1987).

in a more-than-human world. Hence, MPAs territorialising practices can be destabilised by diverse assemblages.

The second reading moves away from an understating of MPAs as regulatory tools managing CPRs and focuses more on MPAs as institutional sites where processes of commoning or un-commoning take place. Characterising MPAs as commoning institutional sites means that they may facilitate institutional strategies aimed at social cooperation, at processes of collective decision-making for the production of shared values and responsibilities over a purpose that is not predetermined. Vice versa, MPAs as un-commoning institutional sites mean that they may hinder social cooperation by fostering only certain practices and knowledges of the nature to be protected. Drawing on the more-than-human geography insights, it was also pointed out that commoning is not solely a social production but a social-ecological one and it is constantly negotiated, reproduced and destabilised by the intertwining of human and non-human entities. This point is valuable for two reasons: on the one hand, it allows us to build a wide conceptualisation of environmental democracy, calling for multiple representations of such human and non-human entanglements; on the other, it holds an epistemological value because by including also what is 'in excess of humanism', to use Whatmore's vocabulary,[69] it points to the importance of perspectives and knowledges that may be left out in conservation strategies and calls for a redistribution of expertise in decision-making.

Thus, bringing in discourses on commoning enables one to move beyond a single focus on questions of distribution of resources, dear to CPRs scholars, to questions of procedures and participatory decision-making. However, this does not mean that questions of distributions should be excluded from the analysis and attention given only to procedural issues as that would provide only a partial representation of what the law on MPAs intends to do. It is precisely the multiple, and sometimes, contradictory legal understandings of MPAs that this book tries to uncover and that is why this chapter has used the language of the commons to introduce such complexity. Given the domestic and socio-legal nature of this book, attention will be given to the role of English environmental law and its implementation in characterising and discussing MPAs. The next chapter introduces English marine conservation law's tools and institutions, following the conceptual threads identified here.

[69] S. Whatmore, 'Humanism's Excess: Some Thoughts on the "Post-human/ist" Agenda' (2004) 36 *Environment and Planning A* 1360–1363.

2

Multi-level Regulation of English Marine Protected Areas

An Introductory Map

2.1 Introduction

This chapter continues the discussion on spatialisation of regulation by examining the multi-level regulation architecture at play in English marine conservation law, offering an overview of the various legal instruments and regulatory bodies. The chapter starts by highlighting the role of international legal and policy drivers on domestic conservation law. In a post-Brexit world, the role of international law is bound to become even more significant, hence the fact that the UK is a party to many multilateral environmental agreements setting out conservation obligations is significant. The chapter then moves to the legal regime for the protection of marine biodiversity in England, starting with an introduction into the regulatory bodies and then focusing on the two main legal instruments for the designation and management of MPAs: the Habitats Regulations and the MCAA, offering a comparison between the two in terms of designation and management provisions. Finally, a note on key implementation challenges is offered. The legal map presented is framed using the conceptual categories of new commons and enclosures defined in Chapter 1.

2.2 English MPAs in Context

England has a high number of MPAs, covering 51 per cent of inshore waters, that is waters defined by mean high water and the UK territorial sea limit,[1] and 37 per cent of offshore waters, that is waters between 12 and 200 nautical miles, the limit of the UK xclusive conomic one.[2] Where are the policy drivers and legal obligations for establishing these MPAs coming from? It is useful to start this legal overview by providing a brief presentation of the multiple and complex international legal and policy drivers influencing English marine conservation law, including Decisions of the

[1] Up to 12 nautical miles from charted baseline.

[2] JNCC, UK marine protected area network statistics, last updated March 2021 at: http://jncc.defra.gov.uk/page-7619.

Biodiversity Convention[3] and Sustainable Development Goals under the United Nations Agenda 2030.[4]

These various drivers have similar but not identical objectives. Although they all put marine conservation protection at the core and promote the establishment of MPAs, some focus more on quantitative aspects, while others include also the qualitative dimension of conservation. For example, if Sustainable Development Goal 14, Target 5 shares with Aichi Target 11 under the Biodiversity Convention the goal of protecting 10 per cent of coastal and marine areas, Aichi Target 11 moves beyond a purely quantitative representation of marine biodiversity protection, adding that these areas are to be conserved 'through effectively and equitably managed, ecologically representative and well-connected systems of protected areas and other effective area-based conservation measures, and integrated into the wider landscapes and seascapes'.[5]

To comply with international and regional conservation obligations, namely the Biodiversity Convention, the OSPAR Convention, the Ramsar Convention, the Habitats and Birds Directives and the Marine Strategy Framework Directive (MSFD),[6] the UK has designated MPAs. Briefly, the Biodiversity Convention contains specific references to protected areas under article 8(a), which encourages parties to establish a system of protected areas where special measures need to be taken to conserve biological diversity. The OSPAR Convention, Annex V requires parties to take the necessary measures to protect and conserve the ecosystems and the biological diversity of the maritime area and to restore, where practicable, marine areas adversely affected. Under article 2.1 of the Ramsar Convention, parties are to designate suitable wetlands in their territories and may incorporate coastal zones adjacent to wetlands and islands or bodies of marine water deeper than six meters at low tide lying within the wetlands. As for EU law, article 3 of the Habitats Directive requires the establishment of a network of protected areas, known as Natura 2000, which comprises both SACs designated under article 4 of the Habitats Directive and SPAs designated under article 4(1) of the Birds Directive. Marine SACs and SPAs are

[3] United Nations Environmental Programme (UNEP) (2004), Decision adopted by the Conference of the Parties to the Convention on Biological Diversity at Its Seventh Meeting, UNEP/CBD/COP/DEC/VII/5, paragraph 19; UNEP (2011), Decision adopted by the Conference of the Parties to the Convention on Biological Diversity at Its Tenth Meeting, Annex, paragraph 13; UNEP/CBD/COP/DEC/X/2. UNEP (2011), Decision adopted by the Conference of the Parties to the Convention on Biological Diversity at Its Tenth Meeting, UNEP/CBD/COP/DEC/X/29, paragraph 2.

[4] UN (2015) GA Resolution *Transforming Our World: The 2030 Agenda for Sustainable Development,* 25 September 2015 A/Res/70/1. Sustainable Development Goal 14, Target 5 reads: 'By 2020, conserve at least 10% of coastal and marine areas, consistent with national and international law and based on the best available scientific information' Indicator 14.5.1 reads: 'Coverage of protected areas in relation to marine areas'.

[5] UNEP/CBD/COP/DEC/X/2, paragraph 13.

[6] Council Directive 2008/56/EC of the European Parliament and of the Council of 17 June 2008 establishing a framework for community action in the field of marine environmental policy, OJ L 164/19 (the MSFD).

collectively referred to as European Marine Sites. Due to Brexit, the Habitats Regulations, which transpose the Habitats and Birds Directives into English law, have been recently amended by EU Exit Habitats Regulations.[7] When references are made throughout this book to the Habitats Regulations, they are to the original 2017 version, and when references are made to the Habitats Regulations, as amended, they are to the amendments brought about by the EU Exit Habitats Regulations to the Habitats Regulations in 2019.

Finally, article 13(4) of the MSFD requires that any programme of measures to achieve or maintain good environmental status of EU waters[8] include spatial protection measures to contribute to coherent and representative networks of MPAs. In addition, paragraph 6 of the Preamble of the MSFD states that MPAs, including those designated under the Habitats and Birds Directive and other international or regional agreements to which the Member States are parties, are an important contribution to the achievement of good environmental status, hence making explicit links to other commitments and allowing Member States to use MPAs designated under other legislation to fulfil obligations under the MSFD, which has been transposed in England by the Marine Strategy Regulations 2010,[9] amended[10] due to Brexit.

By contrast, domestic primary legislation on marine conservation has been dormant until recently, given that the attention of the principal English statute on nature conservation, the Wildlife and Countryside Act 1981, is on terrestrial protected areas, known as SSSIs, and only provides for the establishment of MPAs very close to shore.[11] The passing of the MCAA has made an important contribution to the English protected areas seascape, introducing a new type of designation, the MCZs[12] and requiring the creation of a network of

[7] The Conservation of Habitats and Species (Amendment) (EU Exit) Regulations 2019 (SI 2019/579).

[8] Good environmental status is the key objective of the MSFD, and it is defined under Article 3 as 'The environmental status of marine waters where these provide ecologically diverse and dynamic oceans and seas which are clean, healthy and productive'. Annex I of the MSFD sets out eleven descriptors to help interpret the meaning of good environmental status and a Commission Decision 2017-848 of 17 May 2017 lays down criteria and methodological standards for determining good environmental status in relation to the eleven descriptors and also contains specifications for monitoring and assessing marine waters. The MSFD has been transposed in English law by the Marine Strategy Regulations 2010 (SI 2010/1627), amended by Part 3 of the Marine Environment (Amendment) (EU Exit) Regulations 2018 (SI 2018/1399).

[9] SI 2010/1627. [10] SI 2018/1399, Part 3.

[11] The Wildlife and Countryside Act 1981 provided for the establishment of Marine Nature Reserves and SSSIs. More specifically, under the Wildlife and Countryside Act 1981, Section 36 Marine Nature Reserves could be designated stretching only up to 3 nautical miles from the coast, and under Section 28 of the SSSIs with a marine component could be established. The Marine and Coastal Access Act 2009 amended the Wildlife and Countryside Act 1981 with schedule 12 allowing for the conversion of Marine Nature Reserves into Marine Conservation Zones and schedule 13 clarifying the normal seaward limit of SSSIs as being mean low water mark or land covered by estuarial waters.

[12] Section 116 of the MCAA.

MPAs including Ramsar sites, the marine component of SSSIs, MCZs and European Marine Sites.[13] All of these MPAs meet the international definition of MPAs by the IUCN as they are primarily designated for the purpose of nature conservation.[14]

Thus, on paper, the Aichi Target 11 to conserve at least 10 per cent of coastal and marine areas by 2020 has been significantly exceeded domestically. European Marine Sites and MCZs are the main designations setting out clear legal obligations, and the UK has nominated them (together with parallel designations in devolved administrations)[15] as OSPAR MPAs, contributing to the wider MPA network in the North-East Atlantic under the OSPAR Convention.[16] The legal analysis that follows will therefore be confined to European Marine Sites and MCZs.

2.3 Regulatory Bodies for Marine Conservation Law in England

There are several actors with statutory responsibilities concerning marine conservation in England, namely the Marine Management Organisation (MMO), the IFCAs, Natural England and the Joint Nature Conservation Committee (JNCC). The public and environmental NGOs are also important actors in marine conservation regulation, and their role will be discussed at length in the chapters on the democratisation of regulation in Part III of the book. The Secretary of State for the Environment, Food and Rural Affairs has also a number of statutory powers, which will be discussed in due course when reviewing the law.

The MMO is an executive non-departmental public body and the key regulatory authority under the MCAA, discharging many marine functions on behalf of the UK government.[17] Its general objective is to make a contribution to the achievement of sustainable development taking any action which it considers necessary or expedient for the purpose of furthering any social, economic or environmental purposes.[18] The Secretary of State is to give the MMO guidance as to the manner in which the MMO is to fulfil its general objective.[19] The MMO, in addition to incorporating the work of the former Marine Fisheries Agency, also acquired functions previously associated with the Department of Energy and Climate Change and the Department for Transport. Thus, its responsibilities and powers are wide ranging, including marine planning, marine licensing, nature conservation and also responding to marine emergencies. The IFCAs, previously known as the Sea Fisheries Committees (SFCs),

[13] Section 123 of the MCAA. [14] Day, IUCN Guidelines.

[15] For example, Nature Conservation MPAs under the Marine (Scotland) Act 2010.

[16] OSPAR Recommendation 2003/3 adopted by OSPAR 2003 (OSPAR 03/17/1, Annex 9), amended by OSPAR Recommendation 2010/2 (OSPAR 10/23/1, Annex 7).

[17] The MMO was established by Section 1(1) of the MCAA.

[18] Sections 2(1) and (2) of the MCAA. [19] Section 2(4) of the MCAA.

have also been established under the MCAA, Part 6 and have duties and powers in relation to fisheries management and conservation in MCZs within the 6 nautical miles.[20] IFCAs membership and operations will be explored in Chapter 6 and linked to a discussion on environmental democracy.

Natural England and JNCC are Statutory Nature Conservation Bodies (SNCBs).[21] Natural England was constituted by the Natural Environment and Rural Communities (NERC) Act 2006, Section 1 and amalgamated the functions of English Nature and the Countryside Agency, in response to the Haskins Review that had suggested a restructuring and streamlining of agencies to simplify the delivery of rural and environmental policy and to avoid blurred accountability.[22] Natural England took the conservation powers and duties of English Nature as well as the landscape, recreation and public access responsibilities of the Countryside Agency. This resulted in Natural England having a wide general purpose. Section 2 of the NERC Act 2006 states that the general purpose of Natural England is 'to ensure that the natural environment is conserved, enhanced and managed for the benefit of present and future generations, thereby contributing to sustainable development'.[23] JNCC was initially established under the Environmental Protection Act 1990 to ensure consistency in site designation standards, maintaining comparable standards for surveys, providing conservation advice nationally and internationally. It was reconstituted by the NERC Act 2006, which extended its powers from Great Britain to UK for the purpose of nature conservation and fostering the understanding of nature conservation.[24] The Secretary of State may give Natural England and JNCC general or specific directions as to the exercise of their functions,[25] which must be published, thus ministerial powers in relation to SNCBs are broad. In discharging their functions, both Natural England and JNCC must have regard to actual or possible ecological changes and the desirability of contributing to sustainable development.[26] The Conservation (Natural Habitats, & c.) Regulations 1994[27] gave Natural England responsibilities for inshore European Marine Sites, and the Offshore Marine Conservation (Natural Habitats, & c.) Regulations 2007[28] gave JNCC responsibilities for

[20] Sections 153 and 154 of the MCAA.

[21] Natural England has been established under Section 1 of the NERC Act. JNCC has been re-constituted under Section 31 of the NERC Act. There are different SNCBs in the devolved administration (e.g. the Scottish body corresponding to Natural England is known as NatureScot), but JNCC operates at the UK level.

[22] DEFRA, *Rural Delivery Review: A report on the delivery of government policies in rural England by Christopher Haskins* (DERFA 2003) at: www.tgsystems.org.uk/Gefag/haskins_full_report.pdf.

[23] Section 2(1) of the NERC Act 2006.

[24] Section 33(1) of the NERC Act 2006.

[25] Sections 16 and 38 of the NERC Act.

[26] Section 33(2) of the NERC Act 2006.

[27] SI 1994/2716.

[28] SI 2007/1842.

offshore European Marine Sites. With the MCAA, the SNCBs responsibilities were extended also in relation to the MCZs, inshore for Natural England and offshore for JNCC.

2.4 English MPAs as Regulatory Tools

English MPAs support the protection of specific features that are of domestic or international importance. Features range from vulnerable reefs and sandbanks to species such as harbour porpoise, to sandeels and marine birds such as the black-legged kittiwake. MCZs can be designated 'for the purpose of conserving (a) marine flora or fauna; (b) marine habitats or types of marine habitat; (c) features of geological or geomorphological interest'.[29] The references to the conservation of (a) and (b) include conserving their diversity (Section 117(5)), and the references to the conservation of (a) also include the conservation of any species that is rare or threatened (Section 117(4)).

More restrictively, European Marine Sites are designated only for the protection of specific habitats and species listed under Annexes I and II of the Habitats Directive[30] and Annex I of the Birds Directive and migratory species of birds not listed in Annex I.[31] Moreover, no socio-economic interests can be taken into account at the designation stage, as CJEU case law has made blatantly clear.[32] Differently, the MCAA allows for socio-economic interests to be taken into account at the designation stage.[33] Thus, although there are differences in what is protected under European Marine Sites and MCZs and the interests that can be considered at the designation stage, both types of designation are established primarily for the purpose of conserving nature and, in this light, they can be considered new commons, in the sense discussed in Chapter 1, as they are protecting a global common, that is, biodiversity for humankind. This implies that the primary beneficiaries, next to nature, are humanity at large and future generations, rather than local resource users.

Conversely, from the perspective of local sea-users and coastal communities, English MPAs can be perceived as negative enclosure as their establishment may involve restrictions on their activities for the conservation of nature. Indeed, both the laws on European Marine Sites and MCZs provide for restriction on activities through a command and control style of regulation.[34] This is very different from primary legislation regulating land-based protected areas, that is, SSSIs, where partnerships between landowners/occupiers and SNCBs

[29] Section 117(1) of the MCAA. [30] Article 2 of the Habitats Directive.
[31] Articles 4(1) and 4(2) of the Birds Directive. [32] *ex parte First Corporate Shipping.*
[33] Section 117(7) of the MCAA.
[34] Command and control regulation can be defined as direct regulation by the state through legal rules backed by enforcement powers.

are sought and powers to enter into management agreements granted.[35] In the sea, following the designation of a European Marine Site, a management scheme may be established by the relevant authorities under which their functions can be exercised to ensure compliance with the Directives.[36] Exercising 'their functions' include the power to make byelaws for the protection of a site,[37] and the provisions to make byelaws for MCZs under Section 129 of the MCAA apply.[38]

Moreover, to prevent the deterioration of sites and disturbance of species, any plan or project not directly connected with the management of the site but likely to have a significant effect on the site is subject to an appropriate assessment of its implications for the site in view of the site's conservation objectives,[39] known as habitats regulation assessment (HRA) under English law. The relevant SNCB[40] must be consulted for the purpose of the assessment and regard must be had to its representations.[41] Less stringent measures regard the inclusion of public opinion. A competent authority has the power, but not the duty, to take into account the opinion of the public when assessing the implications of a proposed plan or project on a European Marine Site, if it considers it appropriate.[42] If the appropriate assessment is negative, that is to say it has not been ascertained that the plan or project in question will not adversely affect the integrity of the site, consent cannot be granted.

The meaning of plan and project, as interpreted by the CJEU, is extensive as it refers also to ongoing projects, as in the case of fisheries. As will be discussed in Chapter 4, to comply with this provision, a revised approach to the management of fisheries in European Marine Sites was introduced in England. Although the provisions do not require a complete ban on development,[43] they have been interpreted in the light of a very strong precautionary logic by the CJEU. For example, it has been ruled that mitigation measures cannot be taken into account when carrying out screening for appropriate assessment.[44] An appropriate assessment cannot be side-stepped by anticipating the beneficial consequences of a habitat creation mitigating the negative effects of a plan or project.[45] Cumulative effects, resulting from the combination of a plan or

[35] Section 28 of the Wildlife and Countryside Act 1981, as amended by schedule 9 of the Countryside and Rights of Way Act 2000.

[36] Regulation 38 of the Habitats Regulations.

[37] Regulation 40(1) of the Habitats Regulations.

[38] Regulation 40(3) of the Habitats Regulations.

[39] Regulation 63 of the Habitats Regulations.

[40] Natural England for inshore waters and JNCC for offshore waters.

[41] Regulation 63(3) of the Habitats Regulations.

[42] Regulation 63(4) of the Habitats Regulations.

[43] Case C-2/10 *Azienda Agro-Zootecnica Franchini sarl and Eolica di Altamura Srl v Regione Puglia* [2011] ECR I-06561.

[44] Case C-323/17 *People over Wind, Peter Sweetman v Coillte Teoranta* ECLI:EU:C:2018:244 (*People over Wind*)

[45] Joined Cases C-387/15 and C-388/15 *Hilde Orleans and Others v Vlaams Gewest* ECLI:EU:C:2016:583 (*Orleans*).

project with other plan or projects, must be taken into account in the appropriate assessment.[46] Compensatory measures cannot be taken into account as part of the appropriate assessment[47] and in considering whether the integrity of the site will be affected, no reasonable scientific doubt should remain and the precautionary principle should apply.[48]

Derogations apply. Notwithstanding a negative appropriate assessment, the plan or project can be carried out if there are no alternative solutions[49] and there are imperative reasons of overriding public interest (IROPI), including those a social or economic nature.[50] Neither the Habitats Directive nor the Habitats Regulations provide any guidance on the meaning of 'alternative solutions', though CJEU case law has shed some light. In *Commission v Portugal*, the Advocate General stated that if there are several appropriate measures, a proportionality test applies according to which recourse must be had to the least onerous appropriate measure[51] and evidence shown that all alternatives have been considered. However, this does not mean that the option having the least adverse effect on the site must be chosen as a balance between the adverse effect on the site and IROPI must be struck.[52] The interest must be both public and overriding[53] but, although interests of a purely private nature will not constitute imperative reasons, a private plan or project that has public benefit could be considered an imperative reason in some circumstances.[54] The social and economic interest must be 'of such an importance that it can be weighed up against that Directive's objective of the conservation of natural habitats and wild fauna and flora'.[55] As the Department of Environment Food and Rural Affairs (DEFRA) guidance on the Habitats Regulations states 'plans or projects that only provide short-term or very localised benefits are less likely to be able to show imperative reasons of overriding public interest'.[56]

[46] C-127/02 *Landelijke Vereniging tot Behoud van de Waddenzee, Nederlandse Vereniging tot Bescherming van Vogels v Staatssecretaris Van Landbouw, Natuurbeheer en Visserij* [2004] ECR I-07405, para 53 (*Waddenzee*).

[47] C-521/12 *TC Briels and Others v Minister van Infrastructuur en Milieu* ECLI:EU:C:2014:330.

[48] *Waddenzee*; C-258/11 *Peter Sweetman and Others v An Bord Pleanála* ECLI:EU:C:2013 (*Sweetman*).

[49] This includes the option of doing nothing. Case C-239/04 *Commission v Portugal* [2006] ECR I-10183 (*Commission v Portugal*).

[50] Regulation 64(1) of the Habitats Regulations and article 6(4) of the Habitats Directive.

[51] *Commission* v. *Portugal*, Opinion of Advocate General Kokott, para 42.

[52] Ibid, para 44.

[53] Case C-411/17 *Inter-Environnement Wallonie ASBL and Bond Beter Leefmilieu Vlaanderen ASBL v Conseil des ministres* ECLI:EU:C:2019:622, para 155; *Marie-Noëlle Solvay and Others v Région wallonne* ECLI:EU:C:2012:82, para 75 (*Solvay and Others*).

[54] Ibid. [55] Ibid, para 75.

[56] DEFRA, 'Guidance – Habitats regulations assessments: protecting a European site' (DEFRA 2021) at: www.gov.uk/guidance/habitats-regulations-assessments-protecting-a-european-site.

Moreover, if the site hosts a priority natural habitat or species,[57] the imperative reasons are restricted to those relating to human health, public safety or beneficial consequences of primary importance to the environment or any other reason the competent authority regards to be IROPI.[58] If consent for a plan or project is granted on the grounds of IROPI, then the competent authority must secure that any necessary compensatory measure is taken to ensure the overall coherence of the national site network.[59] The opinion of the European Commission before Brexit and, now, of the appropriate authority can be sought in making a decision, and in giving its opinion, the appropriate authority must have regard to the national interest and must consult and have regard to the opinion of JNCC and where, the appropriate authority is the Secretary of State, the devolved administrations.[60]

Therefore, the ways in which plans and projects are assessed in European Marine Sites show a strong presumption in favour of long-term conservation goals, and a command and control style of regulation as decisions are entirely in the hands of public authorities, with the public marginal to decision-making. Evidently, European Marine Sites are 'new commons' if we embrace the perspective of the conservation of biodiversity as the common concern of humankind, but they may turn into enclosures if the perspective is that of local sea-users, whose concerns may be deemed to be short-term and not IROPI, but nevertheless significant for their livelihoods.

Not dissimilarly, the management of MCZs is based on a command-and-control style of regulation. Management varies depending on whether the activity requires licensing authorisation from a relevant public authority or not before it can be carried out. For activities requiring authorisation, it is an offence to carry out a licensable marine activity or cause or permit any other person to carry on such an activity, without a marine licence[61] or fail to comply with any conditions of a marine licence.[62] Section 126 of the MCAA outlines the procedure to be followed by the public authority to determine whether to grant authorisation for the doing of an act that is capable of affecting, other than insignificantly, the protected features of an MCZ or any ecological or

[57] These are defined in article 1(d) and article (h) of the Habitats Directive. Priority natural habitats means those in danger of disappearance and are indicated by an asterisk in Annex I; priority species mean species of community interest that are endangered and are indicated by an asterisk in Annex II.

[58] Regulation 64(2) of the Habitats Regulations. Please note this has been amended by regulation 25 of the EU Exit Habitats Regulations as before Brexit, the appropriate authority should have had due regard to the opinion of the European Commission.

[59] Regulation 68 of the Habitats Regulations. Regulation 68 of the Habitats Regulations refers to Natura 2000 network. The national site network is the new name of the network of Natura 2000 as per regulation 4(2)(a) of the EU Exit Habitats Regulations.

[60] Regulation 64(4) of the Habitats Regulations, as amended by regulation 25(4) of the EU Exit Habitats Regulations.

[61] Sections 65(1) and 85(2) of the MCAA.

[62] Section 85(2) of the MCAA.

geomorphological process on which the conservation of any protected features of an MCZ is (wholly or in part) dependent. If the authority believes that there is or may be a significant risk to the achievement of the conservation objectives of the MCZ, the authority must notify the appropriate SNCB and then wait a period of 28 days before making a decision, unless the authority thinks there is an urgent need to grant authorisation or the SNCB tells the authority there is no need to wait until the end of the period.

There is no requirement to follow the advice of the SNCB, only to have regard to it,[63] effectively weakening the role of the SNCBs compared to the role they have for European Marine Sites. To date, there is no case law elucidating the meaning of 'significant effect' for MCZs. According to the MMO guidance on MCZs and marine licensing, in determining significance, the likelihood and magnitude of that effect is to be considered and the potential risk any such effect may cause on either the protected feature of the MCZs or any ecological or geomorphological process on which the conservation of any protected features is dependent.[64] Authorisation can be granted only if there is no significant risk of the act hindering the achievement of the conservation objectives for the MCZ. Like for European Marine Sites, derogations apply if there are no alternatives, the public benefit of proceeding with the act outweighs the environmental risk and compensatory measures will be taken.[65]

Although there is no case law on the derogations, DEFRA issued guidance specifying that in considering whether there are no alternatives, the authority should consider whether there are other suitable and available sites, and whether different approaches, timings, methods, etc., would create a lower risk.[66] If that is not the case, then the applicant will need to demonstrate that the benefit of carrying out the activity clearly outweighs its environmental costs. The benefit must be a public benefit rather than a private benefit to a small number of individuals, for example, if it is indispensable or desirable within the framework of national policies, or to protect public health and safety or fulfil public service or statutory obligations. Compared to exceptions under regulation 64 of the Habitats Regulations for European Marine Sites, the exceptions related to the carrying on an act significantly affecting MCZs seem more stringent given that Section 126(7) inserts a risk threshold consideration, specifying that

[63] Section 126(10) of the MCAA.

[64] Marine Management Organisation. 'Guidance-Marine Conservation Zones and Marine Licensing' (Marine Management Organisation 2013) at: https://assets.publishing.service.gov.uk/government/uploads/system/uploads/attachment_data/file/410273/Marine_conservation_zones_and_marine_licensing.pdf.

[65] Section 126(7) of the MCAA.

[66] DEFRA, 'Guidance on the Duties on Public Authorities in Relation to Marine Conservation Zones (Note 2)' (DEFRA 2010), p. 13 at: https://infrastructure.planninginspectorate.gov.uk/wp-content/ipc/uploads/projects/EN010080/EN010080-001544-Orsted%20Hornsea%20Project%20Three%20(UK)%20Ltd%20-%20Appendix%2051%20-%20Defra%20MCZ%20Guidance%202010.pdf.

alternatives creating a lower risk need to be considered versus the more generic 'alternative solutions' requirement in the Habitats Regulations, though, as discussed above, the case law of the CJEU has provided some guidance. However, the decision for granting derogations to site management requirements for MCZs does not contemplate seeking a third view, while for European Marine Sites opinions can be sought and consultations carried out, adding an extra layer of decision-making and contributing to collaborative governance.

The requirements for the exercise of public authorities' functions in MCZs are to be found in Section 125. Although public authorities have a duty to carry out their functions in a manner in which they consider 'best furthers',[67] the conservation objectives stated for the MCZ, where that is not possible, they can carry out their functions in the manner which the authority considers 'least hinders' the achievement of the conservation objectives.[68] Consideration should be given to whether there is an alternative way to carry out the activity which may have a substantially lower impact on MCZ. If the authority believes that there is or may be a significant risk of the act hindering the achievement of the conservation objectives of the MCZs, SNCB needs to be notified and must wait 28 days before doing an act but again the only requirement is to 'have regard' to the SNCB's advice, rather than to follow it.[69] The SNCB can ask for a written explanation from the authority as to why its advice has been followed but has no further powers to require compliance with its advice.[70]

Compared to European Marine Sites, provisions related to management of MCZs under the MCAA are weaker from a nature conservation perspective given that public authorities are afforded wide discretion regarding management decisions and the role of the SNCBs is less central.

Activities that do not require licensing are not left unregulated. The MMO has the power to make byelaws to further the conservation objectives of a MCZ.[71] IFCAs have also powers to impose byelaws to further the conservation objectives of a MCZ.[72] Byelaw provisions include prohibiting or restricting entry into the site and in seashore areas adjoining it, prohibiting or restricting the killing, taking, destruction, molestation or disturbance of animals and plants within the site, prohibiting or restricting the doing of anything interfering with the seabed or disturbing any object in the MCZ.[73] Permits to doing an act otherwise prohibited by the byelaw can be issued and conditions attached at

[67] 'Best furthers' means that the 'public authority should proceed in the manner which is most conducive to achieving the conservation objectives of the MCZ'. DEFRA, 'Marine Conservation Zones Designation Explanatory Note' (DEFRA 2013), p. 4 at: https://assets.publishing.service.gov.uk/government/uploads/system/uploads/attachment_data/file/259972/pb14078-mcz-explanatory-note.pdf.

[68] Section 125(2) of the MCAA. [69] Section 125(12) of the MCAA.

[70] Section 128 of the MCAA. [71] Section 129(1) of the MCAA.

[72] Section 155(1) of the MCAA. [73] Section 156 of the MCAA.

the discretion of the regulator. Consultation on the draft byelaws is required[74] as well as confirmation by the Secretary of State, unless the regulator considers that there is an urgent need to protect the site and in that case an emergency byelaw can be made, which can remain in force to up to 12 months.[75] The power to make emergency byelaws is key for making MPAs governance adaptive to changing conditions, and this is a point to which I will return in Chapter 7. The Secretary of State has the power to revoke the byelaw, and any person affected by the making of the byelaw may make representations to the Secretary of State.[76] In addition, interim byelaws can be made by the MMO even before designating an MCZ if there are or may be reasons to designate the area and there is an urgent need to protect the feature.[77]

It is an offence for a person to contravene a byelaw, including failure to comply with it,[78] and fines can be issued[79] as well as fixed monetary penalties.[80] It is also an offence to damage the protected features of MCZs and strict liability applies as it is immaterial if the person doing the prohibited act knew or ought to have known that the feature is a protected feature.[81] Importantly, it should be noted that, regardless of whether a byelaw has been enacted, any person who intentionally or recklessly causes damage to a protected feature of an MCZ, irrespectively of their knowledge that the feature in question was protected, is guilty of an offence.[82]

As for enforcement, the MCAA offers many options. Enforcement is notably difficult in environmental law, and in the marine environment, such difficulties are exacerbated due to the nature of the environment itself making observation and evidence gathering complicated. In relation to licensable activities, the MMO can issue a variety of statutory notices, including variation, suspension, revocation notices[83] as well as compliance[84] and remediation notices.[85] Sanctions for non-compliance can be imposed through the criminal process.[86] Besides, civil sanctions can be used, including fixed and variable monetary penalties.[87]

[74] Section 130(6) of the MCAA.

[75] Sections 130(11) and 1(1) of the MCAA. For IFCAs emergency byelaws, see Section 157 of the MCAA.

[76] Section 131(4)(c) of the MCAA. [77] Section 132(1) of the MCAA.

[78] Section 139(1) of the MCAA. [79] Section 139 of the MCAA.

[80] Section 142 of the MCAA.

[81] Section 140(3) of the MCAA. Though it should be noted that liability applies if the person at the time of doing the act knew or ought to have known that the feature is within an MCZ, as per Section 140(1)(b) of the MCAA.

[82] Section 140 of the MCAA. [83] Section 72 of the MCAA.

[84] Section 90 of the MCAA. [85] Section 91 of the MCAA.

[86] Breach of requirement for, or conditions of, a licence can be punishable with a fine and/or imprisonment not exceeding two years under Section 85(4) of the MCAA.

[87] Sections 90–91 MCAA.

The enforcement body has also a choice between criminal[88] and civil sanctions also regarding marine conservation byelaws.[89]

This legal review shows that, although there are some differences in both designation and management between European Marine Sites and MCZs, both types of MPAs are for the purpose of nature conservation and derogations to protection requirements are limited only to overriding public interest, hence both European Marine Sites and MCZs can be considered new commons, protecting biodiversity and the public interest. At the same time, employing a command-and-control style of regulation, from the perspectives of sea-users directly affected by their designations, they may be perceived as enclosures. However, much depends on how they operate in practice. Do English MPAs deliver on their conservation objectives or are they more akin to paper parks, that is to say lines drawn on a map not offering a high level of environmental protection on the ground? This is a very broad question and will be answered throughout the book considering specific aspects of MPAs law and regulation. For the time being, a note on implementation will be offered below to identify key implementation gaps. If some of these challenges are visible through a desk-based analysis, other have been highlighted by the research participants during elite interviews conducted in May 2021, demonstrating the relevance of conducting empirical work for gaining a more nuanced picture of MPAs regulation.

2.5 Implementation of English MPAs Law: A Note on Key Implementation Challenges

At a broad level, two main lines of critiques can be raised regarding the implementation of MPAs law in England. One regards the slow designation of MCZs and the other the lack of active management in many MPAs, comprising European Marine Sites.

To designate MCZs, in England the Marine Conservation Zones Project, led by SNCBs, was launched in 2008[90] and four regional projects set up in 2009 with the aim to identify MCZs to be recommended for designation.[91] The regional projects, about which more will be said in Chapter 5, comprised a large number of stakeholders from various marine sectors, who met regularly over a period of two years to finalise the list of recommended MCZs (rMCZs). Their work was guided

[88] Sections 139(2) and 163(3) of the MCAA.

[89] Section 142(1) of the MCAA. For fisheries offences, penalty notices can be issued under the Sea Fishing (Penalty Notices) (England) Order 2011(SI 2011/758).

[90] JNCC, 'Marine Conservation Zones: Designation Process' at: https://jncc.gov.uk/our-work/marine-conservation-zones#designation-process.

[91] The four regional projects were: 'Finding Sanctuary' (South-Wet), 'Balanced Seas' (South-East), 'NetGain' (North-East) and Irish Seas. The areas were chosen to reflect social, environmental and economic differences between the seas in England.

by the Ecological Network Guidance (ENG),[92] which had been created by the SNCBs to define the ecological criteria for the MPAs so to meet the 'ecological coherent' requirement of MPAs network under Section 123 of the MCAA. Independent scientific advice and feedback were also provided by a Science Advisory Panel, comprising national and international natural scientists.[93]

Of the 127 rMCZs submitted to DEFRA in 2011 by the regional projects, which included 65 Reference Areas,[94] the government decided to designate only twenty-seven in 2013 and introduced a phased approach to designation. Such designation choice was justified notwithstanding the lack of adequately robust evidence, despite previous government commitment to designate MCZs on the 'best available evidence' and government guidance stating that 'lack of full scientific certainty should not be a reason for postponing proportionate decisions on site selection'.[95] This evidence-intensive approach remained a characteristics of subsequent designation phases, despite reiterating the commitment to use 'best available evidence'.[96] This was described by the Science and Technology Committee as 'shifting the goalposts'[97] and not being underpinned by a very strong precautionary approach, attracting also the criticism of the Environment Audit Committee.[98] Twenty-three MCZs were designated in the second tranche in 2016 and forty-one MCZs and twelve additional features in the third tranche in 2019 to fill the network gaps. None of the MCZs designated are so-called Reference Areas. This is hardly surprising due to the fact that Reference Areas were the 'most controversial' aspects of the recommendations,[99] effectively enclosing the sea by prohibiting commercial and recreational activities.

Regarding management, many MCZs still lack active management, and this is in part a consequence of the sluggish designation process, given that some

[92] Natural England and Joint Nature Conservation Committee. 'MCZ Project: Ecological Network Guidance' (Natural England and Joint Nature Conservation Committee 2010), at: https://data.jncc.gov.uk/data/94f961af-0bfc-4787-92d7-0c3bcf0fd083/MCZ-Ecological-Network-Guidance-2010.pdf.

[93] Natural England and Joint Nature Conservation Committee, 'Fact Sheet: A Stakeholder-Led Process-How Were Sea Users and Other Interest Groups Involved in Recommending Marine Conservation Zones' (Natural England and Joint Nature Conservation Committee 2012) at: http://publications.naturalengland.org.uk/publication/2033479.

[94] Reference Areas were the name attributed to MPAs with the highest level of protection, where greater restrictions on commercial and recreational activities are needed, akin to a no-take zone.

[95] DEFRA, 'Guidance on the proposed approach to the selection and designation of Marine Conservation Zones under Part 5 of the Marine and Coastal Access Act' (DEFRA 2010), p. 8.

[96] Environmental Audit Committee, *Marine Protected Areas Revisited* (2016–2017, HC 597), para 10.

[97] Science and Technology Committee, *Marine Science* (2012–2013, HC 727), para 23.

[98] Environmental Audit Committee, *Marine Protected Areas* (2014–2015, HC 221).

[99] D. Hirst, 'Marine Conservation Zones in England', Briefing paper, number 06129, 17 July 2015. House of Commons Library, at: https://researchbriefings.files.parliament.uk/documents/SN06129/SN06129.pdf.

sites have only recently being designated but is also part of a slow approach to managing sites, also noted by the Environment Audit Committee.[100] Monitoring has also been inadequate, and this is connected to funding issues as explained below. This has negative consequences regarding not only the effectiveness of MPAs but also regulatory certainty and legitimacy as lack of clarity on management measures can contribute to a sense of uncertainty, undermining the legitimacy of the process in the eyes of those affected by it.

Although EU law does not afford Member States any discretion in decisions regarding the designation of SPAs and SACs,[101] thereby avoiding similar problems to those encountered in MCZs designation to date, the management of European Marine Sites is also problematic as many sites do not have management schemes in place. Under regulation 38(1) of the Habitats Regulations, transposing article 6(1) of the Habitats Directive and article 4 of the Birds Directive, a management scheme may be established for a European Marine Site, but, as in EU law itself, it is not a requirement. This leads to many European Marine Sites lacking management schemes, despite their usefulness to aid management of pressures and threats and improve site conditions, generating a more efficient organisation and delivery of responsibilities and operating as conduits for communication to sea-users and the general public.[102] A recent report of the Marine Conservation Society shows that bottom trawling is taking place in ninety-eight per cent of the UK's offshore MPAs designated to protect the seabed.[103]

Until EU Exit, offshore management difficulties were also complicated by the legal requirement under the Common Fisheries Policy.[104] Article 11 of the Common Fisheries Policy specifies the measures necessary to meet the conservation obligations under the Habitats, Birds and MSFD. Where the conservation measures might affect a fishery in which other Member States have a direct management interest, the European Commission can adopt the measure, upon request, by means of a delegated act. A joint recommendation can be submitted by the Member States, and the European Commission shall

[100] Environmental Audit Committee, 'Marine Protected Areas', para 39; Environmental Audit Committee, *Sustainable Seas* (2017–2019, HC 980), para 80.

[101] See for example, Case C-355/90 *Commission v Spain* [1993] ECR I-4221 on Spanish failure to designate an important wetland area as a SPA. More recently, Case C-669/16 *Commission v United Kingdom of Great Britain and Northern Ireland* ECLI:EU:C:2018:844 on the UK failure to designate SACs for the protection of harbour porpoise.

[102] Environmental Audit Committee, 'Sustainable Seas', para 80. See also R. K. A. Morris et al., 'Managing Natura 2000 in the Marine Environment – An Evaluation of the Effectiveness of "Management Schemes" in England' (2014) 87 *Ocean and Coastal Management* 40–51.

[103] F. Dunkley and J. L. Solandt, 'Marine Unprotected Areas: A Case for a Just Transition to Ban Bottom Trawl and Dredge Fishing in Offshore Marine Protected Areas' (The Marine Conservation Society, 2021), at: www.mcsuk.org/media/marine-unprotected-areas.pdf.

[104] Regulation (EU) No 1380/2013 of the European Parliament and of the Council of 11 December 2013 on the Common Fisheries Policy amending Council Regulations (EC) No 1954/2003 and (EC) No 1224/2009 and repealing Council Regulations (EC) No 2371/2002 and (EC) No 639/2004 and Council Decision 2004/585/EC, OJ 2013 No. L 354/22.

adopt the measure within three months from receipt of the request, taking into account scientific advice. In the absence of a joint recommendation, in cases of urgency the Commission shall adopt the measures. The procedural requirements set out in article 11 show how complicated it is to agree to management measures for offshore MPAs, whose boundaries include the water of more than just one Member State. A case in point is the Dogger Bank, an extensive sublittoral sandbank, designated as a SAC and spanning UK, German, Danish and Dutch waters. The SAC was left unmanaged due to the difficulties of reaching agreement among Member States involved. It was only post-Brexit that the UK had the powers to act unilaterally, and, in early 2021, it proposed a byelaw to close all the UK section of the Dogger Bank SAC to bottom trawling.[105] It should be noted that the UK's decision to introduce management measures has been not only an outcome of post-Brexit 'freedom' from article 11 of the Common Fisheries Policy, but it has also been driven by NGOs' threatening judicial review. Inshore, the situation is better with some positive examples of well-managed MPAs, but that is often down to local leadership such as those of individual IFCAs.[106] As it will be discussed in Chapter 6, IFCAs are a robust institution, playing an important role in inshore management of MPAs.

If fishing attracts most of the attention, both in terms of byelaws introduced, NGOs campaigning and Brexit, it should also be noted that there are many other activities impacting on English marine conservation. As explained by a SNCB representative, allowing multiple expansions to developments that receive consent amounts to 'death by a thousand cuts'.[107] By permitting one operation to take place because of IROPI, there is the danger that there will be more expansion in the area in the years to come. This is a point about the aggregate effects of development, a point that has been made also in the academic literature in relation to wind farms developments. Rydin et al. write 'The "creep effect" refers to a common problem in planning regulation whereby decisions are taken project by project and the aggregate impact of several projects is often under-considered'.[108] Moreover, compensatory measures to be undertaken are not necessarily strong. A SNCB representative I interviewed brought the example of Hornsea THREE, a major wind farm development where likely significant effects on fourteen European Marine Sites could not be excluded. The compensatory measures proposed in the HRA for the significantly affected benthic ecology in the North Norfolk Sandbanks and Saturn Reef SAC are weak, amounting only to a removal of the project-related

105 MMO, 'The Dogger Bank Special Area of Conservation (Specified Area) Bottom Towed Fishing Gear Byelaw 2021'.

106 J. L. Solandt, 'A Stocktake of England's MPA Network – Taking a Global Perspective Approach' (2018) 19 *Biology* 34–41.

107 SNCB national representative, online Interview, May 2021.

108 Y. Rydin et al., 'Do Local Economic Interests Matter When Regulating Nationally Significant Infrastructure? The Case of Renewable Energy Infrastructure Projects' (2018) 33 *Local Economy: The Journal of the Local Economy Policy Unit* 269–286, p. 282.

infrastructure and associated deposits that are above or protruding from the seabed within the SAC.[109]

The management challenges highlighted are also exacerbated by funding issues. Monitoring activities in the marine environment are very expensive due to the technology required, especially for offshore sites, so the number of yearly surveys that can be carried out is low.[110] This, coupled with the budget cuts within the public sector and additional pressure on local government finances exacerbated by the COVID-19 pandemic, risks rendering many MPAs paper parks. For example, Natural England's government-funded Grant in Aid budget has declined almost two-thirds over a decade, with serious consequences for the ability to fulfil their statutory duties.[111] As a House of Lords Select Committee report on the NERC Act explained, the question of funding cannot be divorced from the question of independence of the body, as Natural England had to narrow its focus due to the budget cuts, having an impact on the ability to fulfil its general purpose.[112] Natural England is not at arms' length from government, despite being a non-departmental public body. This is because, inter alia, it is fully accountable to DEFRA for funding, and it carries a substantial amount of work for DEFRA under contract.[113]

Funding cuts have also affected the MMOs and especially the IFCAs over the years. IFCAs' funding comes primarily from local government, with the remaining one third from DEFRA. Local authorities were given additional funding to cover the costs associated with the creation of the IFCAs, although it was substantially reduced from what had been indicated in the DEFRA IA on the MCAA.[114] Moreover, the funding is not equally distributed across the ten IFCAs as local authorities have no obligation to allocate the New Burdens' funding[115]

[109] Department for Business, Energy & Industrial Strategy (BEIS), 'Hornsea Project Three: Habitats Regulation Assessment and Marine Conservation Zone Assessment' (BEIS 2020), p. 62.

[110] A SNCB representative interviewed mentioned that they get funding for two surveys a year, lasting around three weeks each. SNCB national representative, online Interview, May 2021.

[111] Natural England, *Natural England Annual Report and Accounts 1 April 2019 to 31 March 2020* (2019–2020, HC 712).

[112] Select Committee on the Natural Environment and Rural Communities Act 2006, *The Countryside at a Crossroads: Is the Natural Environment and Rural Communities Act 2006 still Fit for Purpose?* (2017–2019, HL paper 99), para 96.

[113] Other reasons hindering the independence of Natural England are that many of its statutory responsibilities have an appeal to the Secretary of State and it has lost a distinct online presence and press office with the creation of the gov.uk website back in 2012.

[114] Para 131 of the IA estimated that the reform of inshore fisheries management in England would result in an additional financial burden on constituent local authorities of 5m per year. www.legislation.gov.uk/ukia/2009/282/pdfs/ukia_20090282_en.pdf. According to an Association of the IFCAs representative, the actual funding received was 3m. Interview with an Association of the IFCA representative May 2021.

[115] Department for Communities and Local Governance, 'New burdens doctrine: Guidance for government departments' (Department for Communities and Local Government 2011), www.gov.uk/government/publications/new-burdens-doctrine-guidance-for-government-departments.

to the IFCAs.[116] The funding difficulties IFCAs have encountered over the years are now also exacerbated by the loss of the European Maritime and Fisheries fund due to the EU Exit. These funding issues have clear implications for the ability of the marine regulators to discharge their management and enforcement activities, as noted by the Environment Audit Committee on multiple occasions.[117]

Thus, even if the quantitative goal of Aichi Target 11 has been exceeded with forty per cent of English waters designated as MPAs, continued work to effectively manage and monitor MPAs to ensure the conservation objectives of these sites are met is necessary.[118] Recent developments give a small degree of hope. For example, Natural England has been receiving two consecutive annual boost in funds in 2020–2021 and 2021–2022, although this is unlikely to erase the damage created by a decade of cuts.[119] Besides, the MMO's proposals to introduce management measures in four offshore MPAs, including, as mentioned, the Dogger Bank, is a step towards active management of offshore sites, though there are some limitations explored in Chapter 7 below.

2.6 Conclusion

The legal picture painted in this chapter shows that there are multiple, sometimes overlapping, MPAs designations in English seas that have been established to fulfil international and national obligations. Their management is complex and fragmented with key regulatory roles divided geographically among MMOs and IFCAs as well as Natural England and JNCC. The role of the public is contemplated in the law, but it is not central as for the most part conservation law is a technocratic exercise. Regulatory instruments belong to the command-and-control style of regulation, a case in point being the possibility to introduce byelaws for the regulation of activities in MCZs, backed up by sanctions. The chapter has concentrated on the key MPAs designations in England, namely European Marine Sites and MCZs, highlighting their

[116] Environmental Audit Committee, 'Marine Protected Areas Revisited', para 24.

[117] Environmental Audit Committee, 'Marine Protected Areas Revisited', para 27; Environmental Audit Committee, 'Sustainable Seas', para 77.

[118] Joint Nature Conservation Committee. 'Sixth National Report to the United Nations Convention on Biological Diversity: United Kingdom of Great Britain and Northern Ireland. Overview of the UK Assessment of Progress for the Aichi Targets' (JNCC 2019), p. 8 at: https://data.jncc.gov.uk/data/527ff89f-5f6b-4e06-bde6-b823e0ddcb9a/UK-CBD-Overview-UKAssessmentsofProgress-AichiTargets-web.pdf; Natural England, 'Written Evidence Submission to the Environmental Audit Select Committee: Biodiversity and Ecosystems Inquiry' (Natural England, 2020) at https://committees.parliament.uk/writtenevidence/11571/pdf/, DEFRA, Marine Strategy Part One: UK Updated Assessment and Good Environmental Status' (DEFRA 2019) at: https://assets.publishing.service.gov.uk/government/uploads/system/uploads/attachment_data/file/921262/marine-strategy-part1-october19.pdf.

[119] C. McGlone, 'DEFRA Set to Announce 47% Budget Increase for Natural England'. ENDS Report 2021.

similarities and differences. Overall, with the exception of grounds for derogation from management measures, the level of environmental protection afforded by European Marine Sites is greater than that afforded by the MCZs, with stricter, ecological-only, grounds for designation, a more prominent role given to SNCBs and less discretion afforded to marine regulators, showing a stronger conservation drive. These differences should not be underestimated as varying levels of protection potentially affect conservation outcomes. However, much depends on the implementation of these measures. Only the core implementation issues have been touched upon here, but it will be the task of subsequent chapters to provide an in-depth analysis of selected aspects of the legal implementation and marine conservation actors and actions to analyse the extent to which MPAs law in England delivers its promises.

3

Impact Assessments for Marine Protected Areas

The Costs of Cost-Benefit Analysis

3.1 Introduction

This chapter opens the discussion of the rationalisation of regulation exploring IAs used for designating MCZs. By rationalisation of regulation, I mean regulatory interventions that, in their quest for optimisation, push for streamlining regulation, reducing the regulatory burden to maximise efficiency, minimise costs to business (and society) and promote instruments and approaches for alleged rational and objective analysis such as cost-benefit analysis and risk-based regulation. In England, the Better Regulation framework[1] endorses the use of cost-benefit analysis in IAs, which are always required when proposed regulation is put forward by the government to assess and estimate its likely associate costs and benefits for business, charities, voluntary sector, public sectors or individuals. IAs are portrayed as favouring rational decision-making, effective and efficient policy choices, through a systematic and objective assessment of the costs and benefits of intervention.[2]

IAs have been produced both for the designation of MCZs and are being produced for the introduction of management measures, such as fisheries byelaws. To provide an in-depth discussion of IAs and a reflection on a process that is complete, this chapter confines the discussion to the IAs related to the designation of MCZs, excluding a consideration of IAs related to management measures. The process of designation of MCZs has been conducted over a long period, first through the setting up of four regional stakeholder groups tasked with recommending MCZs to the government. The regional projects' recommendations on MCZs were accompanied by IA material to assess the potential impacts on the UK economy but also on the different sectors over a period of twenty years following the designation and estimated relative to the situation if no MCZs had been introduced. The government then used a phased approach to designation, with the first tranche of MCZs designated in 2013, the second in 2016 and the third in 2019. DEFRA, when producing its IAs to accompany the designation proposals of MCZs, drew on the IA material produced by the

[1] BEIS, 'Better Regulation Framework: Interim Guidance' (BEIS 2020).
[2] Ibid, pp. 11–12.

regional projects so the regional IAs are key documents, given they informed government thinking and approach in the formal IAs. For each tranche, two IAs were presented by DEFRA, the first, subject to public consultation and, the second being the final one. Below references to DEFRA IAs will make it explicit whether they are to consultation IAs or to final IAs. As designation has been completed to comply with Section 123(1) of the MCAA, the IAs accompanying regional stakeholder group recommendations and those accompanying proposals for each tranche can be analysed in their totality, contrary to the management IAs that are still produced every time a new measure is introduced. The fact that the process of designation has been long and phased offers an opportunity also to reflect on the strength of the IAs in a comparative fashion, so this chapter discusses whether DEFRA IAs constitute an improvement compared to the regional projects IAs.

The structure of the chapter is the following: it starts with an introduction to IAs, leading to a theoretical discussion of cost-benefit analysis as a tool for rationalising regulation. It follows with a critical review of IAs produced by the regional projects using umbrella questions derived from the theoretical analysis, and then, it asks if and how the formal IAs produced by the government for the designation of the three tranches constitute an improvement compared to the regional projects' IAs before offering concluding remarks. Throughout the chapter, connections with the concept of commoning are made arguing that IAs for MCZs, by employing economic language in decision-making and focusing on industry costs over benefits, favour the voices of a few over collective ones, highlight interests at the expenses of values and undermine the potential for ethical consideration to play a role in assessment, thereby failing to encourage a shared ethics of care and responsibility towards the marine environment, hence not favouring commoning practices.

3.2 IAs and Cost-Benefit Analysis

IAs are core elements of the UK Better Regulation framework.[3] Better Regulation has been the dominant narrative in the UK regulatory landscape since the mid-1990s.[4] Initially, the Better Regulation agenda was introduced as a move away from the deregulation of the 1980s. This was evident in the emphasis on the benefits as well as risks and costs of regulation and the establishment of the Better Regulation Task Force in 1997, whose role was to offer independent advice to government to ensure proposed regulation was underpinned by principles of proportionality, consistency, targeting but also accountability and transparency. However, more recently, the meaning of Better Regulation seems to have reverted back to deregulation. The Legislative and Regulatory

[3] Ibid, p. 11.

[4] For a fuller history of the development of Better Regulation, see M. Pieraccini and E. Cardwell, 'Impact Assessments for Nature Conservation: Effective and Reflexive?' (2016) (Jan) *Public Law* 93–110.

Reform Act 2006 and the Regulation and the Regulatory Enforcement and Sanctions Act 2008 have put risk-based regulation and cost-effectiveness at the centre of the regulatory agenda. Efforts at reducing the regulatory costs for business have been most evident with the introduction of the red tape challenge in 2011 and the 'One-in, One/Two/Three out' rules.[5] One-in one-out means balancing the introduction of a new regulation with the removal of another to compensate for direct business costs of regulation. This rule was scaled up to one-in three-out in 2016, but, following the Grenfell Tower fire in 2017, it was suspended. Currently, proposals for the reintroduction of one-in, x-out have been set out by BEIS and linked to the Brexit rhetoric.[6] According to the Organisation for Economic Co-operation and Development (OECD), the UK's Better Regulation framework is strong, though the OECD stresses that the UK framework would be strengthen by emphasising non-business elements important for 'inclusive growth'.[7] 'Inclusive growth' is defined as 'economic growth that creates opportunity for all segments of the population and distributes the dividends of increased prosperity, both in monetary and non-monetary terms, fairly across society'.[8] Although the HM Treasury Green Book provides guidance on how analysis of distributional impacts is to be carried out in cost-benefit analysis,[9] in practice the assessment of impacts on specific social groups is rare[10] and, as explained below in the analysis of MCZs IAs, this causes distributive injustice. Nonetheless, the Better Regulation landscape requires targeted and cost-effective interventions, and IAs are proposed as the central tools that can support the regulatory state's drive towards what Moran, following Scott's *Seeing like a State*,[11] termed 'synoptic legibility'.[12] For Moran, the regulatory state emerging at the end of the twentieth century created surveillance systems, standardised and codified knowledge and practices, making explicit (legible) what had been tacit.

IAs enable policy-makers to decide whether and how to regulate to achieve policy goals, helping an *ex ante* identification of the most cost-effective regulatory measures, though some go even further considering IAs to operate neither

[5] One-in one-out means balancing the introduction of a new regulation with the removal of another to compensate for direct business costs of regulation. It was scaled up to one-in three-out in 2016, but, following the Grenfell Tower fire in 2017, it was suspended.

[6] BEIS, 'Reforming the Framework for Better Regulation: A Consultation' (BEIS 2021). The consultation document stresses that the UK's exit from the European Union provides an unprecedented opportunity to deregulate.

[7] OECD, *Better Regulation Practices across the European Union* (OECD 2019).

[8] R. Deighton-Smith, A. Erbacci and C. Kauffmann, 'Promoting Inclusive Growth through Better Regulation: The Role of Regulatory Impact Assessment', *OECD Regulatory Policy Working Papers, No. 3* (OECD, 2016), p. 6.

[9] HM Treasury, 'The Green Book: Central Government Guidance on Appraisal and Evaluation' (HM Treasury 2020), p. 54.

[10] Ibid, p. 21. [11] J. Scott, Seeing Like a State.

[12] M. Moran, *The British Regulatory State: High Modernism and Hyper – Innovation* (Oxford University Press, 2003), p. 4.

ex ante nor *ex post* but to providing ongoing control while regulatory options are being assessed.[13] In this light, IAs are understood not only as a tool but also as a process providing information on the definition of the problem, the range of options, criteria used for choosing in a transparent way. As explained in the Better Regulation Framework guidance, 'A IA summarises the rationale for government intervention, the different policy options (including non-regulatory options) and the impacts of the intervention, as well as quantifying expected costs and benefits'.[14] Cost-benefit analysis needs to be proportionate and directed at providing a clear assessment of the costs of regulation on (primarily) business. The ground rules for cost-benefit analysis are to be found in the HM Treasury Green Book,[15] and the quality of the IAs in England is subject to the scrutiny of the Regulatory Policy Committee (RPC), an independent body, sponsored by the BEIS, tasked precisely with assessing the quality of evidence and analysis used to inform regulatory proposals. The RPC can deem draft IAs unfit for purpose, as it happened with the draft IA for the tranche one of MCZs.[16]

Such independent scrutiny is important for accountability reasons though it must be stated that the RPC has limited powers as it is not permitted to deem an IA unfit for purposes on the ground of inadequate consideration of wider social impacts, as the basis of its decision are confined to the direct effect of new regulation on business.[17] It is interesting to note that the RPC has noted that many IAs actually do not consider those wider impacts and that those wider impacts are an important determinant of a IA's fitness for purpose so it is unsatisfactory that the RPC are unable to rate a IA as unfit for purpose on the basis of the wider societal impacts of regulation. This risks the unintentional discounting of these wider impacts compared to the business impacts.[18] This is a clear limitation of the oversight powers of the RPC and especially relevant in the environmental field, where many regulatory interventions have wider social-ecological impacts.

[13] This is a recurrent observation in Radaelli's scholarly work on IAs. See for example, C. M. Radaelli and F. De Francesco, 'Regulatory Impact Assessment', in R. Baldwin, M. Cave and M. Lodge (eds.), *The Oxford Handbook of Regulation* (Oxford University Press, 2010), pp. 279–301; C. A. Dunlop and C. M. Radaelli, 'The Politics and Economics of Regulatory Impact Assessment', in C. A. Dunlop and C. M. Radaelli (eds.), *The Handbook of Regulatory Impact Assessment* (Edward Elgar, 2016), pp. 3–20.

[14] BEIS, 'Better Regulation Framework', p. 11.

[15] HM Treasury, 'Green Book'.

[16] RPC, 'Opinion Impact Assessment – Designation of Marine Conservation Zones in English Inshore Waters and English and Welsh Offshore Waters – Consultation Stage'. RPC 12-DEFRA-1604.

[17] RPC, 'Securing the Evidence Base for Regulation: Regulatory Policy Committee Scrutiny during the 2010 to 2015 Parliament', (RPC, 2015), p. 38. This remained a problem in subsequent years. See, RPC, 'Regulatory Overview: RPC Scrutiny during the 2015–2017 Parliament' (RPC, 2018), p. 9; RPC, 'Regulatory Overview: June 2017–December 2019' (RPC, 2020), p. 7 where it was stated that: 'we aim to improve the quality and usefulness of IAs by scrutinising and providing comments in our opinions on departments' and regulators' consideration of wider societal impacts'.

[18] RPC, 'Regulatory Overview: RPC Scrutiny during the 2015–2017 Parliament', p. 45 and RPC, 'Regulatory Overview: June 2017–December 2019', p. 7.

The logic of cost-benefit analysis, quantification and the inclusion of the different policy options at the basis of IA recall many aspects of the comprehensive rationality paradigm of administrative law as described by Diver.[19] For Diver, comprehensive rationality requires decision-makers to have specific goals they aim to achieve, the identification of all possible methods of reaching these goals, the comparative assessment of all these methods and the selection of the alternative that will produce the most effective result towards the desired goal. Interests are exogenous to the decision-making process and cannot be subject to much change; they need to be precise and consistent with conflicting goals reconciled by specific trade-off among them.[20] Cost-benefit analysis is indeed cited by Diver as a key tool of comprehensive rationality.[21]

Rationalised and streamlined regulatory approaches embedding cost-benefit analysis have been subject to much criticism by progressive environmental lawyers[22] and regulatory scholars.[23] In the United States, for example, the academic debates have revolved around searching for alternatives such as the precautionary principle as a basis for regulation;[24] in the UK context, the debates have been linked to critiques of high modernism and increased centralisation in the regulatory state.[25] Without restating the positions in these debates, suffice here to consider the key critiques directed at cost-benefit analysis as a primary tool of (environmental) regulation as they serve to extrapolate key questions directing the analysis of the MCZs IAs in Sections 3 and 4 below. Ackerman and Heizerling have been strong opponents of cost-benefit, going as far as saying that it 'promotes a deregulatory agenda under the cover of scientific objectivity'.[26] Defendants of cost-benefit analysis would rebut this by arguing that cost-benefit analysis may help limit regulators' discretion ensuring decisions are made on the basis of a reasoned analysis as far as possible and are available for independent and public scrutiny.[27] Indeed, many proponents of cost-benefit analysis and IA do not only stress

[19] C. S. Diver, 'Policy Paradigms in Administrative Law', (1981) 95 *Harvard Law Review* 393–434.

[20] Ibid, pp. 398–399. [21] Ibid, p. 416.

[22] A. Sienden, D. A. Kysar and D. M. Driesen, 'Cost-Benefit Analysis: New Foundations on Shifting Sands', (2009) 3 *Regulation and Governance* 48–71.

[23] R. Baldwin, 'Is Better Regulation Smarter Regulation?', (2005) (Aut) *Public Law* 485–511.

[24] D. A. Kysar, *Regulating from Nowhere: Environmental Law and the Search for Objectivity* (Yale University Press, 2010).

[25] Moran, 'The British Regulatory State'; J. Black, 'Tensions in the Regulatory State' (2007) (Spring) *Public Law* 58–73.

[26] F. Ackerman and L. Heinzerling, *Priceless: On Knowing the Price of Everything and the Value of Nothing* (The New Press, 2004), pp. 8–9.

[27] R. L. Revesz and M. A. Livermore, *Retaking Rationale: How Cost-Benefit Analysis Can Better Protect the Environment and Our Health* (Oxford University Press, 2008), p. 13. See also, C. R. Sunstein, *The Cost-Benefit State: The Future of Regulatory Protection* (American Bar Association, 2002); M. D. Alder and E. R. Posner, *New Foundations of Cost-Benefit Analysis* (Harvard University Press, 2006).

the efficiency linked to this rational, evidence-based approach but also its democratic potential by rendering regulatory choices fully documented and open to independent and public scrutiny, increasing the accountability of the decision-making process.[28] In this way, cost-benefit analysis in IAs play a role in the 'symbolic dimension' of the regulatory state by producing transparent assessments on the expected impacts of regulation as a means to increase legitimacy.[29] In addition, just like the environmental impacts of economic activities are considered in environmental regulation through environmental IAs, cost-benefit analysis can be a useful tool to consider the economic impacts of environmental regulations.

However, the risk remains that, by subsuming everything under a quantification logic, certain softer variable and values are undermined. In doing so, cost-benefit analyses fail to properly account for distributive justice in the calculation of costs and benefits. For instance, a proposed regulation can have asymmetric costs and benefits to different sectors, and low numerical costs may be high livelihood costs for some while high numerical costs may be internalised effortlessly by those with the ability to pay. Although the HM Green Book provides some guidance on the accounting of distributional impacts, in practice few IAs are able to properly incorporate distributive concerns.[30] Besides, cost-benefit analysis by aggregating the obtained monetary values to calculate the total net benefit and cost of policy options into one single scale of measurement necessarily overlooks questions of justice. Moreover, there are values, such as many environmental values, which defy quantification because they are 'priceless'.[31] Thus, attempting to align diverse values along a single quantitative metric is not always possible.

To provide an example in the context of the marine environment, place attachment, that is the emotional bonds people form with a specific place, is one such priceless value.[32] Place attachment emerges as a result of people's interactions with complex and interrelated social, psychological and environmental processes. Place attachment does not simply derive from being physically located within a place or being able to access the place, as emotional bonds with a particular place can be formed even living far away from it.[33] For example, people living in landlocked urban environments may still have a strong place attachment towards the sea. Thus, place attachment is hard to measure but, as research has shown, it is a key factor influencing marine governance as environmental

[28] Sunstein, The Cost-Benefit State.

[29] Radaelli and De Francesco, 'Regulatory Impact Assessment'.

[30] HM Treasure, 'Green Book'. [31] Ackerman and Heinzerling, Priceless.

[32] Y. F. Tuan, *Topophilia: A Study of Environmental Perception, Attitudes, and Values* (Prentice Hall Inc., 1974); L. C. Manzo and P. Devine-Wright (eds.), *Place Attachment: Advances in Theory, Methods and Applications* (Routledge, 2014).

[33] I. van Putten et al., 'A Framework for Incorporating Sense of Place into the Management of Marine Systems' (2018) 23 *Ecology and Society*.

behaviour and attitudes are shaped by place attachment.[34] Conversely, place attachment is shaped by environmental governance itself as different regulations may contribute to enhance or hinder people's emotional bonds with the marine environment so it can be considered part of the wider social impacts of a regulatory intervention. Given that place attachment is not static but always evolving as part of one person's interactions with social and environmental factors, attempts at measuring it are difficult, so it is safer to calculate it in a qualitative manner, but this has the risk of losing it in the final calculations, dictated primarily by a quantification logic. Assuming measurement would be possible, it is nevertheless problematic as it would reduce complex, evolving relationships into something static that can be expressed through a precise number.

This brings us to another key criticism of cost-benefit analysis, that it constitutes a 'one-shot' guess at regulating.[35] One-shot systems are not well equipped to account for social and environmental changes. Relatedly, settling on numbers for all costs and benefits in one-shot guess is also difficult because it forces to ignore or downplay uncertainties. Lack of data is a recurrent hurdle in the environmental field, meaning that certain benefits of environmental regulation end up being left out because of information deficit. Even assuming one supports the quantification of all values and pricing techniques are refined to capture also values that are harder to quantify, uncertainty due to unavailable data hinders the possibility of cost-benefit analysis to present a comprehensive and systematic method of evaluating policy proposals. As visible from the below analysis on MCZs IAs, uncertainty is not dealt with in a consistent manner and also often reduced by making simplified assumptions. Although IA is portrayed not only as a tool but also as a process, having at its core cost-benefit analysis inhibits its transformative potential because cost-benefit analyses are not a dynamic regulatory approach in which strategies are revised and refined to reflect cultural, political economic and environmental variations and uncertainties and complex social-ecological relationships. At the core of IAs and cost-benefit analysis, little space is left for experimentalism as policy-makers must choose and to do so they need to have a definite picture of what is at stake even if such picture distorts and simplifies complex processes and erases certain key values and parameters that do not fit within the outcome-oriented approach and the single metric employed, subjecting everything to the logic of commensurability and excluding what cannot be subsumed within this logic. Again, the link with Scott's *Seeing like a state*, discussed in Chapter 1, is evident as only certain variables are made legible.[36]

Connected to these critiques, there are of course underlying ethical concerns about the limits of quantification and cost-benefit analysis, especially when

[34] Ibid. [35] Baldwin, 'Is Better Regulation Smarter Regulation', p. 507.
[36] J. Scott, Seeing Like a State.

applied to environmental regulation. Three main ethical questions arise: Is it right to compare and subsume under a single metric plural values? Are values ever exogenous to the decision-making processes? Does cost benefit analysis contribute to a commodification of the environment? The problem of incommensurability is extensive because it is impossible to use monetary units to express intrinsic and hidden values associate with biodiversity.[37] When ecosystems are described as natural capital and services, there is the risk of reducing everything to an instrumental and anthropocentric logic, which from an environmental ethics perspective is problematic as it does not recognise intrinsic[38] or, even more significantly, relational values.[39] Moreover, the values priced and assessed through cost-benefit analyses seem to exist as exogenous interests, not as endogenous to decision-making and co-created by human and more-than human forces. This has the consequence of taking deliberative politics out of policy, which is reduced to a choice among alternatives less detrimental to economic welfare. The irony, of course, is that cost-benefit analyses are highly political tools. In so far as they decide what to include, how to compare and what costs are tolerable, they determine what is politically acceptable from what it is not.

In addition, by separating the economic costs from the environmental benefits, often expressed in the language of ecosystem services as in the IAs to be discussed below, two problems are encountered: on the one hand, the dichotomy between nature and society is re-proposed and exacerbated. This limits the potential for commoning, intended as a collective political act in search of shared values which represent complex encounters between the human and the non-humans, as opposed to a balancing act among pre-existing, given and context-independent interests. On the other, nature risks to be commodified.[40] The two problems join because commodification of nature implies its reification and tradability,[41] disregarding relational values that recognise social and ecological systems as entangled and mutually constitutive. As Chan et al. argue 'relational values are not present in things but derivative of relationships and responsibilities to them'.[42] Returning to the example of place attachment, it is

[37] C. L. Spash, 'Deliberative Monetary Valuation and the Evidence for a New Value Theory' (2008) 84 *Land Economics* 469–488.

[38] For a defence of intrinsic values, see M. Sagoff, *The Economy of the Earth: Philosophy, Law, and the Environment*, 2nd ed. (Cambridge University Press, 2008).

[39] K. M. A. Chan et al., 'Opinion: Why Protect Nature? Rethinking Values and the Environment' (2016) 113 *Proceedings of the National Academy of Sciences of the United States of America* 1462–1465.

[40] K. Polanyi, *The Great Transformation: The Political and Economic Origins of Our Time* (Beacon Press, 1957); E. Gomez-Baggethun and M. Ruiz – Perez, 'Economic Valuation and the Commodification of Ecosystem Services' (2011) 35 *Progress in Physical Geography: Earth and Environment* 613–628.

[41] C. L. Spash, 'Bulldozing Biodiversity: The Economics of Offsets and Trading-in Nature', (2015) 192 *Biological Conservation* 541–551.

[42] Chan et al., 'Opinion', p. 1462.

evident that attachment to place expresses a relationship between the environment and people and places are valued in the context of these relationships, hence it is inherently a relational value. If, following a relational view, we are prepared to accept that many values are about relationships rather than being values *of* separated entities[43] and that such values are formed through ongoing deliberations and interactions rather than existing as fixed, exogenous interests, then the ethical shortcomings of cost-benefits analysis become obvious as complex and evolving social-ecological relations are transformed in simple exchange relations between objects following an instrumental logic.

The above critiques show a number of limitations of cost-benefit analysis and consequently of IAs which, by placing regulatory choices into an economic frame based on quantification and commensurability, simplify complex social-ecological relationship and suppress the possibility for the articulation of relational values. These observations are important because they show that IAs are not and cannot be objective representations of different options and calculations of given existing or projected interests, but they construct what is possible and acceptable by making visible certain elements and not others, by using quantification as the privileged means of representation, thereby minimising what cannot be quantified and by deciding how and what to quantify. Such quantification is then essential for the legitimation of decision-making. In the case of MCZs, it is essential to decide what gets designated as an MPA and what does not. IAs as acts of social and ecological quantification are not only tools to aid policy-makers to make rational and informed decisions but, as mentioned earlier, the quantification itself is a political act in the sense that political judgements are made regarding what to measure, how to measure, which knowledges are relevant in the measurement. If deliberative politics is taken out of policy, the political remains alive in the underlying ontological and epistemological assumptions at the basis of cost-benefit analysis and its methodology.

The vocabulary of the sociology of translation developed by Science and Technology Studies' scholars[44] can prove valuable to describe IAs. Translation does not only have the linguistic meaning of relating versions in a language to another, which indisputably involves some transformation, but also the 'geometric' meaning of moving/mobilising from a place to another.[45] Specifically, Latour writes 'in addition to its linguistic meaning (relating versions in one language to versions in another one) it has also a geometric meaning (moving

[43] K. M. Chan, R. K. Gould and U. Pascual, 'Editorial Overview: Relational Values: What Are They, and What's the Fuss about?' (2018) 35 *Current Opinion in Environmental Sustainability* A1–A7.

[44] B. Latour, *Science in Action: How to Follow Scientists and Engineers through Society* (Harvard University Press, 1987); M. Callon, 'Some Elements of a Sociology of Translation: Domestication of the Scallops and the Fishermen of St. Brieuc Bay', in J. Law (ed.), *Power, Action and Belief: A New Sociology of Knowledge* (Routledge, 1986), 196–223.

[45] Latour, Science in Action, p. 117.

from one place to another). Translating interests means at once offering new interpretations of these interests and channelling people in different directions'.[46] The process of translation shows how complex and distant processes and actors come to be displaced from their localities and inscribed within a singular entity, which is then used to act on them. Translation is a process of 'creating convergences and homologies by relating things that were previously different'.[47] Translation emphasises transformation for legibility, displacement, re-inscription and even power, explaining the way in which only a few people get the right to represent many silent actors of the social and natural world they have mobilised.[48] Reducing the dispersed and multiple relations of government intervention into something that can be measured and calculated allows the governing to take place from the centre and to act simultaneously on many actors and processes through dislocation and mobilisation. Thus, ordering and inscription through centres of calculation such as IAs enable the objectification of the sea, disembedding the multiple, complex and evolving relations between human and non-human actors from their context and rendering them subject to control. But, as translation is not only an exercise of power but also a way of trading between different sectors to provide legibility, the multiple, complex relations end up becoming coherent and commensurable so that simple, 'objective' trading can occur. In doing so, the attempt is also to distinguish between the political and the technical, with the technical embodied by the IA to aid political decision-making. However, this division is fictious. As explained above, the quantification choices in IAs are political as there is much discretion at play in choosing how and what to quantify so the boundary between the political and the technical is blurred.[49]

The next section reflects on whether and how the theoretical critiques that have been advanced here apply to the IAs for MCZs designation in England. The critiques are grouped within three umbrella questions asking whether IAs for MCZs designations (1) are acts of power in the sense of silencing certain actors and voices (2) 'engage simplifications'[50] inscribing evolving complex social-ecological relationship into a standardised form and simplistically dealing with uncertainty (3) contribute to distributive injustices by not paying sufficient attention to how costs and benefits are likely to be distributed among society and how benefits are accounted for as against costs. Given that the formal DEFRA IAs are built on the regional projects IA, each of these three questions is discussed first in relation to the regional projects' IAs and then

[46] Ibid, p. 117.

[47] M. Callon, 'Struggles and Negotiations to Define What Is Problematic and What Is Not: The Socio-logics of Translation', in K. D. Knorr, R. Krohn and R. Whitley (eds.), *The Social Process of Scientific Investigation* (D. Reidel Publishing Company, 1980), pp. 197–219, p. 211.

[48] Callon, 'Some Elements of a Sociology of Translation'.

[49] J. Black, 'Proceduralizing Regulation: Part II', (2001) 21 *Oxford Journal of Legal Studies* 33–58.

[50] This is a phrase I borrow from Li, 'Engaging Simplifications'.

similarities and differences in approach in the DEFRA IAs for each tranche of MCZs designation are highlighted.

3.3 Regional IAs: Acts of Power?

The material for the regional projects' IAs was collected, analysed, and put together by the regional project economists, advised by an economist in Natural England. DEFRA's economists provided feedback on draft material to ensure that it was in line with the government's requirements, as it served then as the basis for the government IAs accompanying MCZs proposals. Annex M of the regional stakeholder project describes the way in which stakeholders were involved in the IAs. Although substantial efforts were made to engage stakeholders, it is evident that, in most cases, they were involved primarily as information providers, rather than as deliberants. Information was gathered during the regional meetings and also in sub-regional stakeholder group meetings and by a liaison officer on the socio-economic activities. This information was fed in the IAs. Notably, though each iteration of the regional stakeholder groups on the recommended MCZs included draft material for the IAs, the submitted IA material was produced at the end of the regional stakeholder projects as it was not possible to quantify the majority of the likely impacts, due to uncertainty surrounding management, erasing opportunities to provide feedback.[51] This practice does not show early and meaningful engagement and opportunities for a proper collective scrutiny of information but shows the adoption of an instrumental understanding of the value of participation in decision-making. It is also indicative of an underlying epistemological dualism, separating conservation advice in the hands of SNCBs from information regarding activities, extrapolated from industry.

Moreover, there are multiple cases in which the voices of certain actors and their value judgements are given much preponderance, raising questions over the degree to which the process was subject to regulatory capture. For example, in relation to aggregates, the fact that the British Marine Aggregates Producers Association was content with conclusions made by the IAs is confirmed on six different occasions in Annex H2, detailing the approach to assess the impacts on MCZs on aggregates.[52] Given that information collected from other stakeholder tended only to be used when determining factual information on the level and type of human activity, and public interest groups simply not mentioned, this raises concern over the objective nature of the process.

[51] Natural England, 'Regional MCZ Projects Impact Assessment Materials: Annex M – Stakeholder Engagement in the Impact Assessment Process' (Natural England 2012), M.6.

[52] Natural England, 'Regional MCZ Projects IA: Annex H2 – Approach for Assessing Impacts on Aggregate Extraction' (Natural England 2012), H2.17, H2.21, H2.24, H2.25, H2.29, H2.30.

3.4 Regional IAs: Engaging Simplifications?

Assumptions were made to develop management scenarios for the regional projects IAs as the management measures required for each site were going to be set by public authorities only after the designation stage. After combining information on the feature sensitivity from SNCBs with the level/type activity from the industry to produce a vulnerability assessment, conservation objectives for each recommended MCZs were developed. Each site was assigned a 'maintain' or 'recover' conservation objective depending on whether the protected features were expected to be significantly impacted.[53] After accounting for protection provided by existing management, if any, additional management was identified and costed, producing a best estimate of costs of designation on different sectors (Aggregates, Aquaculture, Archaeology, Coastal Developments, Commercial Fisheries, Flood and Coastal Erosion Risk Management, National Defence, Oil, Gas, Recreation, Renewable Energy). In many cases, calculations were determined using simplified management scenarios and using midpoint estimates.

For example, in the case of ports, harbours, shipping and disposal sites, the summary of impacts presents two management scenarios reflecting existing uncertainty over the distance at which the smothering effects of dredged material can impact marine features,[54] with the second scenario extending the distance from 1 to 5 km, following concerns raised by eight port operators.[55] When it comes to determining the location of future port and harbour developments, a figure of 50 per cent is given to represent the number of applications that will fall within the 5-km zone. Yet, there is nothing to substantiate this, with Annex H12, assessing the impacts on the port sector, admitting that it is a 'crude assumption'.[56]

Similarly, in the case of fisheries, IAs presented both a low-cost (no additional management) and high-cost scenario, used to determine a midpoint cost as the 'best estimate' using a generic 75 per cent displacement figure irrespective of context,[57] despite the insufficient evidence to suggest that each scenario should be treated as having an equal chance of being implemented and irrespective of whether the conservation objectives had been set as recover or maintain. Having the low-cost scenario for recommended sites with recover conservation objectives is particularly problematic given that some form of additional management is likely to be required to improve the conservation of protected features. The consequence is an underestimation of costs when it comes to the midpoint calculations.

[53] Natural England, 'Regional MCZ Projects IA: Annex H1 – General Assumptions and Approach' (Natural England 2012), H1.39–H1.48.

[54] Natural England, 'Regional MCZ Projects IA: Annex H12 – Approach for Assessing Impacts on Ports, Harbours, Shipping and Disposal Sites' (Natural England 2012), H12.9.

[55] Ibid, H12.9. [56] Ibid, H12.27.

[57] See Pieraccini and Cardwell, 'Impact Assessments', p. 103.

Estimates for other sectors present similar problems resorting to the use of midpoint estimates.[58] However, in cases where the evidence base was deemed stronger, the calculation is less arbitrary. For example, for the oil and gas sector, there was no need to resort to range-best estimates as the evidence provided by the then Department of Energy and Climate Change and the SNCBs was strong enough for the IA to adopt a single management scenario.[59] The scenarios for the aquaculture industry were also more evidence-based and designed to reflect a contentious ongoing debate between industry operators (no additional management/low-cost) and the government (high-cost).[60] Moreover, where the evidence was very strong, the 'mid – point' strategy was abandoned altogether in favour of a more accurate representation of costs, as in the case for renewable energy. There, instead of settling for either an arbitrary midpoint (as in the case of fisheries) or take the industry estimate at face value (as in the case of aggregates), costs were calculated following an adjustment based on advice received from the SNCBs that only fifteen per cent of the additional high-cost mitigation estimate for wind was to be taken account. This is because evidence received from the SNCBs provided proof that the concerns raised by industry – which had formed the basis for the high-cost scenario – were unlikely to come to fruition.[61]

However, while the approach was possible when sufficient evidence was available, the problems arose when assessors were either faced with uncertainty or where there was an imbalance of expertise between those assessors and the industry actors that were supplying information and advice, with a potential for regulatory capture as highlighted above. The difficulties associated with modelling the potential economic impact of designation, in the

[58] See, for example, aquaculture at Natural England, 'Regional MCZ Projects IA – Annex F2 – Finding Sanctuary' (Natural England 2012), F2.31. Cables at Natural England, 'Regional MCZ Projects IA: Annex F1 – Balanced Seas' (Natural England, 2012), F1.50; Natural England, 'Regional MCZ Projects IA – Annex F2 – Finding Sanctuary' (Natural England 2012), F2.38; Natural England, 'Regional MCZ Projects IA: Annex F3 – Irish Seas Conservation Zones' (Natural England 2012), F3.29; Natural England, 'Regional MCZ Projects IA: Annex F4 – NetGain' (Natural England 2012), F4.40–F4.41. Oil and gas at Natural England, 'Regional MCZ Projects IA: Annex F3 – Irish Seas Conservation Zones' (Natural England 2012), F3.94; Natural England, 'Regional MCZ Projects IA – Annex F2 – Finding Sanctuary' (Natural England 2012), F2.91 Recreation at Natural England, 'Regional MCZ Projects IA: Annex F1 – Balanced Seas' (Natural England 2012), F1.132.

[59] Natural England, 'Regional MCZ Projects IA: Annex H11 – Approach for Assessing Impacts on Oil and Gas Related Activities' (Natural England 2012), H11.7.

[60] The debate revolved around the Pacific Oyster's status as an invasive non-native species. The UK government considered its potential spread to be damaging to the condition of protected habitats and species within MCZs and thus backs the compulsory use of sterile triploid stock. Whereas the oyster cultivation industry disagrees with the government's analysis and argues for no additional management. See. Natural England, 'Regional MCZ Projects IA: Annex H3 – Approach for Assessing Impacts on Aquaculture' (Natural England 2012), H3.8.

[61] Natural England, 'Regional MCZ Projects IA: Annex H14 – Approach for Assessing Impacts on Renewable Energy' (Natural England 2012), H14.39 and H.14.7.

absence of accurate knowledge on management measures, contributed to arbitrary decision-making when it came to making cost calculations.[62]

Another simplification at play constitutes the general approach taken for the calculation of additional management and its costs.[63] The regional IA assumed that additional management (i.e. new management measures) will be needed only for species and habitats with a conservation objective of 'recover' to favourable condition, meaning that no costs for additional management were calculated for sites with features with a 'maintain' objective. Given that the IAs cover a period of twenty years, this assumption is underpinned by a static ecological view, not considering that features that are currently at a 'maintain' status may become deteriorated in time due to environmental change and new human impacts, so in need of additional management.

3.5 Regional IAs: Contributing to Distributive Injustice?

Distributive injustice was manifested in the IAs in multiple ways: firstly, through the imbalance between the representation of costs compared to the benefits of designation; secondly, through the dominance of economic interests over environmental interests and thirdly through the non-equal treatment of sectors in deciding whether to quantify highly uncertain costs.

In relation to the first issue, Annex F, which presents the regional summary of impacts for each region, touches on the qualitative environmental benefits, but there is no mention of any potential benefit that could impact an industry on the back of a designation. For example, the discussion surrounding the impact of designation on commercial fisheries is devoid of any acknowledgement of the fact that greater restrictions on certain fishing gear types (especially trawls and dredges) can allow fishing stocks to recover, having positive spillover effects and facilitate sustainable fishing, providing inter-generational socio-economic benefits for small coastal communities. Instead, all four documents seem to be concerned solely with the economic costs that will be incurred by the fishing industry, from the impact that gear restrictions will have on the value of landings,[64] to the damaging impacts arising from mass displacement of the fishing effort (e.g. time spent away from families, steaming costs).[65]

62 See also Pieraccini and Cardwell, 'Impact Assessments'. The discussion in that paper is confined to fisheries.

63 Natural England, 'Regional MCZ Projects IA: Annex H1-General Assumptions and Approach' (Natural England 2012), H.1.49.

64 Natural England, 'Regional MCZ Projects IA: Annex F1 – Balanced Seas' (2012) Table 1; Natural England, 'Regional MCZ Projects IA – Annex F2 – Finding Sanctuary' (Natural England 2012), Table 1; Natural England, 'Regional MCZ Projects IA: Annex F3 – Irish Seas Conservation Zones' (Natural England 2012), Table 1; Natural England, 'Regional MCZ Projects IA: Annex F4 – NetGain' (Natural England 2012), Table 1.

65 Natural England, 'Regional MCZ Projects IA: Annex F1 – Balanced Seas' (Natural England 2012), F1.81–F1.85; Natural England, 'Regional MCZ Projects IA – Annex F2 – Finding Sanctuary' (Natural England 2012), F2.74–F2.78; Natural England, 'Regional MCZ Projects

This imbalance is also observable in relation to other sectors. For example, when comparing the competition that exists between the aggregate and archaeological heritage industries in the Goodwin Sands rMCZ, much emphasis is placed on the economic damage that restrictions on dredging could do the marine aggregates industry, as voiced by the Crown Estate.[66] However, there is no mention of the benefits that restrictions on dredging would have on the archaeological sector.[67] Tellingly, Goodwin Sands was only designated in tranche three of the MCZs designation, indicating the prioritisation of the economic interests in earlier stages of designation.

The lack of due attention to the benefits MCZ designations can bring to social-ecological systems leaves the IAs with a large costs section and an unquantifiable benefits section filled solely with some qualitative benefits. A keyword search of 'costs' and 'benefits' also reinforces this point, with costs mentioned over 600 times against benefits mentioned nineteen times in Annex F.

Regarding the second point, it is often the case that economic interests gain predominance over environmental concerns, with assumptions about economic costs made even in cases in which these are unquantifiable. For example, in the assessment of ports, harbours, shipping and disposal sites within the 'Balanced Seas' regional area, maintenance navigational dredges overlap with three recommended MCZs Reference Areas.[68] Navigational dredges are of course incompatible with the prohibition of extraction within Reference Areas. However, the IA assumes that these activities will be allowed to continue because of their economic importance in maintaining the viability of harbour operations and impacts will not be mitigated.[69] As such, the costs are calculated according to compensatory measures that will be taken by the operator according to Section 126(7) of the MCAA, that is, the cost of the operator in providing benefit equivalent to the impact that continuation of the plan would have on the MCZ's features.[70] On the back

IA: Annex F3 – Irish Seas Conservation Zones' (Natural England 2012), F3.74–F3.76; Natural England, 'Regional MCZ Projects IA: Annex F4 – NetGain' (Natural England 2012), F4.71.

66 Natural England, 'Regional MCZ Projects IA: Annex F1-Balanced Seas' (Natural England 2012), F 1.34.

67 In the south-eastern MCZs, there are twelve designated shipwrecks under the Protection of Wrecks Act 1973, of which Goodwin Sands has a particularly high concentration (5), not to mention countless artefacts that might also be considered part of the historical environment. See. Natural England, 'Regional MCZ Projects IA: Annex F1 – Balanced Seas' (Natural England 2012), F1.38.

68 Reference areas are Highly Protected Marine Areas, akin to a no-take zone.

69 Natural England, 'Regional MCZ Projects IA: Annex F1 – Balanced Seas' (Natural England 2012), F1.118.

70 Section 126(7) states that: 'the condition in this subsection is that, although the person seeking the authorisation is not able to satisfy the authority that there is no significant risk of the act hindering the achievement of the conservation objectives stated for the MCZ,

of this 'significant unknown cost',[71] it is anticipated that the advice provided by Natural England in final designation decisions will suggest that the site recommendation is adjusted to render more likely the achievement of the conservation objectives.[72]

Similarly, in the discussion surrounding the potential impact of Holehaven recommended MCZs on Flood and Coastal Erosion Management within the 'Balanced Seas' project area, the assumption is that the socio-economic risk in question, that is flood risks to economically important properties, would be too high to justify restricting flood defence operations in favour of marine conservation concerns. Therefore, the impact is assessed by identifying the cost of compensatory measures under Section 126(7) of the MCAA.[73] Section 126(7), however, should be triggered only as a last resort mechanisms: that is in instances in which although the doing of an act may bring a significant risk, there are no alternatives and the benefit of proceeding with the act clearly outweighs the risk of environmental damage. Compensatory measures providing equivalent environmental benefit must be taken.

In the Holehaven case, the impact remains unquantified in the absence of information regarding what undertaking will constitute equivalent environmental benefit and again it is anticipated that the advice of SNCBs will suggest that the site recommendations will be adjusted to increase the likelihood to achieve the MCZs conservation objectives.[74] Although it is subsequently stated that including such an adjustment within the summary of impacts would be inappropriate because the IA is an assessment of the regional MCZ projects' recommendations,[75] it is arguable that Annex F has already overstepped its remit by commenting over the viability of site designation rather than providing an assessment of impacts.

Moreover, the explicit reliance on compensatory measures under Section 126(7) to make estimates regarding costs of designation in these cases is also problematic because, instead of accounting for the costs of compliance, it accounts for the costs of derogation. Relying on Section 126(7) side steps the whole legal process, assuming that the three conditions for satisfying the public authority that the act can be carried out will be met, including that there are no

that person satisfies the authority that – (a) there is no other means of proceeding with the act which would create a substantially lower risk of hindering the achievement of those objectives, (b) the benefit to the public of proceeding with the act clearly outweighs the risk of damage to the environment that will be created by proceeding with it and (c) the person seeking the authorisation will undertake, or make arrangements for the undertaking of, measures of equivalent environmental benefit to the damage which the act will or is likely to have in or on the MCZ'.

71 Natural England, 'Regional MCZ Projects IA: Annex F1 – Balanced Seas' (Natural England 2012), F1.119.

72 Ibid, F1.120. 73 Ibid, F1.97. 74 Ibid, F1.98. 75 Ibid.

alternatives even though this is not considered in the IAs. By way of comparison, if we recall how the CJEU has interpreted the parallel provisions under the Habitats Directive in cases related to developments likely to affect the site integrity of European protected site, we see that compensatory measures cannot be relied upon at any stage of article 6(3) because they are 'highly difficult to forecast with any degree of certainty and, in any event, will be visible only several years into the future', thus they can be only invoked only in the derogation provision of article 6(4).[76]

Finally, distributive injustice is visible in the fact that all sectors are not treated equally in deciding whether to quantify or not the costs in the context of uncertainty. As explained above, the IA for the ports, harbours, shipping and disposal sites sector gave a crude fifty per cent figure to represent the number of applications falling within the zone to be affected by the recommended MCZs. Although this is explained on the basis that 'it was not possible to relate the number of historic applications submitted to the MMO to the location of individual r(ecommended) MCZs',[77] this does nothing to explain the decision to make an arbitrary estimate, when there are multiple circumstances throughout the IAs where costs are left unquantified for lack of certainty. A case in point being the archaeology sector, where most costs are expressed in a qualitative way, revolving around the costs to society. Although management assumptions within Annex H, which detailed the approach for assessing impacts on various sectors, take account of the fact that a more obstructive licensing process is likely to impose additional costs upon operators, due to uncertainty over the quantity, location and content of future licence applications, even these costs cannot be quantified.[78] There is therefore lack of consistency for when decisions are made to either produce arbitrary assumptions, as in the case of fisheries' displacement figure or ports or leave costs unquantified as in the case of archaeology. As the IA gives dominance to costs that are quantified, this inconsistency assumes an important weight in the final decision-making process. The following sections consider what changed and what stayed the same in the DEFRA IAs.

3.6 DEFRA IAs: Acts of Power?

IAs for each tranche of MCZs produced by DEFRA followed the formal procedure whereby they were subject to public consultation as well independent scrutiny by the RPC. Such level of scrutiny should in principle help avoiding regulatory capture as well as enabling silenced voices to be taken into account,

[76] *Briels*, at 32.

[77] Natural England, 'Regional MCZ Projects IA: Annex H12 – Approach for Assessing Impacts on Ports, Harbours, Shipping and Disposal Sites' (Natural England 2012), H12.27.

[78] Natural England, 'Regional MCZ Projects IA: Annex H4 – Approach for Assessing Impacts on Archaeological Heritage' (Natural England 2012), H4.32.

hence overcoming some of the shortcomings identified for the regional projects IAs. However, it is debatable whether public consultation is sufficient to be considered a form of strong participation, as Arnestein's ladder reminds us.[79] Indeed, for MCZs, IAs consultation has not often resulted in substantial change. For example, in tranche one, although consultation responses allowed for some total cost figures to be refined[80] and the number of MCZs to be designated reduced from thirty-one to twenty-seven, many responses were considered to relate either to existing information within the regional projects or not attributable to MCZs, being costs associated with other existing legal requirements.[81] The impact of consultation in the second tranche is even more reduced with the final IA representing a very similar set of data to the consultation IA. In the third tranche, the effects of consultation also serve to confirm the designation of the proposed MCZ and are only 'felt' in the adjustment of the boundary of an MCZ (Bembridge) responding to concerns raised about future navigational dredging, hence consultation served to strengthen economic concerns. Although respondents both in the second and third tranches raised concerns over the static ecological approach regarding the measurement of benefits and cots for features with 'maintain' objectives, DEFRA referenced a lack of site-specific information to justify its position.[82]

In regard to the RPC, its role is to be welcome, and this is evidence by the fact that the final IA for tranche one did not pass its scrutiny first time around so required amendments to be approved.[83] However, as emphasised above, the RPC has limited powers to determine when an IA is unfit for purpose. Indeed, the criticisms raised by the RPC at the consultation IAs for tranche one MCZs were about inconsistencies with the 'One-IN, One-Out' methodology, about presentational issues (the length of the IA) and about poor estimations of business costs. Contextual variables such as inadequate consideration of wider social impacts or narratives around values were not discussed.

Moreover, the main data used by the IAs for estimating costs were those collected from the regional IAs. Although the IA for tranche one of MCZs championed the data collection process as 'open policy making' in which a 'diverse range of stakeholders' were able to shape marine conservation,[84] as discussed above, the regional IAs were almost entirely dominated by industry and SNCB

[79] S. R. Arnstein, 'A Ladder of Citizen Participation' (1969) 35 *Journal of the American Planning Association* 216–224.

[80] DEFRA, 'Tranche 1: Impact Assessment: Final Stage. IA No: DEFRA 1475' (DEFRA, 2013), para 4.6.

[81] DEFRA, 'Tranche 1: Impact Assessment: Final Stage', para 6.11.

[82] DEFRA, 'Tranche 2: Impact Assessment: Final Stage. IA No: DEFRA 1810' (DEFRA, 2015), para 8.19; DEFRA, 'Tranche 3: Impact Assessment: Final Stage. IA No.: Defra/MAR/008' (DEFRA, 2018), para 8.20.

[83] RPC 12-DEFRA-1604 shows a red assessment. RPC, 'Opinion – Impact Assessment: Designation of Marine Conservation Zones' RPC 12-DEFRA-1604(2) shows a green assessment, following the amendments.

[84] DEFRA, 'Tranche 1: Impact Assessment: Final Stage', para 1.5.

advice and in cases in which SNCBs did not have sufficient information, the data of industry taken at face value, with the potential for regulatory capture. This is particularly problematic given industry's tendency to overestimate costs, as DEFRA itself acknowledged.[85] The final IA for tranche one explicitly states that 'it has not been possible to verify the cost estimates provided by industry'.[86] This points to the importance of the consultation phase where public interest groups had a chance to feed their expertise and knowledge that could be used to support the scrutiny of industry data, though as mentioned consultation did not often result in substantial changes.

As for tranches two and three, although DEFRA held pre-consultation engagement events through meetings and workshops with representatives of affected industries, conservation NGOs and local stakeholders,[87] at its core the consultation IAs continue to use the same data from the regional IAs as a basis for identifying management assumptions and costs. Notwithstanding, in light of the information collected during the pre-consultation engagement some changes were made, including updates on baseline data to reflect latest best available information and creating new sources of socio-economic information to cross-check existing data. In addition, more specifically for tranche two, another stage was introduced, during which additional information submitted by stakeholders, when raising concerns about draft scenarios, was 'validated through engagement with appropriate experts in DEFRA, Natural England, JNCC, the MMO, Centre for Environment, Fisheries, and Aquaculture Science (Cefas) and the Environment Agency',[88] showing a higher level of engagement and collaborative decision-making. As for tranche three, the voice of environmental NGOs was more prominent as they were given the opportunity to submit sites for highly mobile species, then assessed for their scientific and economic suitability, with other stakeholders able to comment during the formal consultation process.[89] Although only two of the proposed twenty-one sites by NGOs were accepted, this represents some progress from previous assessments.

3.7 DEFRA IAs: Engaging Simplifications?

Simplifications are visible on a number of fronts when analysing DEFRA IAs. Firstly, in relation to assumptions, most of them mimic that which has been described under the regional IAs, with the consultation IA for tranche one explicitly referring to the key assumptions of the regional IAs.[90]

[85] DEFRA, 'Tranche 1: Impact Assessment: Consultation Stage', E.16.

[86] DEFRA, 'Tranche 1: Impact Assessment: Final Stage', footnote 13.

[87] DEFRA, 'Tranche 2: Impact Assessment: Consultation Stage. IA No.: DEFRA 1810' (DEFRA, 2014), Box 2 and Defra, 'Tranche 3: Impact Assessment: Consultation Stage. IA No: DEFRA/MAR/008' (DEFRA, 2017), para 6.2.

[88] DEFRA, 'Tranche 2: Impact Assessment: Consultation Stage', Box 2.

[89] DEFRA, 'Tranche 3: Impact Assessment: Consultation Stage', para 2.11.

[90] DEFRA, 'Tranche 1: Impact Assessment: Consultation Stage', para 3.2.46.

This means that in most cases, arbitrary midpoint calculations remain unaltered. Taking the examples discussed above, in the case of fisheries, the seventy-five per cent displacement figure remains present. Although in the consultation response of tranche two sites, it is noted that some consultees challenged the assumption, no action was taken because no evidence was available from these responses enabling a change to be made.[91] A similar justification is provided in relation to tranche three, stating that no changes were made as consultees were unable to provide an 'alternative viable method'.[92] As for the case of ports, harbours, shipping and disposal sites, again analysis and assumptions are replicated from the regional IA[93] with the best estimate of impact taken to be the midpoint estimate in tranche one and tranche two.

However, certain changes are visible in tranche three given that the IA, differently from the previous tranches, presents four scenarios to capture the range of costs and rather than selecting the midpoint, consultation with the MMO and Cefas led to a decision that the best estimate should be the midpoint between two lowest cost scenarios, in light of the number of historical applications that had been received.[94] If this shows less arbitrary decision-making in place, it should nevertheless be noted that tranche three sites were adapted to reduce or remove the need for port mitigation.[95] This effectively constitutes double-counting of economic considerations, already accounted for in the regional MCZs projects and suggests a degree of regulatory capture within the decision-making process.

Looking at other sectors, some arbitrary decision-making is again visible even without resorting to midpoint calculation. For example, in the case of aggregates, for tranche two, although a high- and low-cost scenario were produced, the high-cost scenario is considered 'most likely' so taken as the best estimate.[96] And, for tranche three, the low-cost estimate is taken to be the best estimate.[97] However, neither in IAs for tranche two nor three, a rationale is provided for these choices.

Secondly, simplifications are present in the split between 'maintain' and 'recover' objectives as part of the general management approach proposed. Like for regional IAs, it is only features that have been assigned a 'recover' objective that are assumed to be additionally impacted by MCZ designation, while it is assumed that those with a 'maintain' objective will not need any additional management following designation.[98] As mentioned in regard to the

[91] DEFRA, 'Tranche 2: Impact Assessment: Final Stage', para 7.26.
[92] DEFRA, 'Tranche 3: Impact Assessment: Final Stage', para 7.33.
[93] DEFRA, 'Tranche 1: Impact Assessment: Consultation Stage', para 3.2.104.
[94] DEFRA, 'Tranche 3: Impact Assessment: Final Stage', para 7.48.
[95] Ibid, para 7.51.
[96] DEFRA, 'Tranche 2: Impact Assessment: Final Stage', para 7.9.
[97] DEFRA, 'Tranche 3: Impact Assessment: Final Stage', para 7.14.
[98] DEFRA, 'Tranche 1: Impact Assessment: Final Stage', para 7.4, DEFRA, 'Tranche 2: Impact Assessment: Final Stage', para 7.7; DEFRA, 'Tranche 3: Impact Assessment: Final Stage', para 7.11.

regional IAs, this is centred on a simplistic and static baseline that assumes that features will remain in their 'favourable' or 'unfavourable' condition for the duration of the twenty-year assessment period. As the Wildlife Trust emphasised during the consultation for the second tranche MCZs,[99] this is problematic primarily because the assumption that there will be no improvement or deterioration in feature condition means that benefits arising from designation will be underestimated. Specifically, those relating to features that are protected from further deterioration under 'maintain' conservation objectives.

This shows that the criticisms raised at the regional IAs remain valid for the DEFRA IAs, whose calculations are not always well evidenced and rational as advocated by the Better Regulation's rhetoric. Nevertheless, if the focus is shifted from the assumptions to the discussion on values, DEFRA IAs present a more nuanced analysis.[100] Specifically, DEFRA recognises a clear distinction between economic and intrinsic, 'non-use' value, but also goes further to distinguish intrinsic values in the anthropocentric and non-anthropocentric sense, with the latter being 'beyond human knowledge'.[101] This constitutes a positive step and, although not going as far as recognising relational values, it acknowledges at least the existence of multiple values, departing from one-dimensional instrumental interpretation of values typical of many cost-benefit analyses. Having said this, the acknowledgement of multiple values changes little in the practical account of values, as discussed below in the section on the imbalance between costs and benefits.

3.8 DEFRA IAs: Contributing to Distributive Injustice?

The way in which the IAs calculated costs arising out of the designation of MCZs was through a mixture of additional costs to industry and costs to public bodies. Additional costs comprise both the costs of making future licence applications (extra time involved in considering the impacts of a proposal on MCZ broad-scale habitats) and costs arising from the need to comply with measures to mitigate human impacts on protected features, such as relocation of an activity or reduction or ban. Public sector costs include those related to monitoring, enforcement and environmental reporting. Industry costs were taken at face value. As mentioned earlier, in the final IA for tranche one, it is admitted that for many sectors, the figures were provided at the discretion of industry showing how the IA process can end up favouring economic interests. The weight assigned to economic interests has evident consequences in the designation of MCZs including the reduction of number of sites, the

[99] DEFRA, 'Tranche 2: Impact Assessment: Final Stage', para 8.19.

[100] See DEFRA, 'Tranche 1: Impact Assessment: Final Stage' (2013), para 2.1 and footnote 13; DEFRA, 'Tranche 2: Impact Assessment: Final Stage', para 3.1 and footnote 17 and DEFRA, 'Tranche 3: Impact Assessment: Final Stage', para 4.1 and footnote 24.

[101] See DEFRA, 'Tranche 2: Impact Assessment: Final Stage', footnote 17.

decision to remove Reference Areas, the adjustments of boundaries to avoid conflicts with existing activities, with IAs effectively double-counting some of the economic impacts that had already been taken into account during the stakeholder regional projects when deciding the list of recommended sites. The bias towards industry costs as against the benefits of protection is a criticism applicable to all DEFRA IAs and also emphasised by the Environment Audit Committee Report on tranche one.[102]

As with the regional IAs, an imbalance between costs and benefits is conspicuous. This is primarily due to the different methods for assessing costs and benefits, with benefits assessed primarily qualitatively and costs quantitatively. Having, on the one hand, costs quantified, often based upon a range of arbitrary midpoint estimates and on highly uncertain data (even in situation of uncertainty through the use of crude assumptions), and on the other hand, benefits not quantified is likely to produce one-sided results in the cost-benefit analysis, given that the qualitative data are not included in the final calculations. DEFRA itself recognises this as a problem, stating that the IAs are likely to result in a relative bias against the benefits versus costs.[103]

Starting with the consultation IA for tranche one, it is visible that benefits are assessed only qualitatively using an ecosystem service approach,[104] whereby a typology of services (provisioning, regulating, cultural and supporting services) is constructed to group together the benefits that can be identified.[105] After a number of consultation responses raising this as a key concern,[106] DEFRA's approach towards benefits improved in the final IA, which displays some monetised benefits that MCZ designation is able to supply.[107] That being said, these benefits are only designed to be illustrative, so as to aid the comparison that takes place with costs. Therefore, when it comes to inclusion in the overall summary of benefits, the IA states that 'there is a lack of scientific and economic research on the marine environment suitable for adapting for use in benefits evaluation'.[108]

The same approach is followed in subsequent tranches with some benefits monetised but only serving an illustrative purpose and not included in the final calculations. DEFRA's justification is the lack of technical evidence to provide

[102] The Environmental Audit Committee report states, citing evidence from the Wildlife and Countryside Link, that little attempt was made to assess the benefits of protection such as sense of well-being, capture and storage of carbon, recreation. Environmental Audit Committee, 'Marine Protected Areas', pp. 10–11.

[103] DEFRA, 'Tranche 1: Impact Assessment: Final Stage', para 7.21, DEFRA, 'Tranche 2: Impact Assessment: Consultation Stage', para 7.20; DEFRA, 'Tranche 3: Impact Assessment: Final Stage', para 8.22.

[104] DEFRA, 'Tranche 1: Impact Assessment: Consultation Stage', para 1.5.26.

[105] Ibid, para 1.5.20.

[106] DEFRA, 'Tranche 1: Impact Assessment: Final Stage', para 7.19.

[107] Ibid, Table 7. [108] Ibid, para 7.6.

sufficient certainty to these calculations that would have allowed for formal quantification to take place[109] and the inherent difficulty that comes with proving causality between the designation of MCZs and benefits that may arise as ecosystem services. For example, the consultation IA for tranche two explains how, even when there is growth in ecosystem services (recreation and tourism in particular), it 'is difficult to attribute to MCZs as there are many factors that contribute to growth'.[110] Meanwhile, a similar argument is used in relation to commercial fisheries to explain how it is 'difficult to attribute [responsibility] solely to MCZs as there are always many contributing factors to fisheries productivity'.[111]

Moreover, in tranche three, we witness a step backwards in regard to the inclusion of benefits as none of the additional sites that were proposed by the SNCBs or NGOs were included in any benefits calculations. This is primarily down to the fact that the majority of DEFRA's monetised data for the benefits comes from a commissioned research that was published in 2013 and therefore only considered sites originally proposed for designation by the regional stakeholder groups.[112] Therefore, while there is no doubting that MCZ designation will enhance ecosystem services – with illustrative studies suggesting that this could be worth as much as £262 m from recreational benefits alone[113] – there has been little progress towards formal quantification since the final IA of tranche one. So long as uncertainty is met with arbitrary estimates regarding industry costs and the benefits section is left entirely unquantified, the decision-making process remains vulnerable to bias and the cost-benefit analysis far from objective.

Finally, like for regional IAs, we see differential treatment regarding how uncertainty was considered. If, for certain sectors, crude assumptions were made regarding additional mitigation costs, for other sectors uncertainty meant that the costs were not monetised. This is visible in relation to the archaeology sector for instance, where the costs to future licence applications are not provided. Similarly, the socio-economic impacts on local communities from the effects of fisheries remain un-costed.[114]

3.9 Conclusion

The chapter has presented a theoretically informed analysis of IAs for MCZs designation. Focusing the discussion on IAs accompanying the process of designation has not been a light task though, as there have been two 'rounds' of IAs: one to accompany the recommendations on MCZs designation made by

109 DEFRA, 'Tranche 2: Impact Assessment: Consultation Stage', para 7.6.
110 Ibid, para 7.7. 111 Ibid.
112 DEFRA, 'Tranche 3: Impact Assessment: Final Stage', para 8.12.
113 Ibid, para 11.1.
114 DEFRA, 'Tranche 1: Impact Assessment: Consultation Stage', E.14.

the regional stakeholder projects in 2012 and the second by DEFRA when formally consulting on the establishment of each of the three tranches of MCZs. Furthermore, for each tranche of MCZs, there have been two sets of DEFRA IAs, either side of the public consultation. This has meant processing a large quantity of technical material, and it has not been possible to provide an in-depth discussion of how each marine sector has been represented in the various IAs but only to extrapolate key examples to evidence the arguments made.

It has been demonstrated how IAs for MCZs are, to use the language of the sociology of translation, centres of calculation, displacing and mobilising complex and evolving series of events, processes and actors into a standardised and homogenous form, which then is used to act on them. In doing so, IAs are acts of power, engage in simplifications and do not foster distributive justice. This is because they privilege particular interests and voices at the expenses of others, they deal with uncertainty by simplifying management scenarios and making crude assumptions, they do not treat in an equal way sectors and do assign more weight to costs than benefits, justifying this on the basis that the quantification logic employed does not work for representing many benefits, though, incongruously, it is used to represent highly uncertain costs. Ultimately, by reducing everything to a trade-off between different interests, they do not help the development of shared ethics of care and commoning practices and are unable to represent relational values and account for complex social-ecological relations and the more than human.

Furthermore, the phased approach to designation has served only partially as a reflective aid to improve the IAs. Indeed, although certain positive developments have been highlighted, for instance the inclusion of pre-consultation engagement activities in the IAs for the second and third tranches, helping certain voices to be heard, key problems have persisted and sometimes a step backwards has been taken, such as in the case of the consideration of benefits in the third tranche MCZs compared to the second tranche. Much has to do with the fact that the DEFRA IAs have heavily relied on the regional projects material, without questioning some of its (flawed) assumptions and simplistic approach to management. A lot has also to do with the lack of evidence available, both ecological and socio-economic and the necessity to rely on industry costs without much external scrutiny. Some has also to do with the fact that certain variables are hard to quantify. However, problems should not only be attributed to technical/methodological faults, lack of evidence or difficulties to quantify but also to ontological, epistemological and ethical assumptions underlying the cost-benefit analysis at the basis of the IAs. Cost-benefit analyses, in order to make comparisons, need to reduce complex social-ecological relationships to interests, understood as pre-existing and somewhat static. Such splitting of benefits versus costs, of the environment versus socio-economic, of industry knowledge versus SNCBs scientific knowledge does not do justice to much more complex and evolving social-ecological processes and erases the possibility to consider relational ethical values. Ultimately, it does not contribute to commoning and does not recognise the sea as a social-ecological system. As a final note, it should be stated that a more nuanced accounting of environmental factors has been developed by the Natural Capital Committee recently.[115] The Natural Capital Committee created a natural accounting framework to track progress of the 25 Years Environmental Plan,[116] and the natural accounting framework has been incorporated in the HM Treasury Green Book,[117] with the aim of strengthening the valuation of environmental costs and benefits. It is too early to know how the natural capital guidance will be considered in future IAs. The Natural Capital Committee end of term report[118] recommends that the RPC red flags those IAs that will result in significant losses of natural capital. In any case, the extent to which the new accounting for natural capital will be able to overcome the more fundamental ontological, epistemological and ethical concerns raised in this chapter remains to be seen.

[115] The Natural Capital Committee was an independent advisory committee which ran from 2012 until 2020. It was established following the HM Government, *The Natural Choice: Securing the Value of Nature* (Cm 8082, 2011). Its role was to advise government on natural capital and helped the development of the government 25 Year Environmental Plan (HM Government, 'A Green Future: Our 25 Year Plan to Improve the Environment', 2018). The Natural Capital Committee's role has come to an end as the scrutiny of the 25 Year Environmental Plan is now in the hands of the Office for Environmental Protection, established under the Environment Act 2021 (see Chapter 8 below for further discussion). It is worth noting, though that the Natural Capital Committee's full remit and functions do not transfer over to the Office for Environmental Protection.

[116] HM Government, 'A Green Future'. [117] HM Treasury, 'Green Book', p. 63.

[118] Natural Capital Committee, 'End of Term Report to the Domestic and Economy Implementation Committee of the Cabinet' (Natural Capital Committee, 2020).

4

Risk-Based Regulation

The Case of the Revised Approach to Fisheries in Marine Protected Areas

4.1 Introduction

This chapter presents another aspect of the rationalisation of regulation by discussing risk-based approaches to regulating fisheries in MPAs. Fishing is presumably the first activity that comes to mind when thinking about the use of marine space and fish stock are an important CPR, as the Brexit debate highlighted. Although the number of fishers and fishing vessels has fallen from the mid-1990s and there is a long-term trend of decline in landings in the UK, the fishing industry remains an important commercial activity.[1] Environmental regulatory control is needed to minimise fisheries' impact not only on fish stock but also on marine ecosystems. However, until recently in England, fisheries were not a key regulatory object of marine conservation law. While most activities affecting MPAs features are regulated through the marine licence regime, fishing activities are not, thus potentially escaping sustained regulatory control.

Over ten years ago, environmental NGOs shed light on this issue, criticising the fact that existing fishing activities in European Marine Sites were, problematically, deemed to be compatible with site integrity. Following pushes from the environmental NGOs, the government introduced a revised approach to inshore fisheries management in 2012 to comply with article 6 of the Habitats Directive, which requires that an appropriate assessment is carried out prior to deciding whether to grant permission to plans and projects that may affect the integrity of the European Marine Site in question.[2] Fishing is now deemed a 'project' as per regulation 63 of the Habitats Regulations, which transpose article 6 of the Habitats Directive into English law and therefore subject to its requirements. As the Habitats Regulations form part of retained EU law, their interpretation should follow retained case law, as per Section 6(3) of the European Union Withdrawal Act 2018 (EUWA), unless interpreted by the Supreme Court and the Court of Appeal, who are free to depart from retained

[1] E. Uberoi et al., 'UK Fisheries Statistics' (House of Commons Library, 2021) at: https://researchbriefings.files.parliament.uk/documents/SN02788/SN02788.pdf.

[2] Article 6 of the Habitats Directive is transposed under regulation 63 of the Habitats Regulations.

EU case law.[3] This implies an interpretation driven by a strong precautionary principle, following *Waddenzee*.[4]

However, rather than producing a complete ban on fishing activities, unless proven not be environmentally damaging, which would have showed a strong precautionary approach, England has adopted a risk-based and phased approach, creating a matrix that divides European Marine Sites into red, amber, green and blue based on the risk degree of gear/(sub)feature interactions. Applying the logic of risk-based regulation has meant that the enclosure of fisheries has been partial and this is a welcome step towards a proportionate response, but it runs the risks of not being sufficiently precautionary to comply with the interpretation of article 6(3) of the Habitats Directive under retained case law. Besides, risk-based regulation is not without its critics[5] and even in this case certain shortcomings are apparent, as will be made clear below. In reviewing the English revised approach, the chapter pays attention also to the actors involved and the knowledges accepted as evidence in developing and implementing the approach and in doing so it also taps into debates of commoning, asking whether the revised approach has facilitated collective problem-solving and epistemic inclusivity.

The chapter begins by introducing the literature on (over)fishing and the tragedy of the commons.[6] Then, it turns to the regulatory history of commercial inshore fisheries operations within European Marine Sites, critically discussing the development of the revised approach. In presenting the case of the revised approach to fisheries in MPAs, the chapter draws on and reflects on key theoretical insights on risk-based regulation for the management of the commons.

4.2 Fishing, the Tragedy of the Commons and MPAs

Fishers are central marine actors, and fishing is a major activity in the marine environment. In the UK, although the industry's value to the UK economy is negligible, many coastal communities depend on it and fishing's significance

[3] See Section 6(4) of the EUWA and regulation 3(b) of the European Union Withdrawal Act 2018 (Relevant Court) (Retained EU Case Law) Regulations 2020 (SI 2020/1525), hereafter EUWA (Relevant Court) Regulations. See also Chapter 8 below for a discussion on retained law and case law.

[4] *Waddenzee.*

[5] J. Black, 'The Emergence of Risk-Based Regulation and the New Public Risk Management in the United Kingdom' (2005) (Aut) *Public Law* 512–549; B. M. Hutter, 'The Attractions of Risk-Based Regulation: Accounting for the Emergence of Risk Ideas in Regulation' (2005) *CARR Discussion Paper 33* at: https://citeseerx.ist.psu.edu/viewdoc/download?doi=10.1.1.125.7494&rep=rep1&type=pdf; J. Black, 'Risk-Based Regulation: Choices, Practices and Lessons Being Learned' in OECD (ed.), *Risk and Regulatory Policy: Improving the Governance of Risk* (OECD, 2010), pp. 185–224; J. Black and R. Baldwin, 'Really Responsive Risk-Based Regulation', (2010) 32 *Law and Policy* 181–213.

[6] Hardin, 'The Tragedy of the Commons'.

in the Brexit debate has showed that it holds a key political value as a symbol of national identity and independence with fishers being vocal leave supporters.[7]

Fisheries are a classic CPR as they are subject to the subtractability and exclusion problems. Fishing by one user reduces availability of fish stock for others, and it is difficult, though not impossible, to exclude users from fishing given that the property rights system in the sea is not as structured as on land. Besides, unsustainable fishing practices do not only affect fish stock but can also have detrimental environmental consequences. It would be erroneous to speak about fisheries' impact on marine ecosystems in the singular, given that fishing activities affect marine ecosystems to different degrees and extent and not all of them require the same type of regulatory control and limitation.

Fisheries' environmental impacts include disturbance to and damage of the pelagic environment, of benthic communities and associated ecosystem services, bycatch (incidental capture of non-target species) as well as the removal of target species. The extent of the impact depends on a number of factors. The type of fishing gear is a key factor as mobile fishing gears, such as dredging or trawling, tend to have a higher environmental impact compared to static gears, such as pots or creels. There are, however, many other variables influencing fisheries' impact, including the size of the fishing fleet, the intensity of fishing and the volume of catches as well as the sensitivity of species, habitats and communities and the background environmental conditions of the habitats impacted. Small-scale fisheries tend to be more sustainable than large-scale fishing fleets, with the former having lower extraction rates and using more static gears.[8]

Over-exploitation of fisheries and related environmental degradation has been subject to much attention in academic literature being a classic example of the tragedy of the commons. To avoid the tragedy, regulation is necessary but there are divergent views among scholars regarding what constitutes the most appropriate regulatory approach. Proposals to avoid tragedies through either direct state regulation or conversion of a CPR into a private good have been met with sustained criticism by the commons' scholars reacting to Hardin. Commons scholars have written critically about enclosures of fisheries commons demonstrating that state regulation or privatisation is not necessarily the most effective tools for the management of shared resources.[9] Studies have ranged from documenting successful cases of community-based

[7] The UK in a Changing Europe, 'Fisheries and Brexit' (2020) at: https://ukandeu.ac.uk/wp-content/uploads/2020/06/Fisheries-and-Brexit.pdf.

[8] O. Guyader et al., 'Small Scale Fisheries in Europe: A Comparative Analysis Based on a Selection of Case Studies' (2013) 140 *Fisheries Research* 1–13.

[9] McCay and Acheson, *The Question of the Commons*; E. Berkes (ed.), *Common Property Resources: Ecology and Community-Based Sustainable Development* (Belhaven Press, 1990).

fisheries management such as the Cree fishery operating in the coastal waters of James Bay, Canada,[10] to co-management approaches such as those established in the well-known case of the Maine lobster fishery studied by Acheson[11] and advocated by other leading fisheries scholars.[12]

MPAs enter into these debates as they can constitute one type of spatial enclosure of fisheries commons. McCay, in a comparative review of measures used to enclose the fisheries commons to avert tragedies, includes MPAs stating that 'from a fisheries perspective, MPAs may be thought of as "exclosures"',[13] where they are set up for the protection of the natural environment limiting or excluding fisheries or other activities. This criticism has been at the core of much parks and people literature, considered in Chapter 1, and it is especially targeted at those MPAs that have been established by the state and substantially limit or prohibit fisheries activities. For example, Christie et al. differentiate, somewhat simplistically, between MPAs established by the state (the 'park model') and those that are community-based, with the former being MPAs where 'a governmental agency declares an area out-of-bounds for some or all activities'.[14] Even if also community-based models of MPAs have been subject to criticisms, much anthropological literature on MPAs has primarily voiced concerns over the 'park model' arguing that state interventions aimed at nature protection can aggravate social injustices by fomenting conflict, disrupting coastal communities' economies and negatively affecting fishers who have no ability to displace when changes to fishing practices are required as part of the management measures.[15]

Fishing displacement can take many forms, for example, from removal of the fishery pressure altogether from the MPAs temporarily or permanently to

[10] F. Berkes, 'Fishery Resource Use in a Subarctic Indian Community' (1997) 5 *Human Ecology* 289–307.

[11] J. M. Acheson, *Capturing the Commons: Devising Institutions to Manage the Maine Lobster Industry* (University Press of New England, 2004).

[12] S. Jentoft, 'Fisheries Co-management: Delegating Government Responsibility to Fishermen's Organizations' (1989) 13 *Marine Policy* 137–154; Pinkerton, Cooperative Management of Local Fisheries; B. McCay and S. Jentoft, 'From the Bottom Up: Participatory Issues in Fisheries Management' (1996) 9 *Society and Natural Resources* 237–250; B. McCay, 'Muddling through the Clam Beds: Cooperative Management of New Jersey's Hard Clam Spawner Sanctuaries' (1988) 7 *Journal of Shellfish Research* 327–340; N. L. Gutierrez, R. Hilborn and O. Defeo, 'Leadership, Social Capital and Incentives Promote Successful Fisheries' (2011) 470 *Nature* 386–389.

[13] B. McCay, 'Enclosing the Fisheries Commons', in D. H. Cole and E. Ostrom (eds.), *Property in Land and Other Resources* 2012 (Lincoln Institute of Land Policy, 2012), pp. 219–258, p. 221.

[14] P. Christie et al., 'Towards Developing a Complete Understanding: A Social Science Research Agenda for Marine Protected Areas' (2003) 28 *Fisheries* 22–25, p. 23.

[15] T. Agardy, 'Dangerous Targets? Unresolved Issues and Ideological Clashes around Marine Protected Areas' (2003) 13 *Aquatic Conservation: Marine and Freshwater Ecosystems* 353–367; M. B. Mascia, C. A. Claus and R. Naidoo, 'Impacts of Marine Protected Areas on Fishing Communities' (2010) 24 *Conservation Biology* 1424–1429; P. West, J. Igoe and D. Brockington, 'Parks and Peoples: The Social Impacts of Protected Areas' (2006) 35 *Annual review* of *anthropology* 251–277.

requiring changes in fishing gear.[16] Displacement is a term used to include both changes to fishing behaviour (substitution of fishing gear) and patterns (change of fishing grounds), and it was something feared by all fishers I interviewed when designation of MCZs was underway in 2013 and management measures still not decided.[17] In this light, it is evident that MPAs can be seen as enclosures with the emphasis being on the negative social impacts and economic dislocations suffered by local fishers in the name of environmental protection. As explained in Chapter 1, highlighting the politicised nature of conservation initiatives and the way in which they produce space and subjectivities restructuring sea-users' interactions with the marine environment permits focusing on the local scale, the material effects of protected areas and the disruptions caused to local actors such as fishers here and now. To avoid such disruptions, a serious consideration of fishers' livelihoods when designating and managing MPAs is needed.

Studies have showed that there is variety in regard to MPAs' effects on fishing with some MPAs having, or with the potential to have, a positive effect on the social well-being of fishers.[18] Positive cases exist displaying the complementarity of MPAs with fisheries management tools[19] or the inclusion of fisheries voices into the development of MPAs establishment and management leading to food security, sustainable livelihoods and social acceptability.[20]

Thus, the relationship between MPAs and fisheries is complex. From a fisheries perspective, MPAs might be considered in a negative light as sites of enclosure and dispossession for local fishers, disrupting livelihoods and offering few tangible immediate economic benefits. However, many MPAs allow for the continuation of some fisheries activities and/or have no negative consequences in terms of income or loss of resource control, often enabled by successful co-management strategies. In any case, the full integration of MPAs and fisheries management remains challenging for a number of reasons. The high variability of marine ecosystems coupled with the lack of full scientific knowledge on many marine ecosystems makes decisions regarding disturbance levels difficult.[21] Besides as MPAs are 'socio-political enterprises'[22] not just technical

16 D. Vaughan, 'Fishing Effort Displacement and the Consequences of Implementing Marine Protected Area Management-an English Perspective' (2017) 84 *Marine Policy* 228–234.

17 As explained in the Introduction of the book, semi-structured interviews were conducted with fisheries communities in England in the South-West and South-East in the lead up to the designation of MCZs as part of an ESRC funded project (ES/K001043/1).

18 Mascia, 'Impacts of Marine Protected Areas on Fishing Communities'; P. J. S. Jones, *Governing Marine Protected Areas: Resilience through Diversity* (Routledge, 2013).

19 L. R. Little et al., 'Complementarity of No-take Marine Reserves and Individual Transferable Catch Quotas for Managing the Line Fishery of the Great Barrier Reef' (2011) 25 *Conservation Biology* 333–340.

20 J. Y. Weigel et al., 'Marine Protected Areas and Fisheries: Bridging the Divide' (2014) S2 *Aquatic Conservation Marine and Freshwater Ecosystems* 199–215.

21 B. J. McCay and P. J. S. Jones, 'Marine Protected Areas and the Governance of Marine Ecosystems and Fisheries' (2011) 25 *Conservation Biology* 1130–1133.

22 R. Chuenpagdee et al., 'Marine Protected Areas: Re-thinking Their Inception' (2013) 39 *Marine Policy* 234–240.

tools, they are embedded within wider (and often contested) political and legal contexts and by redefining space, they construct new relationships between fishers and fishing grounds affecting communities often already limited in resource use and producing new subjectivities.

Where does the English approach to fisheries within MPAs fit in this diverse spectrum? Are MPAs in England used as spatial tools to enclose the fisheries commons causing disruptions to livelihoods and exclusions, or have they managed fisheries in a more constructive way?

To answer these questions, the next section starts with an historical note explaining that until recently, existing fisheries activities within MPAs were untouched. The MPAs in question, European Marine Sites, did not limit or subject existing fishing activities to any regulatory control and/or limitation.

4.3 Commercial Fisheries in European Marine Sites: Background

For many years, in England, fishing within European Marine Sites was exempt from the management controls of article 6 of the Habitats Directive. DEFRA's justification for this, drawing on the goal of sustainable development underpinning the Habitats Directive,[23] was that the protection of biodiversity needs to take into account socio-economic requirements, as per article 2(3). The logic was that, as European Marine Sites had been designated in the light of their conservation value enduring in association with existing activities, these activities were to be left unaffected by designation.[24] For DEFRA, continuing established fishing activity was compatible with the conservation objectives of European Marine Sites and was not to be considered a plan or project under article 6(3), unless demonstrated it was causing damage to the integrity of the site.

However, in the well-known *Waddenzee* case, the European Court of Justice held that an activity (in that case mechanical cockle fishing) which has been carried out for many years but for which a licence is granted annually is a 'plan' or 'project' under article 6(3) of the Habitats Directive[25] and so should be subject to an appropriate assessment of its implications for the site in view of the site's conservation objectives. In that case, mechanical cockle fisheries' licenses could be renewed only after the competent national authority had ascertained that they would not negatively affect the integrity of the site. The *Waddenzee* case has attracted much attention in environmental law because it proposes a strong version of the precautionary principle, stating that a risk exists 'if it

23 The preamble of the Habitats Directive reads: 'Whereas, the main aim of this Directive being to promote the maintenance of biodiversity, taking account of economic, social, cultural and regional requirements, this Directive makes a contribution to the *general objective of sustainable development*' (emphasis added).

24 R. Clark et al., 'Dialectics of Nature: The Emergence of Policy on the Management of Commercial Fisheries in English European Marine Sites' (2017) 78 *Marine Policy* 11–17, p. 13.

25 *Waddenzee*, para 29.

cannot be excluded on the basis of objective information that the plan or project will have significant effects on the site concerned'.[26] For the purposes of this chapter, the case is also significant from a substantive viewpoint because it conceptualises ongoing licensed fishing activities as a project, thus subject to the management provisions under article 6 of the Habitats Directive. Such broad interpretation of what counts as a project has implications for many licensed fishing activities occurring within or near a European Marine Site and it is contrary to the initial DEFRA approach outlined above.

DEFRA's 'reply' to the case was that in England fishing was a common law public right not authorised by any 'competent national authority', as per article 6(3).[27] Such a rationale was challenged by two environmental NGOs in a campaign running from 2008 to 2012 with the threat of a court case. The environmental NGOs contended that fishing required the granting of vessel licences by the MMO, hence fishing was authorised by a competent national authority. As a solution, the NGOs proposed that the MMO would include a prohibition of fishing in European Marine Sites. Fishing would then be allowed only if subject to the requirements of article 6(3), that is, demonstrating that it was not likely to have a significant impact on the integrity of the site following an appropriate assessment, whose costs were to be incurred by the license holder. The NGOs' proposal effectively reversed DEFRA's initial position that had placed the burden of proof on conservation whereby fishing would be stopped only if proven to having a significant effect on the site. The NGOs' proposed approach placed the burden of proof on the licence holders. The MMO refused the NGOs' proposal on proportionality grounds, arguing that a blanket prohibition on all fishing activity in all marine European Marine Sites in England was disproportionate and not in line with risk-based regulation principles.[28] Citing a Natural England review on European Marine Sites' risk, the MMO specified that only a very small proportion of fishing activities could pose a high risk to some sites, with the majority posing low risk[29] and that the blanket ban was disproportionate given the diversities of sites and fishing fleets. The MMO also specified that fisheries had not fallen off the regulatory net because in certain high-risk cases, emergency byelaws or voluntary agreements, where appropriate, had been introduced. As environmental NGOs continued to push the government for a proper engagement with article 6(3),[30] a middle ground between precaution and proportionality was reached with the government's introduction of the revised approach to fisheries in 2012 for European Marine Sites. The revised approach to fisheries has also served as a basis for managing

[26] *Waddenzee*, para 44.

[27] DEFRA correspondence reported by T. Appleby and J. Harrison, 'Taking the Pulse of Environmental and Fisheries Law: The Common Fisheries Policy, the Habitats Directive, and Brexit' (2019) 31 *Journal of Environmental Law* 443–464, p. 447.

[28] MMO correspondence reported by Clark et al., 'Dialectics of Nature', p. 14.

[29] Ibid. [30] Ibid.

MCZs since 2013, following tranche one of MCZs designations. The next session discussed the revised approach showing that the adoption of a careful risk-based and phased approach underpinned by the development of a matrix has meant that MPAs have not been used as spatial enclosures banning all fishing. Moreover, the evidence base for the risk-based framework has been collected in a collaborative way and to provide oversight of the implementation DEFRA established an Implementation Group made of regulators, industry and environmental NGOs. The Implementation Group, originally set up for European Marine Sites, enabled a collaborative approach to regulation. Such institutional development could be considered an example of commoning. Though this is welcome, some shortcomings are present as the matrix is not only a technical tool but a way of seeing the world, defining risk, determining what counts as evidence and who can provide it, with necessary blind spots and omissions.

4.4 Revised Approach to Fisheries within MPAs

The revised approach follows a risk-based and phased approach to the regulation of existing fisheries within MPAs. Risk-based approaches are not novel in the field of environmental law. Due to the complex and fast-changing nature of the subject of regulation, that is, social-ecological systems, risk-based approaches are considered suitable and rational approaches delivering regulation that is proportionate to risk and that is targeted. Besides, in an economic climate where environmental and fisheries regulatory authorities are understaffed and their budgets are stretched,[31] risk-based approaches contribute to an efficient use of regulatory resources. Finally, in a political climate that has for long favoured the cutting of the red tape, risk-based approaches are portrayed as legitimate because they limit state-based regulation. Their cost-effectiveness, focus and proportionality make them an attractive way of rationalising regulation and reducing the regulatory burden. They promise control and clear management of what seems unmanageable by directing attention to what is most risky, rendering decision-making systematic. Risk-based approaches are often underpinned by neat frameworks that synthetise cause-effect relations and categorise what is high risk from what is low risk, facilitating and streamlining decision-making and avoiding over-regulation. This makes them a legitimising device as they are seen as not being over-intrusive, hence not unfairly limiting regulatees' actions, being cost-effective, underpinned by rationality and objectivity.[32]

Risk-based approaches have been and remain a key item in the better regulation agenda, figuring in the Good Regulation principles firstly advanced by the Better Regulation Task Force and enshrined in Section 21(2) of the

[31] See the discussion on Chapter 2 on funding for monitoring and enforcement.

[32] Black, 'The Emergence of Risk-Based Regulation'.

Legislative and Regulatory Reform Act 2006.[33] The proportionality principle, as defined by the Better Regulation taskforce, states that 'Regulators should only intervene when necessary. Remedies should be appropriate to the risk posed and costs identified and minimised'.[34] The principle urges policy solutions to be proportionate to the perceived problem or risk and to justify the compliance costs imposed. Also, principle five 'targeting', which, as defined by the Better Regulation taskforce, states that 'regulation should be focused on the problem and minimise side effects', urges enforcers to focus on activities giving rise to the most serious risks.[35] Thus, risk-based approaches to regulation have come to occupy a central place offering a rational decision-making tool for both the governance of risks to society and to the environment (in our case potentially environmentally damaging fisheries) and for the regulation of risks of the governance systems themselves. Thus, it could be argued that using a risk-based approach to the management of fisheries in MPAs permits the regulator to avoid an enclosure of the commons and limits state intervention to the minimum necessary. This is to be welcome and likely to avoid conflict with fishers, whose fishing grounds remain available wherever possible. It could be concluded therefore that risk-based regulation avoids the tragedy of the commons without dispossessing resource users by protecting habitats and species as it does not require substantial displacement of fishing activities. However, the story is more complicated than that as there are a series of challenges associated with risk-based regulation approaches.

Firstly, risk-based approaches may generate conflict regarding what constitutes a risk and what evidence is required to justify regulatory action or inaction. There may be divergent views regarding risk priorities and risk acceptability between regulators, regulatees and the public. Perceptions of risks are affected by social and institutional factors, and the acceptance of risk is a political issue so that 'using the risk-based framework becomes more of a political art than a technical application'.[36] Should one focus on larger risks with low probability? Should cumulative risks be taken into account? Risks to *what* (e.g. an ecosystem or a particular species) and to *whom* (a specific group of regulatees or the public or future generations) are to be regulated? What level of risk is acceptable and who should define risks? These are all key questions regarding risk definition that may generate conflicting answers. Secondly, risk-based approaches can mask certain uncertainties when they are used in situations

[33] Section 21(1) of the Legislative and Regulatory Reform Act 2006 requires any person exercising a regulatory function to which the section applies to have regard to the good regulation principles in exercising their function. The principles are not defined in the Act.

[34] Better Regulation Task Force, 'Regulation-Less Is More: Reducing Burdens, Improving Outcomes' (2005), p. 51.

[35] Ibid, p. 52.

[36] R. Baldwin, M. Cave and M. Lodge, *Understanding Regulation: Theory, Strategy, and Practice* (Oxford University Press, 2011), p. 283.

where there is limited information and the evidence is poor and/or lacking.[37] Risk-based approaches require understanding and quantification of the likelihood of the harm so they may hide cases in which the likelihood of the harm is unknown and unquantifiable.[38]

Thirdly, when risk-based approaches are applied to complex systemic problems, they often require some simplification and standardisation in order to work. Social-ecological systems are difficult to categorise within clear cut analytical boundaries. Risk-based regulation, underpinned by scientific knowledge, demands some level of simplification and in doing so many parameters as well as uncertainties end up being removed. As Wynne put it, 'the point is that scientific knowledge proceeds by *exogenising* some significant uncertainties, which thus become invisible to it' and thus 'gives prominence to a *restricted agenda of defined uncertainties*' rendering invisible others, with risk defined by freezing part of the surrounding context.[39] Fourthly, the danger is not only that of freezing the surrounding context by excluding some parameters but also of freezing the risk-based framework itself, leading to a static framework that relies on the stability of the risks themselves. However, risks are not stable as something framed as low risk may become high risk for example with changing environmental conditions, or an accumulation of low risks may produce high risks.[40] Is there an ongoing monitoring of the performance of the risk approach itself and scope for revision and inclusion of new/emergent risks in the framework and revisitation of what falls into low/high-risk categories? If so, how and by whom is the performance assessed and risks re-categorised? What timeframe is used for re-assessing risk frameworks? Fifthly, compliance issues may be accentuated by risk-based regulation. For example, certain activities deemed to be low risk may fly under the radar, and the associated regulatees could then become high-risk creators as they are aware they are escaping the regulatory control.[41] And should the likelihood of compliance be taken into account when deciding whether to score a risk high or low? Many of the questions raised require serious consideration and debate as to who is making decisions regarding what is important and what can be left out of the regulatory gaze without blame been attached to the regulatory authority. In the words of Black, risk-based approaches involve a 'new politics of accountability'.[42]

Most of these criticisms are interrelated as it will be seen below in the analysis of the revised approach to fisheries in MPAs in England that starts by

[37] H. Rothstein et al., 'The Risks of Risk-Based Regulation: Insights from the Environmental Policy Domain' (2007) 32 *Environment International* 1056–1065.

[38] D. A Farber, 'Uncertainty' (2011) 99 *The Georgetown Law Journal* 901–960. Farber distinguishes between uncertainty (where likelihood of peril is not quantifiable) and risk (where the likelihood is quantifiable).

[39] Wynne, 'Uncertainty and Environmental Learning', p. 115.

[40] J. Black and R. Baldwin, 'When Risk-Based Regulation Aims Low'.

[41] Baldwin, Cave and Lodge, Understanding Regulation, p. 284.

[42] Black, 'The Emergence of Risk-Based Regulation'.

discussing how risk has been defined and interpreted, it continues with a discussion on how risk has been categorised in the matrix and then with a number of observations regarding the implementation of the revised approach.

4.5 Risk Definition

In line with the common methodology for assessing the impact of fisheries on European Marine Sites developed at the EU level,[43] the main regulatory tool developed by the MMO has been a risk matrix for prioritisation of risk. The matrix relates the sensitivity of features and sub-features for which MPAs have been designated to different fishing activities. The fishing activities are categorised according to gear type only, without considering other variables such as the temporal and spatial intensity of the fishing activity, feature condition and background environmental conditions in MPAs where the feature occurs.

These factors are rendered invisible in the matrix, making the categorisation only based on feature sensitivity. However, the omitted factors can have an important weight in practice as influencing the feasibility of achieving feature-specific management. For example, certain biogenic reefs such as those formed by the *Sabellaria spinulosa* worm have an ephemeral nature, thus a single data point in time might not be enough to decide whether fishing requires to be regulated in that area because the reef may not currently be present. Ongoing fishing activities may hinder the development of the reef, thus having a background historical record on the feature presence and condition is essential to identify the need for management measures.

Although this limitation was recognised by the regulators and justified on the basis that it is a generic matrix,[44] it shows nonetheless that some simplification and reduction has occurred in the representation and calculation of risk. As mentioned earlier, this is fairly typical and a key limitation of risk-based approaches. Making the unmanageable manageable requires simplification and exclusion of certain parameters, though the question which persists is whether what is rendered manageable encompasses everything that requires to be managed or, as in the case of *Sabellaria spinulosa*, may exclude certain more-than human elements. These parameters might be considered only in

[43] The common methodology is a non-binding guidance developed to harmonise at the EU level approaches to assess the impact of fisheries on European Marine Sites to comply with the Habitats Directive and ensuring a level playing field and equal treatment of fisheries in European Marine Sites. The common methodology proposes the use of a conflict matrix of gear used in European Marine Sites and habitats/species for an initial qualitative screening and an impact matrix on data on effort of gears at risk for habitats/species and data on features sensitivity, leading to a more specific quantitative analysis. Please see: The NK2 Group 'Common methodology for assessing the impact of fisheries on marine Natura 2000'. Contract No. 070307/2010/578174/SER/B3 (2012) at: https://ec.europa.eu/environment/nature/natura2000/marine/docs/Fisheries%20methodology.pdf.

[44] Management of fisheries in European Marine Sites Implementation Group. 'Protocol to inform completing the matrix' (Marine Management Organisation, 2014).

subsequent stages of the process, that is, during the site-specific analysis only where deemed appropriate. It is telling that the parameters that have been excluded are those more subject to change. The matrix, by avoiding their inclusion, is producing not only a partial but also a static representation of the relationship between fisheries and conservation and not attending to the complex relationships between the human and the more-than human. Their inclusion would have produced a much more complex matrix and one in need of constant updating. The erasure of these parameters has its advantages, making the decision-making tool simpler. At the same time, it is essential to recognise that the exclusion of these parameters contributes to freezing the background and risking making the matrix rigid. Also, as the matrix represents sensitivity without accounting for the specific conditions of the site, consideration of the feasibility of achieving feature-specific management is not present.[45] On a positive note, the matrix was intended as a live document so could be updated where new or additional evidence becomes available.[46] Conceptualising the matrix as a live document is indicative of a 'really responsive' approach to risk-based regulation, as defined by Baldwin and Black.[47] A key element of the 'really responsive' approach is sensitivity to change due to the emergence or recognition of new risks for example because of new knowledge developing on the issue in question. However, as confirmed by a DEFRA representative I interviewed, the matrix has not been formally amended.[48]

In any case, being sensitive to change by making the matrix a live document would have not necessarily solved all the issues as questions arise regarding the type and level of evidence deemed to be sufficient to make these changes in line with a precautionary approach as required by retained case law on article 6 of the Habitats Directive.

4.6 Risk Categorisation

As with many risk-based tools, a traffic light-type of system has been put in place for the categorisation of risk in the revised approach to fisheries management in MPAs. The matrix categorises the activity/(sub)feature interactions as red (high priority), amber (medium priority), green (low priority) or blue (no interaction). Following a phased approach, activity/(sub)features interactions identified as red had been the first to be subject to regulatory scrutiny with management measures introduced in 2014 as they present cases in which the conservation objectives for a feature would not be achieved due to its sensitivity

[45] S. Jennings, 'Fisheries in European Marine Sites: A Review of "the Matrix" and Associated Documentation Submitted to the Stakeholder Implementation Group (IG)' (Centre for the Environment, Fisheries and Aquaculture Science, 2012).
[46] Management of fisheries in European Marine Sites Implementation Group, 'Protocol'.
[47] Baldwin and Black, 'Really Responsive Risk-Based Regulation'.
[48] DEFRA representative, Written Communication, May 2021.

to the type of fishing in question. At the opposite side of the spectrum lies the blue category representing interactions in which no conflict arises, hence they have not been made subject to further action. The amber category includes interactions in which there is uncertainty as to whether the conservation objectives for a feature will be achieved because of its sensitivity to the type of fishing in question. In order to resolve the uncertainty, the effect of that type of fishing needs to go through a site assessment to ensure compliance with regulation 63 of the Habitats Regulations for European Marine Sites, with management measures introduced depending on the results of the assessment. The amber category is very broad because in cases where the evidence was not clear an assumption was made that the activity would fall into the amber category and assessment at site level would be required. This shows a precautionary approach in line with conservation law.

The green category presents cases where the achievement of the conservation objectives is highly unlikely to be affected by the type of fishing so further action is not required unless there is potential for a combination effect of fishing with other activities and, in that event, an assessment like the one for amber activities needs to occur. The treatment of low risks under the green category is noteworthy because, rather than letting them fall under the radar, the matrix takes into account cumulative effects and makes them subject to an assessment. Thus, it shows that the regulators have been prepared to go 'low'[49] in the regulation of risk, meaning not only tackling high risks, as well as to look beyond sector-specific matters incorporating contextual variables like other activities, taking a more 'ecosystemic' view of marine regulation. As Black and Baldwin argue,[50] choosing how low to go and how to go low is not an easy task for regulators, and in this case, a good compromise has been achieved, though the question remains if this is enough to show high precaution under conservation law.

To allocate categories in the matrix, scientific evidence and expert judgement were used[51] with Natural England tasked with populating the first draft of the matrix, seeking advice from the Implementation Group (see below). Independent review by Cefas was commissioned and the matrix revised accordingly. DEFRA retained the right to determine the final categorisation of fishing activity if the Implementation Group was not able to reach a consensus.

4.7 Implementation of the Revised Approach

The Implementation Group was set up for advising DEFRA and relevant regulators on the implementation of the revised approach to ensure fishing activities affecting MPAs were compliant with conservation law. The

49 Black and Baldwin, 'When Risk-Based Regulation Aims Low'.

50 Ibid.

51 Management of fisheries in European Marine Sites Implementation Group, 'Protocol'.

Implementation Group was chaired by DEFRA and included various representatives from fishing industry (New Under Ten Fishermen's Association, MPAs Fishing Coalition, National Federation of Fishermen Organisation and Sea Fish Industry Authority), marine regulators (MMO, IFCAs and the Environment Agency), SNCBs (JNCC and NE) and environmental NGOs (Marine Conservation Society, Wildlife Trusts and Client Earth).[52] It had an inclusive membership with groups directly affected by and/or responsible for the delivery of the revised approach and a good balance between the various stakeholders, without an overrepresentation of fishing industry interests.

The establishment of the Implementation Group can be considered an example of collaborative governance. Thus, although the risk-based framework was primarily based on scientific evidence and expertise, the Implementation Group played an important role and consensus was sought to make final decisions, pointing to a collaborative, deliberative and participatory process. In this light, the Implementation Group can be seen as a commoning practice. As described in Chapter 1, commoning is about shared practices and the way in which particular institutions, in our case MPAs, facilitate strategies aimed at social cooperation and collective decision-making. This is in line with regulatory literature's suggestion that deliberative and inclusive approaches to defining and managing risks are needed to enhance the legitimacy of risk-based approaches, though there remains the need to have safeguards in place such as public oversight and transparency of decision-making to ensure the legitimacy and accountability of the regulatory framework.[53] Given that the Implementation Group held an advisory role and that decisions rested ultimately with the Secretary of State and relevant authorities, public accountability was maintained. As for transparency, the membership of the group was publicly available listing names and affiliation of stakeholders, but minutes of meetings or advice given not readily available to public scrutiny. Unfortunately, the Implementation Group has been disbanded so the implementation of the revised approach has remained in the hands of individual IFCAs within the 0–6 nm, potentially undermining the coherence of the regulatory approach.

Regarding the choice of regulatory tools and the timing of regulatory action, this has been directly linked to the scoring, following a phased approach with more stringent regulatory measures (i.e. byelaws) introduced in sites most at risk. In the first phase of implementation, that is by 2014, seventeen byelaws, largely working to prohibit bottom-towed fishing in specific areas, had been introduced across twenty-five MPAs. The success of the risk-based, phased approach can partially be measured by the swift introduction of these

[52] Management of fisheries in European Marine Sites Implementation Group, 'Fisheries in European Marine Sites Implementation Group: Terms of reference' (Marine Management Organisation, 2014).

[53] C. Abbott and M. Lee, 'Economic Actors in EU Environmental Law' (2015) 34 *Yearbook of European Law* 26–59.

byelaws.[54] However, many of these byelaws ban bottom-towed fishing in areas where it was not already occurring, hence not adding new regulatory controls as such. On the positive side, they are still useful as a tool for future proofing.[55] Also, this has meant that fisheries displacement has been kept relatively low, avoiding high costs to the fisheries and minimising potential environmental side effects as displaced fishing could render other areas over-fished.

Secondly, although risk-based approaches are advertised to be as objective and neutral as possible, political considerations can still permeate decision-making. A report by Client Earth on the revised approach to fishing in European Marine Sites provides a telling example.[56] The byelaw in question is the 'Bottom Towed Fishing Gear (Prohibited Areas) Byelaw' by Kent and Essex IFCA.[57] Environmental NGOs had made clear that a precautionary approach would require the total closure of the Thanet Coast SAC, due to the wide distribution of protected subtidal chalk reef throughout the site, which is a feature particularly susceptible to bottom-towed trawling. However, the fishing community raised opposition to the closure during public consultation. This led to a 'compromise' whereby the majority of the site would be closed, with only a small area left open to bottom-towed trawling. The small area in question, known as the 'Gore Channel', was the key fishing ground within the SAC and was allowed to remain exposed to fishing activity in spite of the fact that predictive surveys conducted by Natural England had indicated that the protected feature was also likely to extend into this area.[58]

Similarly, the Easter IFCA approved a byelaw for the Wash and North Norfolk Coast SAC[59] requiring spatial closures to prohibit any bottom-towed gear so as to mitigate the risks of shrimp fishing to the most sensitive sub-features (sub-tidal mixed sediment, sub-tidal mud and biogenic reef). The fishing community raised objections in the consultation phase, which led to the removal of two spatial closures in the north Norfolk coast section.[60] Although

[54] Another key factor for success is effective enforcement, though this is linked more to other factors such as the drafting of the byelaw (is it written in a way that facilitate the production of evidence sufficient to satisfy a court?), the availability of resources for monitoring non-compliance, etc. In relation to the first point, enforcement challenges appear evident in the fact that in twelve of the seventeen byelaws introduced during phase one that prohibit the use of bottom-towed fishing gear, there is no requirement for gear to be 'lashed and stowed' when vessels are transiting through the MPA. It becomes difficult for enforcement bodies to establish, and then prove, that a vessel transiting through a closed area is actually fishing, and therefore causing illegal damage.

[55] Client Earth, 'Revised Approach to Fishing in European Marine Sites: A Status Report' (Client Earth, 2014).

[56] Ibid.

[57] Client Earth, 'Revised Approach to Fishing in European Marine Sites', para 31–40.

[58] Ibid, para 7. [59] Easter IFCA, The Marine Protected Area Byelaw 2018.

[60] Eastern IFCA, 'Summary of the Eastern IFCA Formal Consultation on the Marine Protected Area Byelaw 2018 and the Shrimp Permit Byelaw 2018', at: www.eastern-ifca.gov.uk/summary-eastern-ifca-formal-consultation-marine-protected-area-byelaw-2018-shrimp-permit-byelaw-2018.

regulation 64 of the Habitats Regulations provides the opportunity to consider an overriding public interest, including that of a socio-economic nature, it is questionable whether the economic damage to fishing in these areas would have been enough to engage this provision. This leaves us with an example showing that the attitude of regulators towards the precautionary principle, even under the revised approach, remains conditional. A new proposed Marine Protected Area Byelaw 2019 aims to re-introduce these two spatial closures on the basis that more evidence has been provided to the Eastern IFCA.[61] This is a welcome step, though it can still be argued that in order to trigger the protection afforded by regulation 63, no need for more evidence was required if a strong precautionary logic had been adopted from the start.

Thirdly, risk-based approaches are favoured for streamlining decision-making, but it is evident that this particular risk-based approach has not always produced a standardised response in terms of management. For example, the management of mosaics of gravel and soft sediment has been managed differently by the different IFCAs, with some putting byelaws in place protecting the whole site, while other protecting only a smaller portion of the site from bottom-trawling.[62] This divergence in approach is not only determined by different fishing intensity in the MPAs in question but also by the lack of data on the habitat condition in the absence of trawling. The lack of inclusion of background environmental conditions in assessing risk, in this case due to a lack of baseline data, has consequences for the application of the management measures even if the interaction is at the same level. The lack of a streamlined approach among the IFCAs is also visible in the different levels of progress made regarding the implementation of the revised approach and the varying levels of information available on their websites on such progress. The revised approach does not appear to offer any kind of joined-up implementation approach that would help with streamlining decision-making and also with public accountability.

Streamlining decisions is also difficult due to the different site assessments processes in place for MCZs and European Marine Sites. As discussed above, amber interactions (and green, where cumulative impacts are present) require a site assessment to decide whether to introduce regulation. After the same initial screening to understand whether the activity is already managed or the interaction possible, tests for MCZs differ from those of European Marine Sites. For European Marine Sites, the 'likely' significant test is conducted and if the likelihood cannot be excluded an appropriate assessment follows and management is introduced unless it can be demonstrated that the activity will

[61] Eastern IFCA, 'Marine Protected Areas Byelaw 2019-Proposed Additional Restricted Areas', at: www.eastern-ifca.gov.uk/wp-content/uploads/2019/06/2019_06_12_Two_page_summary.pdf.

[62] J. L. Solandt et al., 'Revisiting UK Marine Protected Areas Governance: A Case Study of a Collaborative Approach to Managing an English MPA' (2020) 30 *Aquatic Conservation Marine and Freshwater Ecosystems* 1829–1835.

have no adverse effect on site integrity, unless exceptions in article 6(4) of the Habitats Directive are present. For MCZs, the test revolves around the question whether the activity is capable of affecting other than insignificantly the protected features (Section 126(1)(b) of the MCAA) and if there is or may be a significant risk of the activity hindering the achievement of the conservation objectives (Section 126(2) of the MCAA). In that case, the appropriate SNCB is notified but the ultimate decision whether to grant authorisation rests with the regulatory authority. Thus, the environmental protection afforded through the type of site assessment for European Marine Sites is stronger than for the MCZs as the test is stricter and the regulatory authority has less discretion, as discussed in Chapter 2. This means that, although the interaction in question may be the same according to the matrix, theoretically the type of protection for the feature or sub-feature offered will depend on the typology of the MPA and the underlying conservation law establishing it. In practice, though, this is not necessarily the case. As expressed by a SNCB national representative during an interview, the advice SNCBs offer is similar irrespective of the type of designation that is in place.[63]

These points show that risk-based approaches do not happen in a vacuum. Their success is based on a number of contextual factors such as political judgement and culture as well as legal frameworks already in place and background environmental conditions. This is perhaps an obvious point, but it is useful to lower the expectations and the promises of a risk-based approach of streamlining and simplifying decision-making to make them more effective without being burdensome.

Having said this, from interviews I conducted with DEFRA, regulators and SNCBs at the national level, it was made abundantly clear that the matrix has not being as central to their advice and decisions as policy documents would indicate. Indeed, the matrix was only a starting point for regulators and SNCBs, who used the information it contained in whichever way they found it useful to fulfil their statutory duties. The matrix helped prioritising where interventions were needed but, in order to act, regulators relied on local and site-specific advice from SNCBs as well as views and opinions of the local communities. As an Association of the IFCAs representative summed it up 'the primary focus of IFCAs was on conservation advice and legal duties so the risk matrix became less important as there was far greater reliance on conservation advice locally and what the local community through its understanding of risk and scientific evidence said'.[64] Where departure from the matrix has occurred, it was to make sensible local interventions to reconcile best available evidence produced by the SNCBs with communities' knowledge and priorities, while fulfilling legal duties.

[63] SNCB national representative, online Interview, May 2021.

[64] Association of the IFCAs representative, online Interview, May 2021.

This displays an admirable attempt at epistemic inclusivity, visible also in the way in which evidence has been collected for site assessment. If information on the protected feature and its sensitivity is obtained from Natural England and peer-reviewed scientific publications, a variety of sources has been used to determine the levels of fishing activities, showing an inclusive methodology, especially for vessels under 12 m given that vessel monitoring system (VMS) data are generally not available as they have not been required to date.[65] For those smaller vessels, Fishermap data have been used, which are data arising from interviews with fishers, as well as fisheries sightings data from the regulators and expert opinion from MMO, IFCAs and fishing industry representatives. In addition, there have been calls for evidence sessions open to the public to complete the MPAs site assessments. Evidence submitted by the public had to follow the MMO quality assurance process.[66] A pool of different knowledges has been used to determine the fishing impact illustrating a collaborative effort in knowledge production. This collaborative attempt at knowledge production has been fundamental also to overcome evidence gaps and to ensure the buy-in of the fishers affected by the introduction of the measures.[67]

Nevertheless, in relation to site assessments, a distinction between conservation and fishing knowledge is visible, with the former arising solely from SNCBs and scientific papers. This shows that, although the regulators have favoured the inclusion of the views of industry and the wider public in producing the fisheries' knowledges, conservation is understood primarily to be the remit of SNCBs only and of science. This is indicative of a broader tendency of conservation law and regulation to decide and separate what is science from non-science, with decisions about science to be left in the hands of recognised experts, with no intrusion of 'lay experts'.[68] This issue will be considered in more depth in Chapter 5, when discussing epistemologies at play in the designation

[65] Legislation will be introduced in late 2022, which will make it a legal requirement for vessels under 12 m in length to have an inshore VMS installed. See MMO, 'Inshore Vessel Monitoring (I-VMS) for under-12 m Fishing Vessels Registered in England' (2022), at: www.gov.uk/guidance/inshore-vessel-monitoring-i-vms-for-under-12m-fishing-vessels-registered-in-england. To date only vessels of 12 m or over are required to report their position, course and speed at regular intervals through the VMS data. This was a legal requirement under EU law (Commission Implementing Regulation (EU) No 404/2011 of 8 April 2011 laying down detailed rules for the implementation of Council Regulation (EC) No 1224/2009 establishing a Community control system for ensuring compliance with the rules of the Common Fisheries Policy OJ 2011 No. L112/1) and post-Brexit maintained through the Fisheries Act 2020.

[66] MMO, 'Process for Evidence Quality Assurance' at: https://webarchive.nationalarchives.gov.uk/20140305093254/http://www.marinemanagement.org.uk/evidence/documents/qa-evidenceprocess.pdf.

[67] Association of the IFCAs representative, online Interview, May 2021; NGO n 1 representative, online Interview, May 2021.

[68] B. Wynne, 'May the Sheep Safely Graze? A Reflexive View of the Expert-Lay Knowledge Divide' in S. Lash, B. Szerszynski and B. Wynne (eds.), *Risk, Environment and Modernity: Towards a New Ecology*, pp. 44–83.

of MCZs. Here, it is sufficient to note the following observation. The critique to be raised about the confining of the scientific evidence to the SNCBs is not simply that other actors may also have interesting scientific insights gained from their practical engagement with the marine environment, thus their knowledge on conservation should be incorporated as complementary. More crucially, what is missing from this simple demarcation is a lack of acknowledgement of the social underpinning of scientific knowledge. As science and technologies scholars have pointed out, knowledge, including scientific one, is co-produced within the social order,[69] it is embedded in a specific lifeworld, which entails a specific understanding of uncertainty and risk. Thus, by confining decisions on the scientific evidence in the hands to the SNCBs, what is happening is that a preferred way of seeing conservation, stemming from a particular lifeworld, is championed, neglecting other conservation knowledge stemming from other experiential contexts.

4.8 Conclusion

The English risk-based and phased approach to inshore fishing within/affecting European Marine Sites and then extended to MCZs has been an interesting example for discussing the potential for MPAs to act as a regulatory tool for enclosing CPRs. Reviewing the approach taken in England for the management of fisheries within MPAs, we have seen that such enclosure has happened only in a limited form due to the adoption of a risk-based approach to management.

The approach, aimed at rationalising the regulation of fisheries, has attempted to build a bridge between the strong precautionary approach required under conservation law and a proportionate response to avoid substantial disruptions to fishers' livelihoods. Besides, this example shows that some steps have been taken at commoning, especially through the establishment of the Implementation Group and the incorporation of multiple knowledges for understanding fisheries activities, though the same cannot be said for what counts as conservation knowledge.

Rendering the decision-making inclusive is an important way to enhance the legitimacy and accountability of risk-based regulatory frameworks, given that they are not neutral, technical instruments but are based on a set of value choices and in managing risk they necessarily require simplification, excluding certain elements. The matrix has indeed rendered certain important variables invisible focusing only on gear/(sub)features interactions, and as discussed, this can have negative consequences for the protection of some habitats and species. The political nature of this alleged objective and rational tool needs to be

[69] S. Jasanoff (ed.), *States of Knowledge: The Co-production of Science and the Social Order* (Routledge, 2004).

acknowledged to soften the promises of this risk-based approach. Similarly, the implementation of the approach shows that political judgement contaminates management choices and that a complete streamlining of regulation has not necessarily happened due to disbanded Implementation Group, differences in IFCAs' approaches as well as the limited knowledge on marine ecosystems and their high variability.

5

Marine Conservation Zones Designation

Whose Voices Have Been Included?[*]

5.1 Introduction

This chapter begins the discussion of the democratisation of regulation. By democratisation of regulation, I simply mean regulatory processes and institutions that contribute to the opening of decision-making. I am particularly interested in the way in which different voices are represented and accounted for in conservation intervention and focus primarily on the participation pillar of democratic decision-making. This chapter considers the process of designation of MCZs in English waters at the basis of MCZs designation, while Chapter 6 considers the issue of democratisation from an institutional perspective, exploring two key actors in MPAs regulation.

The designation of MCZs is a very interesting case to study attempts at democratising conservation regulation as it has contemplated extensive participation. Departing from the technocratic and purely science-based approach to site selection typical of domestic and European nature conservation law, socio-economic considerations and participatory techniques have been key elements of the designation process of MCZs in England from the start. This is partly due to what the law permitted[1] and partly to the way in which England decided to implement it, as compared to the devolved administrations. The bottom-up approach to designation embraced by England seems to satisfy academic calls for co-management of shared resources,[2] subscribing to an ethics of commoning.

[*] This chapter is an adapted and updated version of a journal article I wrote in the *Journal of Environmental Law* in 2015 (Pieraccini, 'Rethinking Participation in Environmental Decision-Making').

[1] Section 117(7) of the MCAA allows socio-economic interests to be taken into account during designation.

[2] S. Jentoft, 'Fisheries Co-management as Empowerment' (2005) 29 *Marine Policy* 1–7; S. Jentoft and B. J. McCay, 'User Participation in Fisheries Management: Lessons Drawn from International Experiences' (1995) 19 *Marine Policy* 227–246; P. J. S. Jones and J. Burgess, 'Building Partnership Capacity for the Collaborative Management of Marine Protected Areas in the UK: A Preliminary Analysis' (2005) 77 *Journal of Environmental Management* 227–243; A. Thorpe, M. Banvick and S. Coulthard, 'Tracking the Debate around Marine Protected Areas: Key Issues and the BEG Framework' (2011) 47 *Environmental Management* 546–563;

However, a critical reading of the participatory approach reveals certain weaknesses, mainly to do with the choice of an aggregative rather than a deliberative model of democracy or, in the words of Black, a 'thin' rather than a 'thick' form of proceduralisation.[3] Rather than being a space for deliberation, the participatory arena was reduced to one of bargain and compromise between the ecological and socio-economic interests and knowledges to be represented by different groups, who were reduced to stakeholders. The effects of this largely failed attempt to achieve environmental democracy and commoning are grounded in a case study, drawing on interviews with affected and dissatisfied fishers in South-East England, who participated in the process of designation. The case study shows that three factors contributed to a 'thin' proceduralisation, namely the framing of the process in implementation documents along problematic dichotomous socio-economic versus ecological lines, the rigid, predetermined representations of interests as stakes and the types of discourses/knowledge considered legitimate. Advocating for a relational ontology and epistemology, the chapter ends with a call for bringing forth new, 'thicker' models of participation that are more attentive to multiple forms of communication and identities.

5.2 Designation of MCZs

As explained in Chapter 2, MCZs are a key component of the network of MPAs in UK waters. The appropriate authority, that is, DEFRA, may designate MCZs by order.[4] The order must state the protected features and the conservation objectives for the MCZs.[5] In considering whether it is desirable to designate MCZs, the appropriate authority may have regard to any economic and social consequence of doing so.[6] This provision is notable as it departs from the strict ecological basis for designation of other MPAs, such as European Marine Sites, explicitly introducing socio-economic issues. However, these are kept separate from ecological considerations that drive the designation as the purpose of MCZs is to conserve marine flora or fauna, marine habitats, features of geological or geomorphological interest. It will be argued below that such separation between ecological and socio-economic interests has been maintained, if not reinforced, during the implementation of the law in England and it has created tensions among sea-users and public bodies.

The MCAA is silent regarding who can participate in the process of designation, except for the standard requirement of consultation before designation to

M. B. Mascia, 'The Human Dimension of Coral Reef Marine Protected Areas: Recent Social Science Research and Its Policy Implications' (2003) 17 *Conservation Biology* 630–632.

[3] J. Black, 'Proceduralizing Regulation: Part I' (2000) 20 *Oxford Journal of Legal Studies* 597–614.

[4] Section 116 of the MCAA.

[5] Section 117(2) of the MCAA. [6] Section 117(7) of the MCAA.

be found under Section 119.[7] Similar provisions are in place for the devolved administrations. For example, the Scotland (Marine) Act 2010 states that the Scottish Ministers may designate by order a nature conservation MPA (equivalent to an English MCZ) and in considering whether to designate the area they may have regard to any social or economic consequences of designation.[8] Analogously to English MCZs, there are publicity and consultation requirements before designation.[9] However, if in Scotland, the implementation of nature conservation MPAs was scientifically led, with a central role played by the Scottish SNCB,[10] in England, in early 2010s, a participatory, bottom-up approach to designation was introduced by the DEFRA guidance on the selection of MCZs published in 2010. The guidance stated:

> Social and economic impacts will be taken into account in designating MCZs, as provided for in the Act (Section 117(7)). The Government wants sea-users, environmental bodies and other interested parties to have a prominent role in formulating advice to Government on the creation of MCZs and which will contribute to an ecologically coherent and well-managed network of Marine Protected Areas.... That is why it has put in place a different approach and has asked its statutory nature conservation advisors to come forward with advice by Nov 2011 that is accompanied by propositions drawn up and supported by sea users.[11]

The DEFRA guidance made an explicit link between Section 117(7) of the MCAA and stakeholders' participation in the selection of MCZs, delegating the structuring of the process to the SNCBs. Accordingly, the SNCBs drafted the project delivery guidance[12] that detailed the process of MCZs designation, and this process is summarised below.

Four regional MCZ stakeholder groups[13] were set up in 2010 to identify and recommend regional MCZs to the SNCBs prior to their submission to the government. The regional stakeholder groups comprised over twenty representatives from various marine sectors. These included fishermen, marine

[7] Section 119 states that the appropriate authority must consult any person likely to be interested in or affected by the making of the designation order as well as publish notice of its proposal to make the order.

[8] Section 68 (8) of the MCAA. [9] Section 75 of the MCAA.

[10] Opportunities for the public and affected sea-users to contribute their views were offered through workshops and meetings, but the initial choice of sites was led by Naturescot, as explained by a SNCB representative I interviewed in 2015 (Scottish SNCB national representative, face-to-face Interview, August 2015).

[11] DEFRA. 'Guidance on Selection and Designation of Marine Conservation Zones (Note 1)' (2010) http://archive.defra.gov.uk/environment/biodiversity/marine/documents/guidance-note1.pdf.

[12] Natural England and JNCC, 'Marine Conservation Zone Project: Project Delivery Guidance on the Process to Select Marine Conservation Zones' (2010) at http://jncc.defra.gov.uk/pdf/Project%20Delivery%20Guidance%20FINAL%20020710%20secure.pdf.

[13] The four regional projects were Irish Seas, Net Gain, Finding Sanctuary and Balanced Seas, each with one regional stakeholder group.

industries, recreational groups, environmental NGOs and SNCBs. IFCAs and MMO, though present during the stakeholder groups meetings, did not have an active role in site selection to maintain regulatory impartiality. Independent facilitators were present in the meetings to make sure that all available evidence was considered and to manage potential disagreements arising between stakeholders. Each regional stakeholder group had the opportunity to set up smaller local groups to feed local knowledge and views into the process, though the responsibility to provide final recommendations rested entirely with each of the regional stakeholder group. For commons scholars, this large exercise in participatory decision-making is a notable step forward as it puts collaboration at the core of MPAs planning from the start. However, the extent to which this participatory decision-making process amounted to a commoning practice and helped constitute a community of interest around MPA is highly debatable.

Firstly, the regional stakeholder groups were not choosing the sites autonomously but operating within certain ecological and scientific parameters as well as in the midst of management uncertainty. Management uncertainty refers to the fact that the activities that would be restricted in each MCZ were unknown and therefore stakeholders operated using assumptions of likely management scenarios, as discussed in Chapter 3 when reviewing the IAs accompanying designations. With regard to the ecological/scientific parameters, these were embodied in the Ecological Network Guidance (ENG),[14] a technical document written by the SNCBs. The ENG outlined the ecological criteria for the selection of MCZs and the establishment of an ecologically coherent network of MPAs. More specifically, the ENG identified a number of network design principles[15] and considerations[16] to be followed by the stakeholder groups. The ENG set most of the parameters around which the ecological discourse of designation took place but was not subject to public consultation. This is something I will return to in the case study discussion below asking whether the public, and sea-users in particular, should have had the opportunity to engage at this policy level.

After the final recommendations from the regional stakeholders' groups were submitted to Natural England and JNCC on 8 September 2011, the regional groups ceased to exist. A Scientific Advisory Panel, composed of independent scientists, reviewed the final recommendations and required more work to be done to fill the gaps in the scientific evidence provided so that DEFRA commissioned additional work and also decided to designate MCZs in different tranches, with the first tranche to be designated in 2013. The final formal

14 Natural England and JNCC, 'Marine Conservation Zone Project: Ecological Network Guidance' (2010) at http://jncc.defra.gov.uk/pdf/100705_ENG_v10.pdf.

15 The design principles were: representativity, replication, adequacy, viability, connectivity, protection and best available evidence.

16 The considerations included: areas of additional ecological importance, impacts and features vulnerability, scientific value, MCZs boundaries and geological and geomorphological features of interest.

recommendations, together with the IAs, were submitted to DEFRA by the SNCBs in July 2012. A formal public consultation on proposed designations, with accompanying IAs already discussed in Chapter 3, was then undertaken by DEFRA at the end of 2012. On the 21 November 2013, DEFRA disappointingly announced the designation of only twenty-seven MCZs (out of the 127 that were proposed by the regional stakeholders' groups), thereby shifting goalposts and not following a strong precautionary logic.

The subsequent MCZs tranches came in 2016 and in 2019. These subsequent tranches drew extensively on the material and recommendations made by the regional stakeholder groups and did not require large-scale participatory exercises like the one at the beginning of the process. More specifically, the second tranche's aim was to fill the ecological gaps in the MPA network,[17] which were identified by the SNCBs. The new sites that could fill these gaps were selected from the list initially provided by the regional stakeholder group. Meetings with interested parties were held to discuss the sites suggested by the SNCBs in a pre-consultation phase and new social and economic evidence was gathered. The additional information submitted by stakeholders, when raising concerns about draft scenarios, was scrutinised and validated through engagement with experts in DEFRA, Natural England, JNCC, MMO, Cefas and the Environment Agency. Next to the new sites, additional features for tranche one sites were selected by the SNCBs.[18] Overall, then, the approach was more scientifically driven and expert led than for the first tranche.

There was another significant change to the methodology used to identify these designations in tranche three. Whereas sites in the second tranche were selected by the SNCBs exclusively from the Regional MCZ Project recommendations (albeit with their ability to fill big ecological gaps in the network as a primary consideration), nine of the recommended sites for tranche three were the product of studies by the JNCC and NE conducted with the sole intention of filling the remaining gaps in the network. Like for tranche two, SNCBs held pre-consultation engagement activities – in the form of a two-day workshop and a webinar with the purpose of making compromises where possible (e.g. boundary changes), while at the same time creating a new source of socio-economic information to cross-check and update existing data. Arguably, tranche three went a step further in the scientifically led designation by allowing SNCBs to select sites that were not listed in the original stakeholder recommendations. Nevertheless, a novel effort to involve the public voice in the designation was made by giving NGOs an opportunity to submit recommendation for sites

[17] For example, features that are not currently protected in a region or only a small proportion are protected.

[18] These were features that did not have sufficient scientific evidence when the first tranche was designated but subsequent surveys improved the evidence or features that were subject to a change in the general management approach (i.e. a change from 'maintain' to 'recover') following the first tranche consultation and additional consultation.

which would provide protection to highly mobile marine species, such as dolphins, birds or sharks. This move is indicative of an attempt at democratising decision-making, even though NGOs were operating using principles developed by the SNCBs for identifying the suitability of MCZ protection for highly mobile species and only two of the twenty-one sites proposed by NGOs were included in the consultation.

Thus, even if opportunities for involving interest groups were present in the second and third tranches beyond standard consultation procedures, large-scale participatory experiment happened only at the start of the designation process, that is before tranche one – with the regional stakeholder working groups. Besides, given that the majority of proposed sites in tranches two and three were drawn from the original list proposed by the stakeholder working groups, in order to investigate the democratic potential of MCZ designation, it is appropriate to concentrate on the initial process. To ground the discussion, the next section presents the findings from the qualitative research conducted in relation to the South-East stakeholder regional project. The case study helps in providing a more in-depth consideration of the form the participation process took and considers its social effects.

5.3 The South-East Case Study and 'Thin' Proceduralisation

In the South-East, the regional project took the name of 'Balanced Seas' and covered inshore and offshore UK waters stretching from north of the Suffolk/Essex border to the Hampshire/Dorset border in the southwest. The total area of this project was smaller compared to the other three regional projects, but this did not simplify the situation as the South-East sea extends to the English Channel, one the busiest shipping lanes in the world. Institutionally, the Balanced Seas project followed the tripartite national format outlined in the JNCC and Natural England Project Delivery Guidance summarised in the section above. In the South-East, the project board consisted of two representatives from Kent County Council, an academic from the University of Kent, two representatives from Natural England, one from JNCC and the project manager of Balanced Seas. The project team consisted of a project manager, two facilitators (known as 'communication coordinators'), an economist, an MPA planner, two Geographic Information System (GIS) technicians and two stakeholder engagement officers (one specifically for fisheries).[19] Regarding the regional stakeholder project, the stakeholders were subdivided into six categories to make sure all the different interests were represented: livelihoods (comprising mainly fisheries but also a representative from offshore renewables and one from marine recreational industry), leisure (comprising angling, diving, canoeing and other

[19] Balanced Seas, 'Meet the Team' at: http://webarchive.nationalarchives.gov.uk/20120502155440/http://www.balancedseas.org/page/team.html.

water sport representatives), national/strategic (comprising representatives from shipping, ports, aggregates and defence), marine ecology (i.e. a number of environmental NGOs), public/policy-makers (i.e. the two SNCBs – JNCC and NE), regulators (MMOs, IFCAs, etc.) and others (comprising a representative of French fishing interests, local government and a representative from the crown estate).[20] The website for the Balanced Seas project listed a number of objectives that were at the basis of stakeholders' engagement. These are reported below in bullet points as they appeared in the website:

- engage with regional, sub-regional and local communities of interest (stakeholders) who may be impacted by the recommendations
- ensure that all stakeholder interests are understood and considered
- access stakeholders' experience and knowledge
- maximise areas of agreement, so achieving support for and/or understanding of the
- recommendations and how they have been developed
- acknowledge and clarify areas of outstanding disagreement
- establish and maintain an open and transparent process through information sharing, reporting and communication.[21]

As visible from the above, the rationales for participation listed seem to revolve around a transparent consideration of different interests to minimise disagreement as well as to improve the substantive quality of decision-making by virtue of the fact that all stakeholders' interests must be considered. From a procedural viewpoint, the framing of the stakeholders' engagement process was such that legitimacy was guaranteed by taking into account different, already existing, interests to reach a compromise. The participants were in fact defined as stakeholders, hence people called to represent a particular, exogenous interest located by the project within defined and bounded categories. Differentiation between categories of actors is the premise upon which the participatory process unfolded in an attempt to coordinate a plurality of interests.

In April 2013, I conducted in-depth semi-structured interviews with eight fishers in the South-East of England (all face to face, except one via written correspondence), in an area stretching from Hastings to Folkestone. The choice of this case study area was the result of a number of conversations with the fisheries' engagement officer of the Balanced Seas team, who recommended this area primarily because it hosted a controversial proposed MCZ (Hythe Bay)

[20] There were two additional forms of stakeholder engagement: named consultative stakeholders, who could not attend the meetings and therefore participated via correspondence, and three local groups, who would raise local issues regarding the likely impacts of the MCZs on their activities as well as feeding local knowledge to the regional stakeholder group, Balanced Seas, 'Regional Stakeholder Group' at: http://webarchive.nationalarchives.gov.uk/20120502155440/http://www.balancedseas.org/page/rsg.html.

[21] Balanced Seas, 'Our Stakeholders', at: https://webarchive.nationalarchives.gov.uk/ukgwa/20120502155616/http://www.balancedseas.org/page/ourstakeholders.html.

that, if designated, could have had detrimental effects on local small-scale fishers.[22] The fishers that were interviewed had participated at least in one of the regional and/or local stakeholders meetings of the Balanced Seas project. The majority of the interviewees were small-scale commercial fishermen, though I also interviewed a fisher with a boat over 10-m and a recreational angler. Interestingly, irrespective of their fishing interests and methods, all of them expressed disappointment with the process of selecting MCZs. There were two main interrelated critiques raised by the fishermen, revolving around a critique of the production and role of ecological knowledge and of the ecologists from various angles.

Firstly, the fishermen were not satisfied with the fact that the ecological framework supplied for establishing MCZs was unilaterally set by the SNCBs in the ENG.

As one fisherman put it:

> we were hassled, almost, straight into 'let's find the ENG percentages and try to work out our network' and everybody started to look at their own areas and getting a bit nervous … so quite rapidly we were being like a pack of dogs well trained to go down certain routes and we did.[23]

Another fisherman talked about the ENG as 'dictat of what you must and must not protect'.[24]

Although the participants were supposed collectively to draw the boundaries of the MPAs, the scientific framework of these representations was set from the outside of the participatory process and never questioned. By outlining the ecological criteria, the ENG canonised the kinds of conservation designation that were acceptable, encouraging a particular understanding of the MPAs' network by outlining the design principles and the features of ecological importance. The blind reliance on the ENG meant that the process of designation was understood by fishermen more as a process of incorporation, framing different interests within a pre-existing ecological project constructed from the outside, hindering participation at this initial level. As Lee and others have argued, participation at early stages in decision-making, such as the strategic level, is very important as participation loses its meaning if key decisions have already been made and the public can only determine the 'how' and not the 'whether'.[25] Early and effective participation is also a key requisite of the Aarhus Convention.[26]

22 Hythe Bay did not end up being designated in the first tranche.

23 Fisherman n 7, face-to-face Interview, April 2013.

24 Fisherman n 4, face-to-face Interview, April 2013.

25 M. Lee et al., 'Public Participation and Climate Change Infrastructure' (2013) 25 *Journal of Environmental Law* 33–62.

26 Article 6(4) of the Convention on Access to Information, Public Participation and Decision-Making and Access to Justice in Environmental Matters (Aarhus) 25 June 1998, in force 30 October 2001, 38 ILM 517 (1999) (Aarhus Convention).

Not only were the ecological criteria already pre-established by the SNCBs but, according to the fishermen interviewed, the scientific evidence used to support the site designation was limited, outdated, not rigorous enough and easily disputable by local knowledge and experience. As a fisherman put it:

> the evidence they presented us with we had to take on board at face value.... Now, some of us who are fairly experienced in what we do realised that the evidence was not solid, it was flawed ... so you had science driven evidence conflicting with experience.[27]

Another fisherman said:

> science is and still remains to be lacking ... when they say 'let's use best available', I don't think that is good enough because the best available on this site out here was from a 1981 spotting of a sea horse. Now, I am sorry, I don't know how long they live, I haven't got a clue, but I bet he is dead anyway, you would not have to tow a trawler to kill it, he died of old age.[28]

This point was reiterated by another fisherman:

> the lack of science is also a major point. I was talking to an environmental NGO representative, we were talking about the mantis shrimp and she was saying that it is only in one area in the South-East but my son took it up on the sand at Dungeness two days ago after a breeze, so I asked her: what is the credibility of your record?[29]

Moreover, the fishermen argued that situated ecological knowledge and experience was not sufficiently considered during the process as fishermen were asked to represent the socio-economic interests rather than their ecological viewpoint. The ecological knowledge seemed to rest solely in the hands of the ecologists during the process. The following quotes clearly make this point:

> Everything that was promoted by the ecologists was good evidence and everything else was bad evidence.[30]
>
> We work in a balance with nature for many many generations and to tell us that we don't know about conservation is annoying because conservation is in our mind all the time.[31]

Besides these explicit critiques of the process raised by fishermen, it is also interesting to note that, during the interviews, the fishermen kept positioning themselves in opposition to those they sometimes derogatively called 'tree-huggers'. The 'tree-hugger' category in the discursive framework of the fishermen comprised Natural England and JNCC but also environmental

[27] Fisherman n 7, face-to-face Interview, April 2013.
[28] Fisherman n 4, face-to-face Interview, April 2013.
[29] Fisherman n 1, face-to-face Interview, April 2013.
[30] Fisherman n 7, face-to-face Interview, April 2013.
[31] Fisherman n 1, face-to-face Interview, April 2013.

NGOs. According to the fishermen, these groups were at the meetings all united to represent the ecological interest against the fishermen, who were called to defend their livelihood by emphasising the socio-economic negative consequences of possible designations. The meetings were portrayed by the fishermen as a trade-off between the conservationists and the fishermen with the sea as the element of dispute. In this sense, the meetings became an instance of 'thin' proceduralisation where pre-existing stakes were to be traded. The quotes below are a clear articulation of this issue:

> At the meetings we were outnumbered by the tree huggers … we gave them some areas in exchange of number 26 but they did not listen to us.[32]

And again:

> there were so many under the banner of green … so if you pulled all these people together then it became conservationists against others and the conservationists always outnumbered you.[33]

This clear-cut dichotomy between conservationists and fishers, and between scientific reasons for designation and socio-economic ones mirrors the MCAA's distinction between ecological reasons and socio-economic consequences in listing the grounds for designation consequences that were primarily defined in the negative during the stakeholder process. It also reflects Balanced Seas' categorisation of stakeholders in separate boxes and is in line with Balanced Seas' representation of the process of participation as a space where different stakes were to be represented to reach a compromise, clearly indicative of an aggregative model of democracy.

It can therefore be argued that the dichotomous framing between the ecological and socio-economic interests to be found in implementation documents and strategy, linked to the selective choice of which discourses were legitimate for representing conservation goals, played a role in the articulation of interests during the process, and contributing to tensions, rather than building a community of interest around MPAs. The fishers sensed that their ecological perspective was not asked for as the ENG was 'dictating' the ecological discussion, so that their role was to only defend the socio-economic interest against the ecological interest represented by experts. The key point to extrapolate from this is that the way the participatory process was legally framed and implemented allowed fishermen to express only a particular knowledge and a particular interest, in direct contrast with the ecological one. The stakeholder process in this case study could be represented as the very opposite of a commoning process, given that it fomented opposition among participants, rather than building communities, producing particular environmental subjectivities.

[32] Fisherman n 5, face-to-face Interview, April 2013.
[33] Fisherman n 3, face-to-face Interview, April 2013.

Drawing on an influential paper written by Black, the South-East stakeholder participatory process can be described as a 'thin' form of proceduralisation. Black made a useful analytical distinction between 'thin' and 'thick' proceduralisation in a paper published in the *Oxford Journal of Legal Studies* (OJLS) back in 2001.[34] The scholar associates 'thin' proceduralisation with liberal democratic processes where participatory procedures are resolved in bargains and trade-offs between the various participants, whose preferences are considered to be exogenous and unchanged by the participatory process. 'Thick' proceduralisation, on the other hand, drawing on a Habermasian conceptualisation of deliberative democracy envisions the participatory process as a space for reaching consensus, rather than compromise. The participatory space serves to transcend actors' preferences in their respective lifeworld, stimulating processes of collective reflection leading to both legitimate and improved outcomes. Black herself favours the 'thick' conceptualisation of proceduralisation from a normative perspective, arguing that the 'thick' conceptualisation, based on deliberative democracy, ensures legitimacy.

In addition, as the case study here discussed demonstrated, 'thick' proceduralisation does not only find its justification on normative grounds but also pragmatically and substantively, as 'thin' forms may have un-commoning effects, exacerbating divisions and distancing actors, in this case sea-users, from conservation policies and goals. Understanding which form of participation prevails in a particular context – and whether its rationale is underpinned by a deliberative or aggregative/liberal understanding of democracy – has substantive pragmatic implications as it may contribute to the way participants perceive the process and position themselves in relation to the decision in question and to the other actors involved. Citing again the paper by Lee and others, the sense of 'hollowness in participatory exercises' risks transforming participation only into a bureaucratic hurdle, increasing frustrations on the part of the public who perceive the meaninglessness of the exercise and on the part of the policy-makers who approach participation only as a tick box exercise.[35] Substantive pragmatic effects stemming from particular articulations of participation processes need, therefore, to be taken seriously. If commons scholars call for participation and cooperative management of natural resources and find these to be prerequisites for building common ownership over conservation decisions, what this study has shown is that participation may end up fomenting conflict and antagonism. Serious attention needs to be paid to the form participation take given that 'thin' forms of proceduralisation have negative consequences normatively and pragmatically.

[34] Black, 'Proceduralizing Regulation: Part I'.

[35] Lee et al., 'Public Participation and Climate Change Infrastructure', p. 60.

5.4 Theoretical Reflections: Moving towards 'Thicker' Proceduralisation

If 'thin' proceduralisation is dangerous, how can we move towards 'thicker' forms? In a subsequent paper published in the OJLS, Black goes on to explain her vision of 'thick' proceduralisation, which is not merely a restatement of the Habermasian conception of deliberative democracy.[36] Drawing on various critical social theorists (from Bourdieu[37] to Teubner[38] and feminist scholars), Black rightly points out that the Habermasian ideal speech situation may be difficult to materialise in practice when participants do not share the same communicative rationality because of the different modes of discourse employed depending, inter alia, on their different *habitus*, to be understood in Bourdieu's sense. To overcome these communicative blockages, Black's solution lies in developing techniques of mediation, including translation and the mapping of different discourses deployed by the deliberants. These techniques are to be included in the communication process to account for differences of power, modes of argumentations, etc, as actors seldom approach the participatory forum denuded of their histories and the power relations in which they are entangled. In Black's words:

> if a thick model of proceduralization is to be realised, the nature of the dispute and the differences between and positioning of participants may need to be mapped, and strategies deployed in an attempt to overcome or resolve difference.[39]

According to Black, a move towards thick proceduralisation involves an acknowledgement of participants' differences (of modes of discourses, powers, etc) and an effort to enable participants who do not share the same communicative rationality to communicate through techniques of mediation. However, what Black is not concerned with is the way in which knowledge and interests are produced, what regimes of truth are considered valid sources of authority to make decisions, and which actors are considered the legitimate carriers of such knowledges in participatory contexts. These are important points in complex environmental scenarios, like the MCZs designation one, where decisions to be made on ecological issues still heavily relied primarily on scientific validations and other ways of acquiring ecological knowledge were silenced.

Commons' literature has considered precisely the relationships between expert-driven discourse and 'traditional ecological knowledge' (TEK), in an attempt to revalue the latter for natural resources management. In his seminal

36 Black, 'Proceduralizing Regulation Part II'.

37 P. Bourdieu, *The Logic of Practice* (Stanford University Press, 1990).

38 G. Teubner, 'De Collissione Discursuum: Communicative Rationalities in Law, Morality, and Politics' in M. Rosenfeld and A. Arato (eds.), *Habermas on Law and Democracy: Critical Exchanges* (University of California Press, 1998), pp. 173–189.

39 Black, 'Proceduralizing Regulation: Part I', p. 47.

Sacred Ecology monograph, Berkes defines TEK as 'a cumulative body of knowledge, practice, and belief, evolving by adaptive processes and handed down through generations by cultural transmission, about the relationships between beings (including humans) with one another and with the environment'.[40] TEK is conceptualised as a source of knowledge based on contextual practices and beliefs, an alternative to the more established Western science, rooted in positivism. The attempt of Berkes and many others[41] has been to rediscover its value in making decisions related to the environment and to individuate ways in which TEK can complement scientific knowledge. Although this body of literature has made important advances in the way we think about environmental decision-making by emphasising the value of non-science-based knowledges, there is the hidden risk of being caught up in a romanticism about indigenous knowledges and in a caricature of the rationality of scientific knowledge. This is evident, for example, in Berkes' attempt to individuate some of the substantive differences between TEK and Western science. For Berkes, TEK 'is holistic (as opposed to reductionist), in TEK mind and matter are considered together (as opposed to a separation of mind and matter), TEK is spiritual (as opposed to mechanistic)'.[42]

However, a number of scholars caution against the fallacy of such dichotomies reclaiming relatedness against Cartesian dualism[43] or pointing out the 'boundary work'[44] at play in demarcating science and lay knowledges and stabilising some forms of authority and decision-making. The problem lies not (only) in the expert-lay contrasting and essential epistemological divide but more in the 'discursive and technical constraints of the professional subcultures which organize the most significant share of our social agency', as Hornborg puts it.[45]

[40] F. Berkes, *Sacred Ecology: Traditional Ecological Knowledge and Resource Management* (Taylor and Francis, 1999), p. 8.

[41] For a revaluation of traditional knowledge in conservation decision-making, see W. Adams and C. Sandbrook, 'Conservation, Evidence and Policy' (2013) 47 *Oryx* 329–335.

[42] Berkes, Sacred Ecology, p. 4.

[43] For example, T. Ingold, *The Perception on the Environment* (Routledge, 2000); T. Ingold, *Being Alive: Essays on Movement, Knowledge and Description* (Routledge, 2011); A. Escobar, *Designs for the Pluriverse: Radical Interdependence, Autonomy, and the Making of the Worlds* (Duke University Press, 2018).

[44] Boundary work is a concept from Science and Technology Studies (STS) first developed by Gieryn in 1983. See T. G. Gieryn, 'Boundary-Work and the Demarcation of Science from Non-science: Strains and Interests in Professional Ideologies of Scientists' (1993) 48 *American Sociological Review* 781–795. Gieryn used it to point out that the boundary between science and non-science is a social construction serving aims and objectives of the scientific community. Boundary work has become a key term in Science and Technology Studies literature. For example, Wynne has pointed out the need to recognise that the boundary between lay and scientific knowledge is a socially constructed one and serves the political purpose to suppress non-expert knowledge giving authority to science. See Wynne 'May the Sheep Safely Graze?'.

[45] A. Hornborg, 'Knowledge of Persons, Knowledge of Things: Animism, Fetishism, and Objectivism as Strategies for Knowing (or Not Knowing) the World' (2006) 71 *Ethnos* 21–32, p. 24.

Therefore, participation goes wrong when embedded within particular regulatory discourses and processes that rigidly codify what counts as knowledge and who can represent it, erasing the fluidity and multiplicity of each participant's knowledges because they are based on a ontological divide between nature and culture, between ecological factors and socio-economic considerations. It follows that rendering the space of participation a truly deliberative one does not necessarily entail what Black suggests, that is, mediating different rationalities among participants and it does not even entail simply reclaiming TEK. Rather it requires going a step backward to understand the ontological foundations upon which the (legal) discourses and practices are predicated. What the MCZs designation process shows is that the grounds for designation of MCZs as well as the implementation of the designation process framed conservation decisions around a clear-cut ontological distinction between socio-economic and ecological ground and stakes, and accordingly categorised people and their knowledges within this framing, following a reductionist logic.

It is claimed here that a move towards relational ontology is a prerequisite for 'thicker' proceduralisation. Relational ontology is an umbrella term within which a variety of social sciences and philosophical approaches can be located, ranging from actor-network theory[46] to new materialism,[47] to phenomenology[48] as well as indigenous cosmologies outside Western thinking.[49] What these approaches have in common is an understanding of beings as relational rather than as separate entities, given that no being pre-exists the relationships that constitute it.[50] So, rather than thinking about entities like a seagrass bed or a fish, an ecologist or a fisher, relational ontology gives primacy to relations. The relevance of relational thinking was already touched upon in the critique of IAs presented in Chapter 3 when it was argued that relational values could be a better way to capture variables such as place attachment that otherwise remain unacknowledged. In the present case, relational ontology would have avoided the framing of socio-economic interests as divorced from ecological

[46] B. Latour, *Facing Gaia: Eight Lectures on the New Climatic Regime* (Polity Press, 2017, transl. by C. Porter).

[47] K. Barad, *Meeting the Universe Halfway: Quantum Physics and the Entanglement of Matter and Meaning* (Duke University Press, 2007); J. Bennett, *Vibrant Matter: A Political Ecology of Things* (Duke University Press, 2010).

[48] M. Heidegger, *Being and Time* (Blackwell, 1996, transl. by J. Macquarrie and E. Robinson). Heidegger speaks of *Dasein* (being-in-the-world) as the existential condition. It is from this embedded, situated condition that one knows and access other beings.

[49] Ingold, The Perception of the Environment; K. H. Basso, *Wisdom Sits in Places: Landscape and Language among the Western Apache* (University of New Mexico, 1996); N. Bird-David, '"Animism" Revisited: Personhood, Environment, and Relational Epistemology', (1999) 40 *Current Anthropology, Supplement*, S67–S91; E. Viveiros de Castro, 'Exchanging Perspectives: The Transformation of Objects into Subjects in Amerindian Ontologies' (2019) 25 *Common Knowledge* 21–42; Escobar, Designs for the Pluriverse.

[50] See also the discussion on the 'more-than-human' in Chapter 1.

ones, a division present in the grounds for designation enunciated in the law and in the way in which the legal implementation was carried out in England.

Relational ontology is useful not only in overcoming Cartesian dualisms but, as Sidorkin put it, it also helps in abandoning the idea of 'monological identity formation and of the authentic self'.[51] Assuming that the boundaries of belonging are rigid fails to acknowledge the fluidity of identities. Recognising identity as situational, multiple and achieved, rather than fixed, is something that anthropologists have done for a long time. From Mauss's argument that notions of the person have complex social origins and are historically and culturally constructed,[52] anthropologists have investigated ethnographically the meaning of the person, even disrupting the notion of the individual. In a seminal study on Melanesia gender relations, Strathern showed how the singular person is a social microcosm and individuality is achieved rather than a starting point.[53] It is worth quoting at length Strather's definition of the person as it well captured the multiplicity and relationality I am referring to:

> Far from being regarded as unique entities, Melanesian persons are as dividually as they are individually conceived. Indeed, persons are frequently constructed as the plural and composite site of the relationship that produced them.[54]

Understanding identities not as monadic, but as contingent, evolving and multiple would have permitted in the present case to understand participants not as stakeholders, representing a predetermined interest, but rather as people able to bring to the deliberative forum a variety of knowledges and understandings. Indeed, the way in which belonging is understood impacts also the way in which knowledge is understood, that is it has epistemological consequences. Fixing the boundaries of belonging fixes also the boundaries of knowledge. Relegating participants in predetermined and bounded categories such as 'livelihood', 'ecology' and so forth limited the opportunity of people to express their multiple identities and knowledges, producing conflicting interests and validating certain regimes of truth. Recognising that each of the participants has multiple knowledges to draw upon and to offer to the decision-making process is key to beginning to rethink the contours of a thick deliberative space as the acknowledgement of multiplicity allows participants to free themselves from the categories in which they are located and that they are supposed to represent and defend. It is when these multiplicities are suppressed on the assumption that those peoples and their interests are separate

[51] A. M. Sidorkin, 'Ontology, Anthropology, and Epistemology of Relation' (2002) 173 *Counterpoints* 91–102.

[52] M. Mauss, 'A Category of the Human Mind: The Notion of Person the Notion of Self', in M. Carrithers, S. Collins and S. Lukes (eds.), *The Category of the Person: Anthropology, Philosophy, History* (Cambridge University Press, 1985, transl. by W. D. Halls), pp. 1–25.

[53] Strathern, The Gender of the Gift.

[54] Ibid, p. 13.

and hence separable in distinct categories, that problems arise as particular knowledges are attributed only to particular actors. The participants may then internalise these discourses and carry forth these dichotomies and essentialisations so that a paradox, as in the case of MCZs designation, is reached: the participatory process that aimed at achieving agreement fortifies difference and antagonism.

5.5 Conclusion

This chapter has focused on the process of implementation of MCZs' designation in England. It has provided a summary of the designation process for each of the three tranches that have been introduced, focusing on issues of participation. Special attention has been dedicated to the stakeholder working groups that were created at the beginning of the process of designation, also explored through empirical data arising out of interviews with fishers from one of the stakeholders working groups (the South-East). The chapter has argued that the democratic effort has not succeeded in creating a commoning space, given that participation has been 'thin', drawing on the distinction between 'thin' and 'thick' proceduralisation proposed by Black. If Black favours a move towards 'thick' proceduralisation on normative grounds, here it has been argued that it should be favoured also for pragmatic and substantive reasons, due to the effects the form of participation can have on people's understandings of the process and on the issue in question.

Secondly, it has been argued that moving towards 'thicker' forms of proceduralisation requires the acknowledgement of the multiplicity and fluidity of identities and knowledges, in short a move towards relational thinking. Accepting the fluidity and processual character of identities enable us to deconstruct simplistic associations, such as those between fishers and fishing interests/knowledges, appreciating that participants can bring multiple knowledges to the table because their identities are manifold, complex and evolving. Embracing multiplicity, rather than trying to overcome it or resolve it through trade-offs, would allow deliberative practices to be thicker.

The case of MCZs designation in England shows how we should be wary of certain institutional processes that rigidify identities and create dichotomies. Reflecting on these issues by developing an awareness of the reductionist risks embedded in particular regulatory framings that become internalised by the subjects and recognising the multiplicity of each participant's knowledge as a primary category of 'thick' proceduralisation could be beneficial in a creating a truly deliberative, commoning space.

6

Environmental Democracy in Marine Protected Areas Management

The Role of Inshore Fisheries Conservation Authorities and Environmental NGOs

6.1 Introduction

Chapter 5 demonstrated, using the example of designation of MCZs, that participation in conservation decision-making is not straightforward and that 'thin' forms of proceduralisation can be damaging. It argued for a pluralisation of perspectives and a recognition of the multiple identities of each actor to help rendering participation experiments thicker and better contribute towards environmental democracy.

This chapter continues the discussion on environmental democracy focusing on two crucial actors in the institutional conservation landscape, environmental NGOs and IFCAs. These two actors have been selected because they both display democratic characteristics, but at the same time have different relationships to the state: one, allegedly, operates in a space external to the state and the other is a statutory regulator working at the local level. The legal and regulatory mapping in Chapter 2 showed that many actors and regulatory tools in marine conservation law conform to a command-and-control style of regulation. However, this chapter problematises the reading showcasing, critically, institutional examples of environmental democratisation.

Environmental NGOs are the 'usual suspects'[1] when discussing environmental democracy. They are the voice of the more-than human, operating as a proxy, or as a 'friend of the natural object' as Stone put it,[2] and they are defending the environmental rights of present and future generations through a variety of strategies, more or less confrontational. They are indeed afforded a special place in the Aarhus Convention. Thus, NGOs are an obvious subject in discussions of environmental democracy. For radical scholars, IFCAs may seem less interesting. After all, their transformative potential is tamed by the statutory obligations governing their behaviour; they are local arms of the state. However, the chapter will reveal that their set up and operation display

[1] M. Lee and C. Abbot, 'The Usual Suspects? Public Participation under the Aarhus Convention' (2003) 66 *Modern Law Review* 80–108.

[2] C. D. Stone, 'Should Trees Have Standing? Towards Legal Rights for Natural Objects' (1972) 45 *Southern California Law Review* 450–501, p. 464.

important democratic aspects. Although both organisations contribute to the democratisation of regulation, they also experience some challenges and constraints, which will be discussed.

6.2 Environmental NGOs

Environmental NGOs are important actors in marine conservation in the UK. They are a broad church, of different sizes, with different funding availability, focus and expertise. Some specialise entirely in marine protection, such as the Marine Conservation Society, the Blue Marine Foundation and Oceana, others have a wider environmental remit, such as the Wildlife Trusts or Greenpeace and, finally, others primarily employ legal experts, such as Client Earth. Their strategies are also varied, from protests, to campaigns, to carrying out research, to engaging in policy-making to legal action. It is not the purpose here to discussing environmental NGOs comparatively or to provide a review of the extensive literature on NGOs in environmental management,[3] but to outline some general points regarding their role in democratising marine conservation regulation, participating in the commoning of MPAs.

Arguably, environmental NGOs fill the gaps left by the hollowing out of the state[4] and its institutions through monitoring sea-user activities, campaigning, carrying out scientific research and education activities, translating technical reports into more digestible formats for the public and, at the same time, holding the government to account, through lobbying, legal mobilisation as well as using nonviolent sensational confrontation tactics. To provide an example, environmental NGOs' tactics to push for the protection of a large offshore SAC (the Dogger Bank) from damaging bottom-towed fishing gear have consisted in a mixture of approaches ranging from the consultative and collaborative to the direct and combative. As an NGO representative put it:

> you got to have all approaches from NGOs: we did a technical report on trawling and climate change, Greenpeace was dropping blocks [in the sea], Blue Marine and Oceana were threatening judicial reviews [...]because of these different tactics we saw a big statement [from the government] on trawling and MPAs so it has been a successful enterprise.[5]

Many scholars consider NGOs as democratic actors, guarding against command-and-control state regulation, encouraging wider citizen participation

[3] See, for example, C. Abbott and M. Lee, *Environmental Groups and Legal Expertise: Shaping the Brexit process* (University College London Press, 2021); P. B. Larsen and D. Brokington (eds.), *The Anthropology of Conservation NGOs: Rethinking the Boundaries* (Palgrave, 2018); S. Jasanoff, 'NGOs and the Environment: From Knowledge to Action' (1997) 18 *Third World Quarterly* 579–594.

[4] R. A. W. Rhodes, 'The Hollowing out of the State: The Changing Nature of the Public Service in Britain' (1994) 65 *Political Quarterly* 138–151.

[5] NGO representative n 1, online Interview, May 2021.

and facilitating public understanding of environmental matters, contributing to the public scrutiny of the state, speaking for the voiceless environment and future generations and increasing transparency of expert decision-making.[6] Citing Jasanoff:

> standing outside the peripheries of official, usually state-sponsored, knowledge production, NGOs are particularly well-situated to observe the limitations of dominant expert framings, to question unexplained assumptions, to expose tacit value choices, and to offer alternative interpretations of ambiguous data.[7]

For Jasanoff, environmental NGOs sit at the knowledge-action nexus, criticising accepted framework of environmental knowledge and policy, creating more inclusive epistemic networks, bridging lay-expert knowledges, disseminating information, supplementing existing, and often poor, monitoring and enforcement approaches.[8] It follows that NGOs can be seen as vehicles for commoning MPAs regulation, pluralising the institutional arena, pressing for radical alternatives and paving the ground towards greater inclusiveness and cooperation in conservation discourses and practice.

Environmental law has followed suit affording environmental NGOs important rights. The main instrument remains the Aarhus Convention that has conferred a wide range of environmental rights on the public and especially the 'public concerned', which includes NGOs promoting environmental protection and meeting certain thresholds.[9] There has been substantial academic commentary on the Aarhus Convention so suffice to write here that rights include access to environmental information under article 4, rights to participate in environmental decision-making under articles 6–8 and access to justice under article 9.[10] NGOs are thus key actors in mitigating the democratic deficit and providing legitimacy in environmental decision-making.

However, over the years, a body of work has emerged problematising the link between democracy and NGOs.[11] Drawing on this literature, it will be

[6] See for example, M. Bratton, 'Beyond the State: Civil Society and Associational Life in Africa' (1989) 41 *World Politics* 407–430; J. S. Dryzek, 'Global Civil Society: The Progress of Post-Westphalian Politics' (2012) 15 *Annual Review of Political Science* 101–119.

[7] Jasanoff, 'NGOs and the Environment', p. 582.

[8] Ibid. [9] Article 2(5) of the Aarhus Convention.

[10] For commentary, see Lee and Abbott, 'The Usual Suspects'.

[11] See, for instance, M. Edwards and D. Hulme (eds.), 1995. *Non-Governmental Organisations: Performance and Accountability. Beyond the Magic Bullet* (Earthscan, 1995); C. Mercer, 'NGOs, Civil Society and Democratization: A Critical Review of the Literature' (2002) 2 *Progress in Development Studies* 5–22; M. Edwards, *Civil Society* (Polity Press, 2004); E. Swyngedouw, 'Governance Innovation and the Citizen: The Janus Face of Governance-beyond-the-State' (2005) 42 *Urban Studies* 1991–2006; P. Jepson, 'Governance and Accountability of Environmental NGOs' (2005) 8 *Environmental Science and Policy* 515–524; F. R. Baumgartner et al., *Lobbying and Policy Change: Who Wins, Who Loses and Why* (University of Chicago Press, 2009); T. Bernauer and C. Betzold, 'Civil Society in Global Environmental Governance' (2012) 21 *The Journal of Environment and Development* 62–66; N. Berny and C. Rootes, 'Environmental Politics Environmental NGOs at a Crossroads?' (2018) 7 *Environmental Politics* 947–972.

showed here how too favourable a reading of NGOs as vehicles for commoning and environmental democracy may be overly simplistic. As Swyngedouw has pointed out, NGOs have a Janus-face:[12] on the one hand, they contribute to the empowerment of the public and nature, democratising environmental decision-making; on the other hand, they may contribute to the democratic deficit. This is because only certain, bigger and well-resourced NGOs end up emerging and consolidating their position, excluding other actors. The exercise of procedural rights guaranteed by the Aarhus Convention as well as by administrative law at the national level may be only a theoretical possibility for smaller, under-funded NGOs. This may in turn legitimise existing power relations rather than facilitate a move towards democratisation of environmental decision-making.

The expansion of NGOs in environmental decision-making is not socially neutral, and NGOs are far from representing the public interest in the environment, but they represent a particular view of the public interest, especially single-issue campaigning groups. As Lee and Abbott wrote a long time ago, even if there are powerful and legitimate incentives to empower NGOs, we must not mistake their involvement for improved democracy.[13] Moreover, the democratic deficit is evident in the lack of formal accountability of NGOs. Although a key role of NGOs is holding the government to account, their own accountability is more open to question. Given that many environmental NGOs receive funding from private parties and enter into strategic partnerships with corporations, the transparency and accountability of their operation become opaque.

The question of accountability is also a question of accountable to whom. NGOs can be deemed to be accountable to many constituencies: donors for carrying out a particular project, staff and members, scientific communities when working in partnerships but, given the lack of formal accountability lines, they may direct their accountability structures towards powerful stakeholders, rather than members from the public.[14] This is possibly more acutely the case of NGOs operating in the global South, where cooperative games between NGOs and states and corporations often take place. By receiving funding from states in the global North, turning big and siding with powerful interests, NGOs operating in the global South may distance themselves from local communities and participate in what has been called 'green grabbing'.[15]

[12] Swyngedouw, 'Governance Innovation and the Citizen'.

[13] Lee and Abbott, 'The Usual Suspects', p. 108.

[14] Jepson, 'Governance and Accountability of Environmental NGOs', p. 521.

[15] C. Corson and K. I. MacDonald, 'Enclosing the Global Commons: The Convention on Biological Diversity and Green Grabbing' (2012) 39 *The Journal of Peasant Studies* 263–283; A. Escobar, 'Whose Knowledge, Whose Nature? Biodiversity Conservation, and the Political Ecology of Social Movements' (1998) 5 *Journal of Political Ecology* 53–82; J. Fairhead, M. Leach and I. Scoones, 'Green Grabbing: A New Appropriation of Nature?' (2012) 39 *The Journal of Peasant Studies* 237–261; J. Igoe and D. Brockington, 'Neoliberal Conservation: A Brief Introduction' (2007) 5 *Conservation and Society* 432–449; C. Corson, 'Shifting Environmental Governance in a Neoliberal World: US AID for Conservation' (2010) 42 *Antipode* 576–602.

Although this issue is less relevant for NGOs concerned with marine conservation in the global North, nevertheless, the portrayal of NGOs as participating in the commoning of environmental issues, highlighting the shortcomings of state regulation and offering alternatives to top-down models of conservation, risks being too naive.

Adopting a Gramscian view of civil society, the claim that environmental NGOs are autonomous actors, existing outside the periphery of the state, does not necessarily hold true. This is simply because civil society and state are mutually constitutive, rather than complete separate entities. Civil society is an arena in which hegemonic ideas concerning conservation are both reinforced and contested. Environmental NGOs as central civil society actors are not simply institutional vectors for democratic transformations, but, sometimes, they contribute to the reproduction of current hegemonic discourses regarding conservation. For example, much of the work of NGOs actively involved in marine conservation in the UK focuses on disclosing patterns of violations and legal non-compliance of sea-users or the state, rather than, let us say, questioning ontological assumptions at the basis of legal frameworks and envisaging alternatives to existing models of conservation. As an NGO representative put it, 'our role is to ensure that the laws are properly implemented and applied, and when not, there is a very compelling case in bringing legal action for non-compliance.'[16] Of course, much depends on the type and expertise of NGO as the example of the Dogger Bank demonstrated earlier, but arguably, marine conservation NGOs in England have been primarily preoccupied with making sure that conservation law is prioritised and properly implemented. Their critiques have been directed more at the poor implementation of conservation law by the government or local regulators than at the key concepts underpinning conservation law itself. As explained by the NGO representative just cited, the lack of environmental NGO advocacy for changing conservation laws is often based on pragmatic choice, as with the re-opening of these laws there is a significant concern that they will be watered down.[17]

However, regardless of the reasons, NGOs may rely quite heavily on scientific knowledge and on existing conservation law provisions and approaches, taking for granted certain concepts and targets set out in international or domestic law and policy. As Chapter 4 discussed, environmental NGOs had a key role in pushing for a revised approach to commercial fisheries in European Marine Sites, threatening legal action against the UK government for failure to comply with article 6 of the Habitats Directive in its management of fisheries. Again, NGOs have had an important role to play in the government announcements post-Brexit in relation to the introduction of byelaws in four offshore MPAs to mitigate impacts of damaging fisheries activities, using similar arguments to those for the revised approach. The examples shows that what the

[16] NGO representative n 2, online Interview May 2021. [17] Ibid.

NGOs have been doing is pointing to the failure of the state to comply with EU legal standards, taken as a given by the NGOs. In this instance, as in many others, we see NGOs as opposed to the state not because they are disrupting existing frameworks of conservation but because they are operating as watchdogs of established legal frameworks. Critical scholars see the incremental institutionalisation of NGOs as problematic because it circumscribes the range of environmental issues deemed worthy of attention and risks excluding issues and perspectives that are more radical.[18] For such scholars, environmental NGO democratic potential is weakened by entering into partnerships with powerful actors and ideologies. An 'agonistic' approach to democracy, which emphasises, following Mouffe, the value of conflict in democracy,[19] is seen as more conducive to reclaiming alternative views, rejecting existing legal frameworks and state institutions to achieve profound transformation. Not dissimilarly, radical commoning scholars portray the struggle for the commons and democracy as a rejection of neoliberal capitalism and state law, which are seen as part of a controlling process inextricably linked to Western imperialism, victimising weaker actors and perspectives.[20] It seems that strategies for radical democracy must be adversarial and militant in character in order to be truly emancipatory.

However, it will be explained below that there are also cases in which environmental NGOs have questioned the hegemonic view of marine conservation, highlighting the limitations of existing management approaches, without embracing an agonistic approach and/or dismissing completely the existing legal frameworks. For example, research led by the Marine Conservation Society, in tandem with academics, proposes a move from a 'feature-based' towards a 'whole site approach' for effective MPAs management.[21] The 'whole site approach' is an innovative, comprehensive approach delivering ecosystem-based conservation across whole suites of habitats. Rather than focusing on individual features, the whole site approach better accounts for movement of species (e.g. crabs) associated with specific features (e.g. reefs or sandbanks) by ensuring their protection even when migrating temporarily outside the habitat feature. Besides, ecologically

[18] A. P. J. Mol, 'The Environmental Nation State in Decline' (2016) 25 *Environmental Politics* 48–68.

[19] C. Mouffe, 'Delibrative Democracy or Agonistic Pluralism' (2000) 72 *Political Science Series* 1–17; C. Mouffe, *On the Political* (Routledge, 2005). Mouffe moves beyond the search for consensus in democratic politics, and she urges to acknowledge the antagonism inherent in politics and claims that agonistic pluralism provides a better framework for expressing differences in democratic systems. Her position is in contrast with that of Habermas on deliberative democracy. See J. Habermas, *Between Facts and Norms: Contributions to a Discourse Theory of Law and Democracy* (MIT Press, 1996, transl. by W. Rehg).

[20] U. Mattei and L. Nader. *Plunder: When the Rule of Law Is Illegal* (Blackwell, 2008); Federici, Re-enchanting the World.

[21] Solandt et al., 'Managing Marine Protected Areas in Europe: Moving from "Feature-Based" to "Whole-Site" Management of Sites', in J. Humphreys and R. Clark (eds.), *Marine Protected Areas: Science, Policy and Management* (Elsevier, 2019), pp. 157–182.

defining where a feature starts or stops is not always straightforward, for example it is not always clear where a biogenic structure is developed enough to be considered a reef. Thus, the whole site approach, by ensuring wider protection, permits a more precautionary strategy to habitats conservation. Interestingly, the approach advocated by the Marine Conservation Society does not require a complete re-writing of the legal framework but a different, more encompassing interpretation of broad scale feature protection for MCZs and of the 'site integrity' provision in the Habitats Regulations, allowing regulators to be ambitious within the existing legal parameters. The approach suggests a reframing of MPA management, exposing the weaknesses of accepted methods of conservation law and questioning its boundaries, thus proposing a counter-hegemonic discourse, following a more holistic interpretation of conservation law, which is also supported by case law from the CJEU. In the case of *Sweetman*, for instance, a more encompassing interpretation of site integrity was offered that can be used to reinforce the argument for the whole site approach.[22]

Another example of environmental NGOs pushing for alternative methods of conservation and, in doing so, enlarging the epistemic community is the work conducted by the Blue Marine Foundation in relation to Lyme Bay, an MPA in south-west England with reef habitats and pink sea fans of international conservation importance. The area became a de facto MPA when bottom-towed fishing gear was prohibited in 2008, and in 2011, a large part became a candidate SAC, with designation as the Lyme Bay and Torbay SAC in 2017. The banning of bottom-towed gear had the consequence of substantially increasing static gear fishing and, to manage changes, the Blue Marine Foundation set up the Lyme Bay Fisheries and Conservation Reserve Working Group in 2011 to provide a forum for discussion and develop a series of voluntary best practices management measures. Fishers adhere to a voluntary code of conduct on fishing and under the guidance of the Blue Marine Foundation, the Working Group has undertaken many initiatives towards sustainable fishing. The Blue Marine Foundation also established a Consultative Committee for Lyme Bay in 2013 bringing together fishers, regulators, local councils as well as scientists, with other organisations such as charities and fish merchants providing advice. The environmental NGO in this instance has been seminal in proposing a collaborative model of governance that put the fishers at the centre of management. Such a project supplements the management under statutory legislation, and although the group has not legal powers, it has promoted

[22] Para 39 of the *Sweetman* judgement reads as follows:
Consequently, it should be inferred that in order for the integrity of a site as a natural habitat not to be adversely affected for the purposes of the second sentence of article 6(3) of the Habitats Directive the site needs to be preserved at a favourable conservation status; this entails, as the Advocate General has observed in points 54–56 of her Opinion, the lasting preservation of the constitutive characteristics of the site concerned that are connected to the presence of a natural habitat type whose preservation was the objective justifying the designation of that site in the list of SCIs, in accordance with the directive.

discussions and initiatives, broadening interpretations and practices of conservation and offering a complementary avenue to top-down knowledge making and management.[23]

Both these examples show that environmental NGOs are not necessarily participating in the reproduction of the current conservation hegemonic practices and discourses but are in fact challenging existing approaches to conservation, proposing alternatives and pluralising knowledges. In this way, they are commoning marine conservation, deepening the possibilities for re-thinking the boundaries of conservation policy. This, however, does not result in an agonistic approach to the state or to science, but often is based on a creative interpretation of the law and on collaboration. Collaborative forms of governance can work and do not necessarily imply a depoliticisation and the silencing of expressions of dissent. Thus, in thinking about the democratisation of decision-making, it is important to not only to consider actors' strategies that directly attack key institutions and legal frameworks of conservation but also to consider ways in which alternative discourses and practices are put in a dialogue with more orthodox discourse and practices, it is to be hoped constructively, as democratic politics requires a commitment to engagement with pluralism and the encounter with the other.

Another example of this sort is the Start Point to Plymouth Sound and Eddystone SAC that lies in inshore Cornish waters. There, a partnership between MCS, Cornwall IFCA and the University of Exeter has been established to monitor the impacts of demersal trawl closures in the Eddystone Reef. If, historically, there had been conflict between the Marine Conservation Society and the Cornwall SFC over management measures in the area, the evolution of the SFC into a IFCA with an explicit requirement to consider fisheries and conservation measures has facilitated the current partnership and it is one of the few examples of UK MPAs where close monitoring takes place to test the ecological impact of closing an area to bottom-towed gear.[24] This last example offers a good way of introducing the second actor discussed in this chapter, the IFCAs. Evidently, IFCAs are institutions even more closely linked to the state than NGOs, but it will be argued that they can be considered, to a certain extent, commoning experiments with the capacity to contribute to the development of the democratisation of conservation regulation.

6.3 An Historical Contextualisation: Sea Fisheries Committees (SFCs)

As mentioned in Chapter 2, IFCAs have been established under Part 6 of the MCAA and been given responsibilities regarding fisheries and conservation between 0 and 6 nm. They became fully operational in 2011. IFCAs are an

[23] R. Singer and P. J. S. Jones, 'Lyme Bay Marine Protected Area: A Governance Analysis' (2021) 127 *Marine Policy* 103201. See also Blue Marine Foundation, 'Lyme Bay: Project Overview' at: www.lymebayreserve.co.uk/about/overview.php.

[24] Solandt et al., 'Revisiting UK Marine Protected Area Governance'.

interesting example of statutory authorities that operate at the local level and rooted in local representation, displaying many characteristics of local communal management institutions proposed by commons scholarship.[25] Local management of inshore fisheries has a longer history than the IFCAs in England. Prior to the IFCAs, SFCs existed, which were established originally under the Sea Fisheries Regulation Act 1988, consolidated by the Sea Fisheries Regulation Act 1996. When initially established, the SFCs did not have any powers in relation to conservation matters. Their powers related exclusively to fisheries management and included the powers to make byelaws,[26] subject to confirmation by the Minister.[27] Byelaws could be made for various purposes including the restriction or prohibition of the fisheries for taking sea fish during specific periods, or using specific gears, for regulating fisheries for shellfish, etc.

The members of the SFCs were split in two: half were elected council members by the constituent local authorities and the other half comprised one person representing the national river authority and persons 'acquainted with the needs and opinions of the fishing interests' of that district, appointed by the Minister.[28] Fishing interests meant persons interested in fisheries as owners of fisheries or interests therein but were not to represent any sectorial fishing interests, though commercial fishers were the dominant appointees. Ministerial appointment, compared to appointment by or including fisheries organisations themselves, reduced the possibility for the Committees to be highly politicised and be subject to regulatory capture, though it was unpopular with fishers as considered to fall short of co-management principles.[29]

The Environment Act 1995 made a number of environmental amendments to the Sea Fisheries Act 1966.[30] The representative of the National Rivers Authority became a representative of the newly constituted Environment Agency, and together with persons acquainted with fishing interests, Committee's membership could include persons having knowledge of, or expertise in, marine environmental matters.[31] Powers to make byelaws to control fisheries were also extended to marine environmental purposes, which included conservation of flora and fauna dependent on, or associated with, a marine or coastal environment.[32] Prior to making such byelaws, the SFC was required to consult with the SNCB and it could appoint other marine

[25] Ostrom, Governing the Commons.
[26] Section 5 of the Sea Fisheries Regulation Act 1996.
[27] Section 7 of the Sea Fisheries Regulation Act 1996.
[28] Section 2 of the Sea Fisheries Regulation Act 1966.
[29] D. Symes and J. Phillipson, 'Inshore Fisheries Management in the UK: Sea Fisheries Committees and the Challenge of Marine Environmental Management' (1997) 21 *Marine Policy* 207–224.
[30] Section 102 of the Environment Act 1995.
[31] Section 102(2) of the Environment Act 1995. The section was repealed by the MCAA.
[32] Section 5A inserted by the Environment Act 1995.

environmental experts at its discretion.[33] Thus, the Environment Act 1995 was significant in bringing environmental concerns into fisheries management, locating part of the responsibility to conserve the marine environment in the hands of SFCs that, to date, had responsibilities concerning fishing only (except for the Devon and North Eastern SFC that had appointed members with conservation interests prior to the Environment Act 1995).[34] However, it should be noted that the byelaws for environmental reasons were confined only to the regulation of fishing activities, that is to cases in which fishing was likely to have an adverse environmental impact, keeping fisheries management central to the SFCs' duties.

It is only with the MCAA that a more substantial conservation turn in inshore management has been made, with the establishment of the IFCAs under Section 149, as explained below.

6.4 Part 6 of the MCAA and the IFCAs

There are ten IFCAs in England covering districts of various sizes and geographies, with different types and numbers of protected areas, structure of the fishing fleet, ports' size, etc. There is also an Association of the IFCAs, tasked with assisting IFCAs in their role and promoting them. Like their predecessors, the IFCAs have inshore fisheries management duties under Section 153 of the MCAA, but they have also explicit duties concerning the conservation of MCZs under Section 154. This is perhaps the most notable addition and change brought in by the MCAA on inshore fisheries management. Section 154 of the MCAA requires IFCAs to ensure that the conservation objectives of any MCZ in their district are furthered, and the performance of this duty cannot be affected by their parallel duty to ensure sustainable exploitation of sea fisheries activities, balancing social and economic interests with environmental ones, under Section 153(2) of the MCAA.

For the purpose of performing the fisheries and conservation duties imposed by Sections 153 and 154, IFCAs can make byelaws for their district that must be confirmed by the Secretary of State before having effect.[35] More specifically, byelaws can be made, inter alia, for permitting, monitoring of sea fisheries, for prohibiting or restricting the exploitation of sea fisheries resources and for requesting information from people involved in sea fisheries exploitation.[36]

[33] Section 5A(3)(a) of the Environment Act 1995.

[34] It should be noted also that domestic and EU conservation legislation had already imposed some environmental duties on the SFCs. More specifically, Section 1(1)(a) of the Sea Fisheries (Wildlife Conservation) Act 1992 imposed a duty on SFCs to have regard to the conservation of marine flora and fauna when exercising their functions and the Regulations transposing the Habitats and Birds Directives required regulatory authorities, including the SFCs, to exercise their function as to secure compliance with EU-derived conservation law.

[35] Section 155 of the MCAA. [36] Ibid.

DEFRA issued guidance on the byelaw making powers of the IFCAs.[37] The guidance stresses that, in line with Better Regulation principles, byelaws should be a last resort when considering options for regulation, and indeed, there are many examples of voluntary codes of conduct introduced by the IFCAs to close areas to fishing, resolve conflicts between commercial and recreational fishers, etc.[38] Interestingly for the present purposes, the guidance includes the requirement for the MMO to act as a policy and legal advisor on the process of making IFCA byelaws and quality assure IFCA byelaws, before they are submitted to the Secretary of State for confirmation. The Secretary of State has also powers to amend or revoke byelaws if it is satisfied that any byelaw provision is unnecessary, inadequate or disproportionate.[39] These powers and duties do not apply in the case of emergency byelaws, which can be made by the IFCAs without confirmation by the Secretary of State if there is a urgent need to make a byelaw and the need to make it could not reasonably have been foreseen.[40] The IFCA must notify the Secretary of State within 24 hours of making the emergency byelaw.[41] Emergency byelaws can remain in force for a period not exceeding 12 months,[42] unless the Secretary of State gives written approval for their extension.[43]

Natural England has a duty to provide guidance and conservation advice on byelaws, and this also explains why a Natural England representative sits in each IFCA committee, as discussed below. But, as highlighted in Chapter 2, the regulators are not under an obligation to follow the SNCB advice, but merely to 'have regard to it' when deciding on management measures for MCZs. Other actors, including Natural England, fishers, other sea-users and any other with an interest in the marine environment, can provide evidence to IFCAs to improve the quality of IAs and can have their voice heard through consultations on byelaws and supporting IAs. These mechanisms render the decisions more democratically accountable both upwards due to the role of the MMO and the Secretary of State and downwards due to public consultation for draft byelaws and accompanying IAs that can also be subject to judicial review. The shortcomings identified in Chapter 3 in regard to IAs still apply but to a lesser extent because the level of knowledge is generally higher, hence with less necessity to rely on assumptions, rendering the documents more accurate. Accountability of IFCAs activities is also reinforced by the provisions in

[37] DEFRA, 'IFCA Byelaw Guidance: Guidance on the Byelaw Making Powers and General Offences under Part 6, Chapter 1, Section 155–164 of the Marine and Coastal Access Act (2011)', at: www.association-ifca.org.uk/Upload/About/ifca-byelaw-guidance.pdf.

[38] See DEFRA, 'Inshore Fisheries and Conservation Authorities: Conduct and Operation Report 2014–2018' (2018) https://assets.publishing.service.gov.uk/government/uploads/system/uploads/attachment_data/file/919059/ifca-conduct-operation-2014-2018.pdf.

[39] Section 159(1) of the MCAA.

[40] Sections 157(1) and (2) of the MCAA.

[41] Section 157(7) of the MCAA.

[42] Section 157(3)(b) of the MCAA.

[43] Section 157(4) of the MCAA.

Section 183 of the MCAA, which requires a quadrennial report by the Secretary of State to Parliament on IFCA conduct and operations as well as provisions under Sections 177 and 178 of the MCAA which require each IFCA to make, respectively, an annual plan before the commencement of the financial year and an annual report at the end of the financial year.

The IFCAs are relatively independent from one another in their decision-making. On the one hand, this independence risks regulatory fragmentation as ecological boundaries do not often equate with administrative ones. Indeed, divergent byelaws between neighbouring IFCAs have been noted to adding complexity to the regulatory landscape and rendering it more difficult to navigate for fishers.[44] On the other hand, individual IFCAs' high degree of independence is positive in enabling them to be more attuned to local conditions and to use the legal tools at their disposal creatively, going beyond the minimum national requirements. For example, Devon and Severn IFCA requires an Inshore-Vessel Monitoring System (I-VMS) unit on all registered commercial fishing vessels between 6.99 and 15.25 metres with a valid Mobile Fishing Permit. This requirement has been introduced as a permit condition under the Mobile Fishing Permit Byelaw.[45] This is an important step to ensure better monitoring of smaller vessels as currently the national requirement is that only fishing vessels with an overall length of twelve metres are required to have VMS units fitted on board.[46] Another notable example is the Sussex IFCA Nearshore Trawling Byelaw banning trawling with bottom-towed fishing gear around the coast of West Sussex to allow for the recovery of kelp forests. Such a byelaw permits large-scale protection of kelp and dependent species, enhancing fisheries and sequestering carbon in a district where the number of MPAs is low, rendering difficult habitat protection through place-based conservation. There are many other examples, ranging from the effective use of emergency byelaws by the North Eastern IFCA to deal with high levels of nomadic scallop dredging over the years to Kent and Essex IFCA whelk fishery permit byelaw that enables flexible management, having been amended to respond to new whelk stock information.[47]

The IFCAs score high also in terms of participation as they have an inclusive and broad membership, escaping the narrower commercial fisheries interest that was found predominant in the SFCs.[48] Besides, none of the IFCAs members are selected by existing IFCAs members, rendering selection more

[44] DEFRA, 'IFCA Conduct and Operation Report 2014–2018', p. 3.

[45] Devon and Severn IFCA Mobile Fishing Permit Byelaw, The Permit Conditions (Category 1 – At Sea), Section 2.5.

[46] For the rationale behind the decision, see Devon and Severn IFCA, 'Mobile Fishing Permit Byelaw: Development Report for Additional Changes to Permit Conditions' (2nd ed., 2017) at: https://secure.toolkitfiles.co.uk/clients/15340/sitedata/byep/consultation_/2nd-edit-Mob-fish-permit-devel-Sept-2017.pdf.

[47] DEFRA, 'IFCA Conduct and Operation Report 2014–2018', p. 43.

[48] J. Eagle, *Democracy and Natural Resources: British and American Approaches to Public Participation in Fisheries Management* (British Council, 2004) cited by T. Appleby and P. J. S. Jones, 'The Marine and Coastal Access Act', p. 75.

legitimate and less prone to regulatory capture. The number and members of individual IFCAs are described in Statutory Instruments that established the authority, so there are variations from district to district depending on the local environmental, social and economic circumstances. For all IFCAs, though, members include local councillors, persons appointed by the MMO and statutory members, comprising one representative from the Environment Agency, one from Natural England and one from the MMO. The Isle of Scilly is the only IFCA without a representative from the Environment Agency, for obvious reasons.

Having democratically appointed councillors on the IFCA committee is a powerful route for local accountability, enabling local interests to be represented. Having said so, the risk of councillors privileging their own political interests and displaying bias exists, as found in relation to the SFCs by Eagle,[49] where local councillors were primarily defending local commercial fisheries interests. Similarly, during an interview with an environmental NGO, I was told of a strong opposition towards an European Marine Site by an IFCA councillor because it had the word Europe in its title and the councillor was anti-European and needed to represent a far-right anti-European political party[50]. More generally, the second quadrennial report on the IFCAs found that, in certain IFCAs, councillors were viewed as being more concerned with the financial implications that IFCA work was presenting to their funding authorities than with marine policy and some conflict of interest existed. As Appleby and Jones discuss, bias is unconstitutional and incapacitates public ownership of marine resources.[51] At the same time, it would be idealistic to think that pure technical decision-making can exist in any setting. Although political considerations and bias cannot be removed, councillors are roughly one-third of the members on the IFCAs committee and the democratic voting system in place reduces the possibility for particular biases to prevail.

The figure of MMO appointees is also very interesting from a democratic perspective. They are members of the public who must be acquainted with the needs and opinions of the fishing community of the district and have knowledge of, or expertise in, marine environmental matters.[52] The term 'fishing communities' is broadly defined comprising 'all persons with any sort of interest in the exploitation of sea fisheries resources or in fisheries for such resources'. Similarly broad is the definition of 'marine environmental matters', meaning either the conservation or enhancement of natural beauty or amenity of marine or coastal areas, or the conservation of flora or fauna of marine or coastal environment.[53] Balancing conservation and fisheries interests is at the core of the MMO appointees as the terms and conditions for MMO appointees stress that:

[49] Ibid. [50] NGO representative n 1, online Interview May 2021.
[51] Appleby and Jones, 'The Marine and Coastal Access Act'.
[52] Section 151(2) of the MCAA. [53] Section 151(8) of the MCAA.

> Appointees to IFCAs are legally required to take into account all the local fishing and marine conservation interests in the waters of the IFCA district, in a balanced way, taking full account of all the economic, social and environmental needs of that district. Appointees should recognise that they are part of a committee and should not regard themselves as representing solely one particular interest within the IFCA district.[54]

This is of course in line with the government's vision for the IFCA, which is that they will 'lead, champion and manage a sustainable marine environment and inshore fisheries, by successfully securing the right balance between social, environmental and economic benefits to ensure healthy seas, sustainable fisheries and a viable industry'.[55]

The opportunity for any person with fisheries and conservation local knowledge to apply to becoming an MMO appointee aligns well with a pragmatic view of democracy in the Deweyan sense. Indeed, as Dewey points out, the public is not preformed but emerges around a particular problem to identify solutions.[56] The public interest that democratic systems should take into account is not a given but it is a contextual, specific occurrence emerging out of a specific problem. The task for democracy is then to ensure that the various emerging perspectives around an issue to be solved are well integrated in the decision-making. The public concerned is not always a pre-existing category of people, such as an environmental NGO with an established mandate to conserve the oceans, but it is an assembly of people called into being by being affected by a particular problem and spontaneously deciding to identify as concerned parties. As MMO appointees self-nominate to become part of the IFCA committee, they are a Deweyan public and an embodiment of a pragmatic view of democracy. By becoming MMO appointees, people are given opportunities to participate in collective action and environmental democracy that go beyond their role as voters, contributing to commoning practices. As Bollier writes, 'the real significance of commoning may be that is not ultimately about a fixed philosophical vision or policy agenda, but about engaged action in building successful commons.'[57]

To sum up, the IFCAs are locally accountable public decision-making bodies, they have a unique structure and their duties and powers span conservation to fisheries management, providing a basis for commoning, being rooted in local representation and knowledge. This view is also shared by the IFCA members themselves. An empirical study consisting of interviews with IFCA

[54] MMO, 'Appointment as an IFCA General Member Terms and Conditions' (2016), para 4, at: https://assets.publishing.service.gov.uk/government/uploads/system/uploads/attachment_data/file/637592/IFCA_General_Member_Terms_and_Conditions__updated_April_2016.pdf.

[55] Defra guidance to the IFCAs at: www.association-ifca.org.uk/about-us/defra-guidance-to-the-ifcas.

[56] J. Dewey, *The Public and Its problems* (Holt and Company, 1927).

[57] D. Bollier, 'Commoning as a Transformative Social Paradigm' (2018), p. 4 at: https://thenextsystem.org/node/187.

members found that the members themselves, on the whole, regard the IFCAs as a locus for democratic decision-making and inclusivity.[58] In this sense, IFCAs seem to fall into the category of the small scale, local, autonomous self-governing institutions that have been praised in the commons literature for supporting collective action and ensuring the sustainable governance of common-pool resources.[59] The emerging publics embodied in MMO appointees also confer on the IFCAs a dynamic quality and point to the commoning qualities of the IFCAs in the sense that they are not made up of fixed pre-given identities but that, through their membership, they take a problem-solving approach through joint action. Such evolving local management and democratic set up can facilitate ownership of decision-making and establish a basis for local environmental justice. It is not surprising then that in my various interviews with both local and national regulators over the years, SNCBs and NGOs, the IFCA model has always been celebrated.[60]

However, the picture is more complicated than this. As already explained, although the IFCAs have wide-ranging decision-making powers, they are not self-governing, having specific statutory duties they are required to fulfil and being subject to the MMO's supervisory functions and Secretary of State's byelaw confirmation, suspension and revocation powers. Secondly, as mentioned in relation to councillors, it is possible that political bias 'contaminates' decision-making. More generally, ensuring a balanced membership has always been regarded as a challenge. MMO appointees do not always reflect the full spectrum of interests in the marine environment, with some IFCAs left with an unbalanced membership, such as overrepresentation of commercial fisheries and an underrepresentation of recreational interests, or an overrepresentation of fishers from some geographical areas of the district compared to others. This is a recurrent problem identified in both the first[61] and second Secretary of State's quadrennial reports to Parliament on IFCAs conduct and operation, with the second report concluding with a recommendation to 'ensure Committee representation is balanced across all fisheries sectors, members are trained in local government procedures and they are clear on their roles, responsibilities and Code of Conduct, especially declaring conflicts of interest'.[62]

Moreover, although the expansion of IFCAs' conservation powers and duties with Section 154 of the MCAA is a welcome addition, it also creates tensions that IFCAs are required to manage. These include tensions between

[58] J. Lowther and L. D. Rodwell, 'IFCAs: Stakeholder Perception of Roles, and Legal Impact' (2013) 15 *Environmental Law Review* 11–26.

[59] Ostrom, 'Governing the Commons'.

[60] Face-to-face interviews carried as part of ESRC project (ES/K001043/1) between 2013 and 2015 in case study areas in the South-East and South-West England; elite interviews carried out with national representatives in May 2021.

[61] DEFRA, 'Inshore Fisheries and Conservation Authorities Conduct and Operation 2010–2014' (DEFRA, 2015) at: www.association-ifca.org.uk/Upload/About/ifca-review-2010-2014.pdf.

[62] DEFRA, 'IFCA Conduct and Operation 2014–2018', p. 76.

local fishery priorities and centralised conservation goals as well as between so-called traditional ecological knowledge and scientific knowledge. As expressed by an Association of the IFCAs representative:

> conservation and fisheries, conceptually, they support one another but the policy origin of the MPAs designation process has been to achieve national level objectives but other rational interventions around fishers management locally have been more difficult because of stakeholders feeling of being put on the side by the focus on conservation [...] that has caused a big tension particularly in certain sectors of the fleet, such as the mobile gear sector inshore feels that their interest have not been well served by the IFCAs as we have restricted their access in many areas.[63]

The process of designating MCZs, coupled with the new duties on the IFCAs since 2014 arising out of the revised approach to commercial fisheries management in European Marine Sites, discussed in Chapter 4, has meant that the IFCAs have been under much pressure and that much of their funding, already not particularly substantial, has been diverted to other fisheries management measures. Such scalar conflict, between local fisheries' needs and global environmental objectives, resonates with the distinction made in Chapter 1 of this book between MPAs as new commons and MPAs an enclosure depending on whether the point of view is that of global conservation or local sea-users. What is interesting in this specific case is that it is the same institution that needs to navigate such conflict, it is within the same institution that such conflict arises, making regulatory decisions complex. To a certain extent, the conflict is tamed by the transparency, openness and democratic character of the decision-making procedure, but, nevertheless, it is one that is ever present.

Relatedly, the other tension regards the relationship between systems of knowledge at play in IFCAs decision-making. On the one hand, there is, on the ground, pragmatic knowledge of local sea-users generated through practical experience and, on the other hand, the more technocratic approach to conservation informed by scientific principles. The ability to reconcile these forms of knowledges is a complex and inherent issue in most environmental regulation and one that has preoccupied environmental social scientists for a very long time.[64] The IFCAs draw extensively on SNCB advice to decide on management measures for MPAs in their district, while also listening to local sea-users' ecological knowledge, which sometimes conflicts with scientific knowledge. The Association of the IFCAs representative I interviewed discussed the protection of *Salmonidae* as an example, stating that the Environment Agency conservation advice is that coastal netting should be banned to protect salmon but long-standing IFCA members participating in these fisheries argue that in over thirty years of fishing in the area, they only caught few salmon, so it seems that

[63] Association for the IFCAs representative, online Interview, May 2021.

[64] See for example, Berkes, Sacred Ecology; Wynne, 'Should the Sheep Safely Graze?'

fishing is the smallest threat to the feature. According to an Association of the IFCA representative, 'the IFCA model does allow that challenge and that goes both ways: conserve more and be more proportionate, so there is the system of sense checking in decision-making process.'[65] Difficult relationships between different epistemologies have already been discussed in Chapter 5, but what is different here, and arguably more positive, is that compared to the process of designation of MCZs, fishers' ecological knowledge is not neglected but internalised as part of decision-making. The fact that IFCA members are conceptualised as more than stakeholders is also facilitated by the law and policy itself. For example, as explained earlier, Section 151(2) defines MMO appointees as people with fisheries and environmental knowledge and the terms and conditions again stress that MMO appointees should not represent only one particular interest, balancing the economic, social and environmental needs of that district.

6.5 Conclusion: Reflections on Institutions, Commoning and Environmental Democracy

This chapter has tackled the question of environmental democracy in relation to MPA regulation from an institutional perspective. Two actors have been identified as conducive to democratisation and commoning of MPA regulation: environmental NGOs and IFCAs. The purpose of the chapter has not been to provide a comparison between the two very diverse institutions but to show that, despite their ties, albeit different, to the state and conservation law, they are contributing to the commoning of MPA regulation. Firstly, the institutionalisation of NGOs has been considered, observing that much of the work of environmental NGOs in relation to marine conservation is not to disrupt and attack state law, but it is actually to re-imagine the boundaries of established legal concepts, such as site integrity under the Habitats Regulations, to push for novel approaches to conservation as well as to collaborate with state institutions and other actors when promoting different management approaches to conservation. This point is significant because it refines the findings of certain radical NGOs and commonning scholarship, showing that the analytical dichotomy between domination and resistance is too simplistic to capture exhaustively what is involved in these relationships, that state law is not necessarily always tied to state domination and power and that NGO collaborations with other actors and creative engagement with the law do not necessarily imply subscribing to a hegemonic paradigm. Concisely, democracy does not have to be necessarily an agonistic practice.

The collaborative aspect at the basis of democracy has also been highlighted in the discussion of the IFCAs. The inclusive membership of the IFCAs shows

[65] Association of the IFCA, online Interview, May 2021.

that MPAs regulation is not solely a choice of conservation technocrats or is dictated by economic priorities. Moreover, the fact that MMO appointees are legally required to consider both conservation and fisheries interest and must not represent a single stake shows that IFCAs call for a deliberative form of democracy, where individual interests are to be transcended through dialogue, moving beyond an understanding of democracy as a trade-off between different, pre-given stakes. Besides, the self-nomination aspect of MMO appointees adds to deliberation an element of pragmatism, as MMO appointees are an emergent public in the Deweyan sense.[66] Although tensions and challenges exist, the relational view of conservation and fisheries championed by IFCAs and the wide and inclusive membership is an important step in the building of environmental democracy.

[66] Dewey, *The Public and Its Problems*.

7

Climate Change and Marine Protected Areas Network

Adaptive Governance in English Marine Conservation Law

7.1 Introduction

This chapter opens the discussion on the last theme of the book, adapting regulation, by providing a critical reading of the current efforts to conserve marine biodiversity in a changing climate. By adapting regulation, I mean efforts that are made at making regulation experimental, reflexive and responsive to changes in circumstances, being these of an ecological or political nature and the way in which the law enables or hinders such adaptation. Political changes and the way in which the law is adapting to them are discussed in Chapter 8 in the context of Brexit, while this Chapter considers adaptation of conservation law and regulation to ecological changes, more specifically climate change.

The relationship between conservation and climate change is a complicated one due to the multiple entanglements between human and more-than human elements. Marine ecosystems play a key role in climate change mitigation as carbon dioxide is captured and stored in sediments and marine habitats, including for instance seagrass meadows and kelp forests. Thus, oceans' sinks are a nature-based solution to climate change. At the same time, climate change has negative impacts on the marine environment, due to the warming of the waters and ocean acidification, that is, the decrease in marine pH due to the increase in dissolved CO2.[1] Variations in temperature and pH affect the survival and development of marine organisms, altering their physiology, behaviour, dispersal patterns and affecting population structure, size and distribution. These shifts at the population level influence the structure of the entire marine community by altering species interactions and trophic relationships.[2] Scientific projections show the loss of some marine and coastal ecosystems, with related

[1] Y. Artioli et al., 'Heterogeneity of Impacts of High CO_2 on the North Western European Shelf' (2014) 11 *Biogeosciences* 601–612.

[2] E. Gissi et al., 'A Review of the Combined Effects of Climate Change and Other Local Human Stressors on the Marine Environment' (2021) 755 *Science of the Total Environment* 142564; S. Baag and S. Mandal, 'Combined Effects of Ocean Warming and Acidification on Marine Fish and Shellfish: A Molecule to Ecosystem Perspective' (2022) 802 *Science of the Total Environment* 149807.

goods, functions and services by the middle of this century,[3] highlighting the need for timely adaptation responses.[4]

This chapter discusses the extent to which the existing legal framework, presented in Chapter 2, promotes adaptative governance to conserve biodiversity in a changing climate and whether management practice follows suit. The chapter is structured as follows: after introducing the concept of adaptive governance for biodiversity conservation in the context of climate change, key provisions of the MCAA and the Habitats Regulations, as amended, are reviewed to identify whether English conservation law displays characteristics of adaptive governance. The doctrinal reading of the law is complemented by empirical insights gained through interviews with SNCBs and environmental NGOs as well as documentary analysis of key policies on implementation measures. It is argued that if the law provides for adaptive governance, its implementation in practice, that is adaptive management, is more problematic. A number of challenges regarding adaptive management tools and practices are identified. Not all is negative, though. Cases of successful adaptive management strategies in specific MPAs are present, and the establishment of HPMAs using the powers under the MCAA is also promising from an ecological perspective, at least. This chapter re-connects with the discussion on the continuous production and reproduction of socio-legal systems and the role of the more-than human in supporting or destabilising the boundaries created, discussed in Chapter 1.

7.2 Biodiversity Conservation in the Context of Climate Change: The Relevance of Adaptive Governance

Climate change presents unprecedented challenges to environmental law and regulation. As Fisher and others have argued, climate change has a 'legally disruptive' nature due, inter alia, to the uncertainty associated with climate change future scenarios, the need to manage a highly dynamic physical environment and the polycentricity of climate change.[5] Specifically in the marine context, the assessment of future climate change is pregnant with uncertainty. The scientific community acknowledges the presence of such uncertainty as evident in the Reports of the Intergovernmental Panel on Climate Change (IPPC), the

[3] H. O. Pörtner et al., 'Ocean Systems' in C.B. Field et al. (eds.), *Climate Change 2014: Impacts, Adaptation, and Vulnerability.* Part A: *Global and Sectoral Aspects. Contribution of Working Group II to the Fifth Assessment Report of the Intergovernmental Panel on Climate Change* (Cambridge University Press, 2014), pp. 411–484.

[4] N. L. Bindoff et al., 'Changing Ocean, Marine Ecosystems, and Dependent Communities' in H. O. Pörtner et al. (eds.), *IPCC Special Report on the Ocean and Cryosphere in a Changing Climate* (IPPC, 2019), pp. 447–587.

[5] E. Fisher, E. Scotford and E. Barritt, 'The Legally Disruptive Nature of Climate Change' (2017) 80 *Modern Law Review* 173–201; R.J. Lazarus, 'Super Wicked Problems and Climate Change: Restraining the Present to Liberate the Future' (2009) 94 *Cornell Law Review* 1153–1234.

United Nations body tasked with providing policy-makers with regular scientific assessment on climate change. Indeed, the recent IPPC Special Report on the Ocean and the Cryosphere in a Changing Climate shows that there is only medium confidence (rather than high or very high) for many projected changes and risks for ocean ecosystems as well as for people and ecosystem services. For example, there is only medium confidence that future shifts in fish distribution and decreases in their abundance due to climate change will negatively impact livelihoods of marine resource-dependent communities,[6] and there is only medium confidence that ocean acidification, oxygen loss and reduced sea ice extent have the potential to exacerbate warming-induced ecosystem impacts, such as a decrease in global biomass of marine animal communities, their production and fisheries catch potential and a shift in species composition.[7]

Regulators have to make decisions in such an uncertain context and are also confronted with the challenge of managing a highly dynamic physical environment. The marine environment has never been static due to its very fluid nature, but anthropogenic climate change exacerbates such dynamism presenting more challenges for regulators from sea level rise to new shifts in species distribution, showing the disruptive nature of the more-than human. Finally, the polycentric nature of climate change means that, as there is no just one identifiable source of pollution, there is not just one impact confined to one scale, but both the causes and impacts are varied, cumulative and multiscalar. In relation to impacts of climate change in the marine environment, these include impacts on coastal communities, on fish distribution, on suitable habitat for species protection, on entire ecosystems, hence ranging from the human to the physical, from the individual to the ecosystemic. Conservation measures in the context of global environmental change must therefore recognise and confront such cross-scalar complexity and uncertainty, thinking beyond the preservationist paradigm in environmental regulation. The preservationist paradigm is based on assumptions of 'ecological stationarity', as Craig would call it.[8] By ecological stationarity, Craig means environmental regulations attempting either at preserving an ecosystem in a more natural state or at reversing the human-induced changes to some more natural baseline, rather than focusing on the adaptive capacity of ecosystems. Similarly, Ruhl writes that a shift from preservationism based on the stationarity premise to transitionalism in environmental law is fundamental in a climate change era.[9]

[6] IPCC, 'Summary for Policymakers' in H. O. Pörtner et al. (eds.), *IPCC Special Report on the Ocean and Cryosphere in a Changing Climate* (IPPC, 2019), para B.8.

[7] Ibid, para B.5.

[8] R. K. Craig, 'Stationarity Is Dead' – Long Live Transformation: Five Principles for Climate Change Adaptation Law (2010) 34 *Harvard Environmental Law Review* 9–75.

[9] J. B. Ruhl, 'Climate Change Adaptation and the Structural Transformation of Environmental Law' (2010) 40 *Environmental Law* 363–435.

Adaptive strategies are thus necessary for law and regulation to grapple with the complexity of conserving biodiversity in the context of climate change. It is here that the concept of adaptive governance becomes relevant. The concept of adaptive governance has gained traction in scholarly work on the sustainability and resilience of complex social–ecological systems.[10] Although no single definition exists, adaptive governance promotes experimentation encouraging flexibility, learning, monitoring and revisions to deal with the inherent uncertainty and complexity associated with environmental change.[11] All of these elements are interlinked and demonstrate the processual and iterative nature of adaptive governance. Experimentation allows to adapt to new circumstances, testing particular assumptions, promoting learning of what works and what does not. Monitoring permits the periodic evaluation of data, critical to understand whether revisions are needed, and in so doing it promotes learning too.

Although adaptive governance may seem to be threatening foundational concepts of legal certainty and stability at the core of the rule of law,[12] procedural guarantees, such as strong participatory provisions, can ensure the legitimacy and accountability of the governance regime and indeed are regarded as a fundamental aspect of adaptive governance in the legal literature on adaptive governance.[13] Participatory decision-making is also essential from an instrumental perspective, due to the complexity of social–ecological systems and the cross-scalar challenges presented by climate change demanding pluralistic knowledges and perspectives and collective evaluations, as no single centre/regulator holds all the information necessary for decision-making. Adaptive governance stresses the relevance of having strategic decision-making happening at various scales and by different actors. Thus, embracing adaptive governance means that the aim of environmental regulation is not to minimise change but to manage uncertainty and complexity in social–ecological systems experimentally and as collectively and collaboratively as possible. Manifestly,

[10] For an introduction see, C. Folke et al. 'Adaptive Governance of Social-Ecological Systems' (2005) 30 *Annual Review of Environmental Resources* 441–473.

[11] T. Dietz, E. Ostrom, P. C. Stern, 'The Struggle to Govern the Commons' (2003) 302 *Science* 1907–1912; B. C. Chaffin, H. Gosnell and B. A. Cosens, 'A Decade of Adaptive Governance Scholarship: Synthesis and Future Directions' (2014) 19 *Ecology and Society* 56.

[12] R. K. Craig et al., 'Balancing Stability and Flexibility in Adaptive Governance: An Analysis of Tools Available in U.S. Environmental Law' (2017) 22 *Ecology and Society* 3.

[13] J. Ebbesson, 'The Rule of Law in Governance of Complex Socio-Ecological Change' (2010) 20 *Global Environmental Change* 414–422; B. A. Cosens et al., 'The Role of Law in Adaptive Governance' (2017) 22 *Ecology and Society* 30; M. Pieraccini, 'Towards Just Resilience: Representing and Including New Constituencies in Adaptive Governance and Law' (2019) 31 *Journal of Environmental Law* 213–234; B. A. Cosens et al., 'Designing Law to Enable Adaptive Governance of Modern Wicked Problems' (2020) 73 *Vanderbilt Law Review* 1687–1732.

adaptive governance shares many features with Dorf and Sabel's democratic experimentalism,[14] with whom environmental law and regulation readership will be familiar. Although it is not the aim of this chapter to discuss the connections between these two strands of literature, it is evident that both schools aim to tackle strategic uncertainty, promoting polycentric decision-making and multiple collective problem-solving and iterative learning with accountability through, for instance, regular monitoring and reporting on performance and periodic revisions. The implementation of the goals is left to local units, afforded some discretion in experimental problem-solving practices and subject to regular reporting obligations to provide feedback on their performance and to adjust if needed. The centre, such as a government agency, facilitates interactions between local units, fulfilling a coordination role and evaluating goals in the light of experience, rather than dictating uniform action from the top. Governance becomes an ongoing practice to respond to social–ecological feedback and, in this context, law itself should be adaptive by facilitating reflexivity and experimentation and putting in place procedural mechanisms allowing for ongoing deliberation between various actors, representing social–ecological relationships and diverse human–non-human entanglements at different scales and times.

The extent to which the existing English framework of marine conservation law displays elements of adaptive governance is discussed below. Given that procedural aspects regarding participatory decision-making have been the subject of discussion in Part III of this book on democratising regulation, the analysis below will not reiterate them, but will focus instead on whether the law contains provisions and tools facilitating flexibility and monitoring, facilitating learning and revisions when needed.

7.3 Adaptive Governance in English Marine Conservation Law

Both the Habitats Regulations, as amended, and the MCAA contain provisions that facilitate adaptive governance. Due to potential changes to the abundance and distribution of species as well as changes in habitats and ecosystems caused by climate change, a flexible process to enable the network of MPAs to evolve is essential. This might require the designation of new sites, changes to boundaries or the declassification of sites no longer supporting important species and/or habitats. Both the Habitats Regulations, as amended, and the MCAA contain provisions of such kind. Section 122 of the MCAA contains provisions for the amendment, revocation and review of orders designating MCZs. Comparably, the Habitats Regulations, as amended, provide for the designation of new sites as well as provisions for managing, and where

[14] M. C. Dorf & C. F. Sabel, 'A Constitution of Democratic Experimentalism' (1998) 98 *Columbia Law Review* 267–473; C. F. Sabel and J. Zeitlin (eds.), *Experimentalist Governance in the European Union: Towards a New Architecture* (Oxford University Press, 2010).

necessary adapting, the network of European sites[15] with a view to contributing to the achievement of the management objectives.[16] As will be discussed at greater length in Chapter 8, the provisions under the Habitats Regulations, as amended, relax the grounds for changes and declassification of sites, compared to what is available under the Habitats Directive, whereby declassification under article 9 is possible only 'where this is warranted by natural developments noted as a result of the surveillance provided for in Article 11'. In any case, changes cannot be based on lack of compliance with the legal provisions. As stated in the CJEU case law, which is still relevant as retained EU case law, declassification cannot be based on the failure to comply with the legal provisions and not all degradation justifies declassification as 'it is essential that that degradation should make the site irretrievably unsuitable to ensure the conservation of natural habitats and of the wild fauna and flora or the setting up of the Natura 2000 network.'[17] This point is essential, as adaptive governance cannot be used as an excuse for not complying with the legal requirements.

Besides, Section 143(2) of the Habitats Regulations confers a further degree of flexibility on environmental protection by enabling the appropriate authority to amend the Schedules of species and habitats in the Habitats Regulations in the light of scientific and technical progress. Similarly, under Section 144(2), the appropriate authorities may make amendments to the Annexes of the Habitats and Birds Directive for adapting them to technical and scientific progress. The 2021 government policy paper explaining the changes to the Habitats Regulations, as amended, following Brexit connects this power directly to climate change, stating that 'it is anticipated that changes will be rare but could, for example, include additions of new species in response to climate change or their successful reintroduction in Great Britain.'[18] Any proposed changes will be subject to public consultation and will be made using statutory instruments. Changes to the Schedules 2 and 5 of the Habitats Regulations, as amended, and to Annex IV of the Habitats Directive will be subject to stringent procedural requirements as they require an affirmative statutory instrument to ensure appropriate scrutiny by both Houses of Parliament.[19] However, the list of marine protected species and habitats under the Habitats Directive is short, and the criteria for the selection of sites do not refer to climate change and are primarily concerned with current numbers and presence of listed species and habitats.

[15] This is known as 'national site network' after Brexit. See regulation 3(1)(a) of the Habitats Regulations, as amended, by regulation 4(2) of the EU Exit Habitats Regulations.

[16] Regulation 16A of the Habitats Rgulations introduced by regulation 13 of the EU Exit Habitats Regulations.

[17] Case C-301/12 *Cascina Tre Pini Ss v Ministero dell'Ambiente e della Tutela del Territorio e del Mare and Others* EU:C:2014:214 (*Cascina Tre Pini*), para 30.

[18] www.gov.uk/government/publications/changes-to-the-habitats-regulations-2017/changes-to-the-habitats-regulations-2017.

[19] Regulation 145(2) of the EU Exit Habitats Regulations.

The same issues are not encountered in relation to MCZs. Differently from European Marine Sites, the ecological grounds for the designation of MCZs are broader in that MCZs can be designated for the protection of any marine flora and fauna and marine habitats to conserve their diversity or because they are rare or threatened,[20] rather than relying on set lists of protected habitats and species. Thus, the wider grounds of designation for MCZs under the MCAA provide more flexibility than those under the Habitats Regulations and can be used also to create HPMAs, given that the law is not prescriptive regarding the level of protection MCZs must afford. Indeed, the section on implementation below will discuss how HPMAs are in the process of being established in England using the designation powers under the MCAA. In any case, although the designation grounds are narrower for European Marine Sites in the Habitats Regulations, the possibility to amend Schedules and Annexes in the light of scientific and technical progress, as discussed above, is a welcome step towards climate-proof conservation of European Marine Sites.[21]

Flexibility is also present in the management of MPAs. Firstly, under the Habitats Regulations, there is an obligation to prevent deterioration of habitats and disturbance of species and there is an argument to say that this includes an obligation for local authorities to put in place measures that are going to prevent or reduce in some way the effects of climate change on those designated features.[22] Similarly, under MCAA,[23] public authorities are under a duty to exercise their functions in the manner which the authority considers best further the conservation objectives stated for the MCZ and again this may include climate-smart measures.[24] Also, there is no reason why management schemes that can be established for European Marine Sites under regulation 38(1) of the Habitats Regulations cannot address the climate change impacts on protected habitats and species. Similarly, under MCAA,[25] public authorities are under a duty to exercise their functions in the manner which the authority considers best further the conservation objectives stated for the MCZ, which could include management schemes and again this may be interpreted as including climate-smart measures.[26]

Secondly, byelaws, which are a key regulatory tool, can be amended and drafted in a way that facilitates adaptive strategies. However, the making of a

[20] Section 117(4) and Section 117(5) of the MCAA.

[21] A. Cliquet et al., 'International and European Law on Protected Areas and Climate Change: Need for Adaptation or Implementation?' (2014) 54 *Environmental Management* 720–731.

[22] Regulation 9 establishes a duty to comply with the requirements of the Habitats and Birds Directive. One of these requirements is to be found under article 6(2) of the Habitats Directive, which requires Member States to take appropriate steps to avoid the deterioration of natural habitats and the habitats of species as well as disturbance of the species for which the areas have been designated in so far as such disturbance could be significant in relation to the objectives of this Directive.

[23] Section 125(2)(a) of the MCAA.

[24] Ibid. [25] Ibid. [26] Ibid.

byelaw is time-consuming due to the procedural requirements that are to be followed from the public consultation measures to the signing of the Secretary of State.[27] Powers to amend the byelaws are present but again that requires time.[28] Although those procedural requirements are positive from the perspective of democratic accountability, they slow down decision-making. However, the power to make emergency and interim byelaws under Sections 131 and 132 of the MCAA provides an avenue towards adaptive governance.[29] Emergency byelaws can be introduced by the MMO if it thinks there is an urgent need to protect MCZs without the need of Secretary of State's confirmation and interim byelaws can be made if the MMO thinks there is an urgent need to protect a feature and there are or may be reasons for the Secretary of State to consider designation of the area as an MCZ. Such powers apply also in relation to European Marine Sites.[30] These powers are important from an adaptive governance perspective as they enable the authorities to respond quickly to unforeseeable social–ecological changes, hence maximising flexibility.

The legal instruments contain also strong monitoring and reporting obligations, essential to promoting learning through the gathering and sharing of information, through critical evaluation of the current progress and through potential revisions. Regarding monitoring, regulation 50(1) of the Habitats Regulations, as amended,[31] requires the appropriate authority to make arrangements for the surveillance of the conservation status of protected species and habitats. The surveillance may be carried out by a SNCB or any other person acting pursuant to, and in accordance with, an agreement with the appropriate authority or SNCB.[32] Similarly, Section 124(3) of the MCAA makes provisions for the appropriate authority to direct SNCBs to monitor MCZs.

Weaker reporting obligations following Brexit were a possibility, given that the requirement under article 17 of the Habitats Directive is no longer applicable. Under article 17(1), Member States are under a duty to submit a report to the European Commission including information about the implementation of the Directive, in particular focusing on the conservation measures established for the sites and the evaluation of impacts of those measures on the listed species and habitats as well as the results of the surveillance. The Commission is under an obligation to draw up a composite report that shall

[27] Section 130 and Section 155 of the MCAA for MCZs and regulation 32 of the Habitats Regulations for European Marine Sites.

[28] The implied power to amend byelaws, which an Act confers powers to make, is set out under Section 14 of the Interpretation Act 1978. On top of this, the Secretary of State has powers to amend or revoke an IFCA byelaw made under Section 155 by order, if it is satisfied that any provision is unnecessary, inadequate or disproportionate. The procedural steps are set out in Section 159 of the MCAA.

[29] Also, the IFCAs have powers to make emergency byelaw under Section 157 of the MCAA.

[30] Regulation 40 of the Habitats Regulations.

[31] Regulation 50(1) of the Habitats Regulations as amended, by regulation 20(2) of the EU Exit Habitats Regulations.

[32] Regulation 50(6) of the Habitats Regulations.

include an appropriate evaluation of the progress achieved.[33] Fortunately, the Brexit amendments to the Habitats Regulations do maintain stringent reporting requirements. Under Section 9A of the Habitats Regulations, as amended, the appropriate authority must publish a report every 6 years on implementation, including information on the conservation measures under article 6(1) of the Habitats and article 12 of the Birds Directive, and its impacts on listed protected species and habitats as well as the results of the surveillance undertaken under Part 4 of the Regulations. Moreover, the Secretary of State is also under an obligation to publish a composite biennial report including an appropriate evaluation of the progress achieved with a special focus on the contribution of the national site network (the new name for the network of European Marine Sites) to the achievement of the objective of enabling the listed protected species and habitats to be maintained at, or where appropriate, restored to, favourable conservation status in their natural range. The report must be submitted in draft to the devolved administrations for verification, showing polycentric governance at play. The provisions under Section 9A mirror those under article 17(1) and (2) under the Habitats Directive and ensure transparency of environmental performance in respect of the retained EU law, though, for obvious reasons, the role of the European Commission is replaced by that of the Secretary of State. Brexit issues are considered in more detail in the next chapter.

Stringent reporting obligations are also present in Section 124 of the MCAA, which contains reporting requirements related to the network of MPAs in the UK, established under Section 123(2). Such a report must also be published every 6 years and include information on the MCZs that have been designated, their conservation objectives, any changes to designation orders made and any further steps required for each MCZ to achieve the conservation objectives stated for it. Besides, it shall contain information regarding the extent to which the objectives of creating a network of MPAs detailed in Section 123(2) have been achieved and any further step required to contribute to their achievement. The MCAA specifies the conditions that the network must satisfy, namely that the network contributes to the conservation or improvement of the marine environment in the UK marine area, that the features protected by the MPAs represent the range of features present in the UK marine area and that the designation of sites comprised in the network reflects the fact that the conservation of a feature may require the designation of more than one site.[34] In the context of climate change, networks of MPAs, rather than individual/isolated sites, are crucial because they enable the protection of biodiversity in more dynamic and connected ways, facilitating cross-scalar interactions. MPAs cannot be thought of as ecological islands that function independently of the broader ecosystem.[35] Networks add the ecosystemic dimension to conservation law needed in the context of climate change

[33] Article 17(2) of the Habitats Directive.

[34] Section 123(3) of the MCAA.

[35] G. S. Cumming et al., 'Understanding Protected Area Resilience: A Multi-scale, Social-Ecological Approach' (2015) 25 *Ecological Applications* 299–319.

to deal with complex social–ecological changes. Having provisions directly addressing the conditions of the network is therefore important.

To sum up, the doctrinal analysis reveals that the Habitats Regulations, as amended, and the MCAA contain provisions facilitating adaptive governance, especially those regarding site designation, management, monitoring and reporting. What about the implementation of the law? The extent to which the implementation of the law also favours adaptive strategies is discussed below. In analysing the legal implementation, the discussion moves from the realm of governance to that of management, considering management strategies employed. Adaptive management can be distinguished from adaptive governance in that it relates to specific tools and management practices, rather than the wider structure of the governance system within which adaptive management occurs.[36] Simply put, adaptive management can be conceptualised as the means by which adaptive governance is operationalised.[37]

7.4 Adaptive Management for English MPAs

If current conservation law is fit in principle for promoting adaptive governance, its implementation tells a different story. Although some positive examples of adaptive management exist, a number of challenges are present. This section discusses both the positive steps and the challenges towards adaptive management.

Interest in adaptive management is fast developing in MPAs practice at the national level. Recently, for example, JNCC run a two-year project on adaptive management, launched in 2018 and funded by the European Maritime and Fisheries Fund. The aim of the project was not to amend measures in place or to influence existing processes to develop management measures, but it was to develop a management toolkit to establish a process for future adaptive management based on a participatory approach. The project was confined to fisheries management in offshore MPAs and, specifically aimed at tackling the uncertainty around fishing impacts on sedimentary habitats. Given its aims and focus, it remained at a theoretical/exploratory level. Nevertheless, the project shows that there is interest from SNCBs in taking adaptive management seriously, integrating various actors (from fishing sector, to NGOs, to academic community) within the management review process and developing an ecological model to predict ecological outcomes of different management scenarios.[38]

[36] For the difference between adaptive management and governance, see L. Gunderson and S. S. Light, 'Adaptive Management and Adaptive Governance in the Everglades Ecosystem' (2006) 39 *Policy Sciences* 323–334; L. Hasselman, 'Adaptive Management; Adaptive Co-management; Adaptive Governance: What's the Difference?' (2017) 24 *Australasian Journal of Environmental Management* 31–46.

[37] Folke, 'Adaptive Governance of Social-Ecological Systems'.

[38] JNCC et al., 'Developing a Participatory Approach to the Management of Fishing Activity in UK Offshore Marine Protected Areas' (2020), at: https://data.jncc.gov.uk/data/f9819ea9-e286-47a6-9e45-08c243dbb0cb/MPA-AdaptiveManagement-ProjectReport-FINAL.pdf.

However, there are also reservations toward adaptive management among some key players. Various actors interviewed expressed concern that adaptive management, though useful from a pragmatic viewpoint, should not be used to water down environmental objectives and, because the term is vague, it may hinder regulatory certainty. As a DEFRA representative put it 'we prefer not to use the term "adaptive management" as there's confusion around what it means (e.g. in case it is used as an argument for delaying implementation of measures while additional data is gathered, which wouldn't be appropriate).'[39] Similarly, an NGO representative described adaptive management as a 'sneaky word' that could be used to get buy in from everyone to an idea that the management of fisheries MPAs could be partial in order to see how the site responds in some areas in comparison to others.[40] Experiments in MPAs are of course problematic from a legal perspective if they risk jeopardising the conservation objectives of sites causing likely significant effects, especially where there are activities with high environmental impact such as bottom-trawl fishing. Again, another NGO representative, speaking in relation to European Marine Sites, though recognising the value of adaptive measures to conserve biodiversity in the context of climate change, reiterated the point that the priority is to maintain site integrity and that adaptive management should be used only if site integrity is not risked.[41]

Looking at a more local scale, it is possible to identify instances of adaptive management in IFCAs' byelaws. For example, Sussex IFCA has introduced the Oyster Permit Byelaw, which establishes a permit-based system for the commercial exploitation of native oyster stocks by dredging.[42] Section 20 of the byelaw sets out flexible permit conditions on catch restrictions and gear configuration. New conditions are reviewed once a year and all permit conditions once every four at the very minimum. Decisions on the flexible permit conditions are taken following consultation with those who are likely to be affected by the changes as well as organisations and drawing on data collected from permit holders, SNCBs advice and scientific data. Similarly, Southern IFCA's Solent Dredge Permit Byelaw allows for adaptive management of the fishery through permit conditions and involving interest actors in the decision-making process.[43] Devon and Severn IFCA's Mobile Fishing Permit Byelaw to protect MPA's features such as seagrass and *Sabellaria* reef provides the framework for fishing permits to be issued, and the conditions of these permits are again flexible and can be adapted should changes in management be required.[44] It should be noted, though, that all these examples concern inshore management

[39] DEFRA representative, Written Communication, May 2021.
[40] NGO representative n 1, online Interview, May 2021.
[41] NGO representative n 2, online Interview, May 2021.
[42] Sussex IFCA, Oyster Permit Byelaw 2014.
[43] Southern IFCA, The Solent Dredge Permit Byelaw 2021.
[44] Devon and Severn IFCA, Mobile Fishing Permit Byelaw 2013.

and depend on individual IFCAs efforts so, albeit positive, they do not show a concerted effort towards adaptive management. However, these are important steps and are in line with an experimentalist attitude that takes polycentricity seriously, being the actions of local units, rather than a top-down blanket policy.

Although tools for adaptive management exist, according to an Association for the IFCA representative I interviewed, often the conservation advice is lacking and, especially in relation to ephemeral features (such as *Sabellaria* reef), it is up to the local regulator to make a case for protection within the context of the tension between precaution and proportion.[45]

The situation is even more complicated for offshore sites. Although interest in adaptive management is present, as demonstrated by the JNCC research project mentioned earlier, most offshore MPAs lack any form of management and current efforts to put in place byelaws are happening in a political context, which is pressing for quick results to protect existing vulnerable species and habitats primarily from bottom-towed fishing, leaving no time for creative, long-term conservation thinking. As a JNCC interviewee put it:

> their [the government] focus is on putting byelaws in as quickly as possible and there is no much thought put on novel and creative ways to do other things. Because of pressure to get results from ministers and pressures from NGOS, threatening judicial review, it [adaptive management] is not a priority even if we [SNCBs] are pushing for those approaches.[46]

In relation to both inshore and offshore MPAs, there does not seem to be consistent thinking about how to internalise future potential ecological changes in decision-making. This was something interviewees regretted. As one interviewee stated in relation to inshore MPAs, 'there has not been the space available to discuss the future of conservation'[47] given that measures introduced with the revised approach to fisheries discussed in Chapter 4 have been about the protection of what is currently present, without taking into consideration potential long-term changes. Not dissimilarly from the situation of offshore sites, the threat of judicial review from NGOs put on pressure for delivering management measures as quickly as possible for the protection of existing vulnerable species and habitats in inshore MPAs, without much room left to think about adaptation measures. This is compounded by political pressures to show green credentials after Brexit, which means acting rapidly to meet government aspirations to maintain high environmental standards, a point to which I will be returning to in Chapter 8.

Moreover, a major challenge is that of monitoring. As mentioned in Chapter 2, monitoring is expensive, especially in offshore sites, and funding is scarce.

[45] Association of the IFCAs, online Interview, May 2021.
[46] SNCB national representative, online Interview, May 2021.
[47] Association of the IFCAs, online Interview, May 2021.

Monitoring is fundamental to understand what works in practice and what can be revised. Although monitoring provisions in the law are present, the lack of resources means that monitoring for each MPA is impossible to achieve. Consequently, as put by a SNCB representative, 'we need to start getting creative on how we use the resources for detecting change that are available and that will be selecting a representative number of sites and using the finding that we see to make more informed judgement around other sites in the network.'[48]

In this context, the introduction of HPMAs is especially relevant. As expressed by a SNCB representative:

> ideally we'd want obviously many more surveys and areas, but it is not possible and HPMAs can help in this respect and are test sites because we can do the design to mimic what we would do under a higher funding scenario.[49]

HPMAs belong to the category of strict natural reserves, excluding extractive and depositional use and preventing damaging levels of other activities. Because of their stringent level of protection, HPMAs offer whole site protection and can be used as test sites to check how biodiversity recovers when there is minimal human impact and what effects climate change is having. HPMAs can provide sound benchmarks against which to test the effectiveness of other, less strictly protected MPAs and for the future evidence-based management of the MPA network. If HPMAs protect different examples of marine ecosystems inshore and offshore, they constitute an important national experimental ground, helping to clarify what recovery to a mature state looks like for marine ecosystems and helping to fill knowledge gaps, especially in relation to representative habitats or species where baseline conditions are not present. The value of HPMAs from a scientific perspective is to ensure recovery of marine ecosystems as well as to be able to monitor and assess what is happening to the various ecological attributes such as the distribution of a particular habitat or species in a site, the biological community composition, the typical species composition. Relative trend information can be gathered for wider biodiversity conservation.

HPMAs are thus a very useful tool from an adaptative management scientific perspective but, of course, they are highly political, in the sense of being subject to very different views from different interests. Being strictly protected marine reserves, they are de facto enclosures, bringing in all the problems of fortress conservation discussed in Chapter 1. It is not the case that the precursor of HPMAs, that is, Reference Areas, proposed during the MCZs designation process, encountered much opposition from sea-users. Of the sixty-five Reference Areas proposed in the initial phase of the MCZs designation, none were designated.

[48] SNCB national representative, online Interview, May 2021. [49] Ibid.

Renewed efforts to put in place HPMAs are present in England, but the government approach is very soft, starting with a pilot of five sites. More specifically, the government asked an expert panel, chaired by the former fisheries minister Richard Benyon, to review if there was a need to introduce HPMAs and provide proposals for their designation. The Benyon review was published in 2020 and recommended that HPMAs are an essential component of the MPAs network and should be introduced by the government in Secretary of State waters.[50] The review did acknowledge the social and economic challenges of HPMAs, especially for the fisheries industry due to the halting and/or displacing of fishing efforts. Displacement is particularly problematic for small-scale fishers, less able to relocate. Although long-term HPMAs can have benefits for fisheries due to, for example, the spillover effect,[51] for current generations of fishers they are threatening, and the panel recommended mitigation measures such as nesting HPMAs within existing MPAs and adopting the principle of transparency and early and continuous engagement with sea-users.

Sea-users were also extensively engaged during the designation of MCZs but as discussed in Chapter 5, participatory decision-making then had many flaws, not generating the expected buy-in from sea-users. This begs the question of what will be done differently in the current HPMA process. The Benyon review stressed that to overcome the problems previously encountered with MCZs designation, it is essential to allow time for sea-users to plan and adapt to the proposed changes, to have clarity in relation to the aims, definition and management of the HPMAs and to encourage continuous engagement of a diversity of actors also post-designation through co-management. It also recommended that the principles to designate HPMAs are of an ecological nature, including ecological importance, naturalness, sensitivity and potential to recover, as well as ecosystem services, with social and economic principles as a secondary filter.[52] Such recommendations help to overcome some shortcomings of the process of designation in MCZs identified in Chapter 5 but not all. As explained in Chapter 5, one of the major issues with the designation of MCZs was the form participation took, which was an example of 'thin' proceduralisation with the participatory space used to trade-off stakes in order to reach a compromise. This was due to the categorical division between socio-economic and ecological variables, reflected in the separation of participants in distinct stakeholders' categories representing different interests. Such separation was internalised by the fishermen, contributing to their negative perception of the MCZs, of the designation process and of the ecological Other. Indeed, paying attention to the form of participation is not only important in order to design

[50] 'Benyon Review Into Highly Protected Marine Areas: Final Report' (2019) at: https://assets.publishing.service.gov.uk/government/uploads/system/uploads/attachment_data/file/890484/hpma-review-final-report.pdf.

[51] The spillover effect refers to movement of individuals from MPAs to outside fishing grounds.

[52] 'Benyon Review'.

procedures that are legitimate but also to avoid the negative substantive/pragmatic effects of 'thin' proceduralisation on the perceptions of the environmental issue in question, as discussed in Chapter 5. 'Thicker' procedural alternatives for the designation of HPMAs would require developing processes and relying on concepts that enable the multiplicity of knowledges to come forth by deconstructing fictitious dichotomies between nature and society and avoiding relegating sea-users in fixed, predetermined stakeholder categories.

The Benyon review remains silent on this issue though, leaving to the government the decision regarding the form participation should take. The government's published response to the Benyon report does not provide any further detail on the form participation will take, however, and it is the task of the implementation team to decide on this matter. What the government's response does is to set a timeline for shortlisting ten HPMAs by the end of 2021, followed by designation of five pilot sites in 2022. It stresses that the pilot has the aims of improving understanding on how the marine ecosystem will recover in the absence of human pressures, how best to monitor and manage MPAs, the suitability of the MCAA for the designation of HPMAs and the effects of HPMAs on sea-users and coastal communities. This is in line with an adaptive management approach, with pilot HPMAs being part of an experimental design for the conservation of biodiversity.

Regarding participation, which is a key element of the adaptive approach, the government response to the Benyon's review states that HPMAs 'should be used to increase engagement with the marine environment' and that 'transparency and early, continuous engagement is essential and have already been applying this principle in developing this response through stakeholder meetings'.[53] In this respect, it seems that HPMAs will not amount to enclosures and could actually contribute to an ethics of commoning. However, nothing is stated in regard to the form of participation or the actors that will be involved in engagement opportunities. Clearly, the law provides opportunities for public participation, such as consultation on draft orders of MCZs under Section 119 of the MCAA, which will also apply to HPMAs, but to what extent the government will go beyond statutory requirements is left in the hands of those implementing the process, rather than detailed in the government's response.

Besides, considering that the government response was published in June 2021 and the shortlisted sites are to be defined by the end of 2021, the timeframe for engagement opportunities at this crucial stage is short. Shortlisted sites are chosen primarily on the basis of ecological criteria, and ecological guidance has been developed in this respect by the SNCBs to start selecting potential

[53] DEFRA, 'Government Response to the Highly Protected Marine Areas (HPMAs) Review' (DEFRA, 2021), at: www.gov.uk/government/publications/government-response-to-the-highly-protected-marine-areas-hpmas-review/government-response-to-the-highly-protected-marine-areas-hpmas-review.

locations.[54] Although third parties can submit proposals, they must do so based on the ecological criteria listed in the ecological guidance, which are rather technical. Moreover, the window to submit third-party proposals is very narrow, with the deadline set less than two months from the government's announcement on committing to designate HPMAs. It will be recalled that third-party proposals were also used for highly mobile species for the designation of second tranche MCZs as explained in Chapter 5, but most of the submissions were disregarded. Furthermore, then as now, due to the technical nature of the third-party proposal submission form, it is unlikely that many sea-users, such as fishers, will fill in the form, making third-party proposal an exercise for elite environmental NGOs. Arguably, more inclusive methods to present ecological evidence could have been designed, enabling more actors from different backgrounds to share their knowledge at this stage. On the positive side, a group leading on stakeholder engagement for HPMAs in DEFRA, advised by an academic board, has been created with the aim to devise engagement opportunities,[55] but these will be set in place after the shortlisted sites have been agreed, which is arguably quite late in decision-making, leaving one to wonder whether the principle of early and continuous engagement is met.

7.5 Conclusion

This chapter has discussed adaptive strategies in marine conservation law and its current implementation which are needed to assist the conservation of biodiversity in a changing climate and enable to take seriously the role of more-than-human components in destabilising legal territories. The analysis has focused on both legal provisions facilitating adaptive governance and on application of adaptive management on the ground, drawing on a mixture of doctrinal research and insights from elite interviews as well as a consideration of current policy documents and practices. The conclusions are straightforward: if the Habitats Regulations, as amended, and even more so the MCAA enable adaptive governance and are sufficient for the establishment of climate smart MPAs, current adaptive management practices are found more wanting. The Habitats Regulations, as amended, and especially the MCAA contain provisions that enable flexibility, learning, monitoring and revisions. In practice, although successful examples of adaptive management in the byelaws of specific IFCAs are present and valuable tools such as HPMAs are in the process of being put in place as part of an experimental design, there are a series of drawbacks for successful adaptive management, ranging from the costs of

[54] JNCC and Natural England, 'Identifying Pilot Highly Protected Marine Areas in English Waters: Ecological Principles and Criteria Guidance Note' (JNCC and Natural England, 2021) at: https://data.jncc.gov.uk/data/47bafb41-05d8-4929-b236-162f4eddd22f/pilot-hpma-ecological-guidance-note.pdf.

[55] DEFRA representative, Written Communication, May 2021.

monitoring, to the lack of strong design principles by the government to establish inclusive participatory opportunities for the designation of HPMAs, to some actors' mistrust of adaptive management for the fear that it could water down conservation objectives. Adaptative governance and adaptive management are not panaceas, and of course, they can bring in risks if they are used to condone activities that may be detrimental to the conservation objectives or site integrity or as justifications to avoid meeting legal obligations. As discussed, declassification, and arguably other adaptations, cannot be based on the failure to comply with legal provisions as decided in *Tre Pini.* Also, case law on the Habitats Directive and Habitats Regulations has made blatantly clear that the integrity of the site should not be compromised[56] and that the precautionary principle should be applied, thus it is highly unlikely that adaptive strategies could in fact be used to water down conservation objectives. However, the weight of the Habitats Regulations, as amended, and related case law is uncertain in a post-Brexit world, as discussed in Chapter 8 below.

To sum up, in a context of scientific uncertainty, rapid physical changes and the polycentric impacts of climate change, flexible experimental strategies and continuous revisions following observations of their consequences constitute a pragmatic solution for the conservation of marine biodiversity, as long as they are not used as excuses to avoid meeting legal obligations and as long as procedural safeguards are put in place to ensure their legitimacy and accountability, such as strong participatory mechanisms. As Cosens et al argue, in considering the role of law in adaptive management, 'integrating reform to achieve adaptation with reform to ensure legitimacy increases the likelihood of both acceptance and success in navigating the changes to come'.[57]

[56] The CJEU as well as domestic courts have held that plans or projects can only be authorised where competent authorities are convinced that they would not adversely affect the integrity of the site. See for instance *R. (on the application of Champion) v North Norfolk District Council* [2015] UKSC 52, para 41. Where doubts remain as to the absence of adverse effects on the integrity of the site, the authorisation must be refused, as per *Waddenzee*, paras 56 and 57. If the plan or project is liable to prevent the lasting preservation of the constitutive characteristics of the site that are connected to the presence of a priority natural habitat whose conservation was the objective justifying the designation of the site, the plan or project is adversely affecting the integrity of the site and the precautionary principle should be applied as held in *Sweetman*.

[57] Cosens et al., 'The Role of Law in Adaptive Governance'.

8

Marine Protected Areas Regulation in the Context of Regulatory Uncertainty and Change

Reflections on Brexit

8.1 Introduction

This is the last substantive chapter of the monograph. It provides additional observations on the theme of adapting regulation. Whilst Chapter 7 focused on adaptive strategies due to the ecological uncertainty brought about by climate change, this last substantive chapter focuses on adaptation to regulatory uncertainty. Previous chapters of the book have already considered dimensions of regulatory uncertainty and change such as management assumptions at the basis of the designation of MCZs or funding cuts experienced by the regulatory bodies. This chapter discusses regulatory uncertainty and change by focusing on a majorly legal and political disruptive force, that is Brexit. The chapter investigates how Brexit is affecting the conservation of marine biodiversity as well as the legitimacy and accountability of marine conservation regulation, thereby potentially impacting on the commoning of conservation law.

The UK left the EU on 31 December 2020, following the outcome of a referendum in 2016 in which 52 per cent of votes were cast in favour of leaving. The UK joined the Common Market in 1973, and it is the first Member State to have left the Union using the powers under article 50 of Treaty on the EU. Such choice is thus unprecedented, and it has created much uncertainty regarding the future of environmental law, especially given that a large part of UK environmental law derives from EU law. Marine conservation law is no exception, exemplified by the fact that, throughout this book, the EU-derived Habitats Regulations have been cited as one of the two key legal instruments for the governance of MPAs, the other being the MCAA.

The chapter, after a note to remind the reader of the multiple entanglements between EU and UK law, introduces key challenges to environmental law due to the changing governance architecture, considering specifically the role of environmental principles as well as that of institutions for ensuring the accountability for environmental standards. A section on the changes brought about by Brexit amendments to the Habitats Regulations follows and precedes the chapter conclusions.

8.2 The Multiple Entanglements between EU and UK Environmental Law

The weight of EU environmental law on domestic law has been considerable with a significant proportion of domestic law deriving from EU Regulations and Directives. Marine conservation law is a case in point, with the Habitats Regulations, transposing the EU Habitats and Birds Directives, being a cornerstone of biodiversity protection and the main instrument for the establishment and management of MPAs prior to the introduction of the MCZs under the MCAA. The MCAA dates back to 2009, while the initial English transposition of the Habitats and Birds Directive dates back to 1994,[1] meaning that for 15 years, MPAs in England were established almost exclusively thanks to EU law. Indeed, as mentioned in Chapter 2, domestic conservation law, embodied by the Wildlife and Countryside Act 1981, was weak in respect of marine spatial protection leading to the establishment of only three small marine nature reserves. Moreover, it was thanks to the enforcement powers of the Commission under EU law,[2] that the Offshore Marine Conservation (Natural Habitats, etc.) Regulations 2007[3] were introduced and the UK was obliged also to designate MPAs offshore, again showing the relevance of EU law.

The EU also brought stability to the environmental policy field, given that changes to EU law are more difficult to make than changes to domestic legislation, the latter being more susceptible to short-term political pressure. For Reid, such stability has clear advantages in the environmental context where long-term planning, goals and investments are needed to tackle major environmental problems and provide certainty to business and other environmental actors.[4] At the same time, as discussed in Chapter 7, adaptive governance is also fundamental in the context of climate change, thus the flexibility to revise and adapt legal provisions to make desirable changes should be seen in a positive light, as long as procedural safeguards to ensure regulatory legitimacy are in place.

Some commentators discussing Brexit caution against constructing a nostalgic narrative idealising the strong ecological nature of EU environmental law and forgetting the economic drives and market-based origins at the basis of EU environmental law.[5] Others have argued, drawing on an historical reading,

[1] The Conservation (Natural Habitats, & c.) Regulations 1994 (SI 1994/2716).

[2] The European Commission can bring infringement action against a Member States for failure to comply with EU law under article 258 of the Consolidated version of the Treaty of the Functioning of the European Union, OJ C 326/47 (TFEU). This is what happened in Case C-6/04 *Commission* v. *UK* [2005] ECR I-9017 in respect of designating offshore European Marine Sites.

[3] SI 2007/1842.

[4] C. T. Reid, 'Brexit and the Future of UK Environmental Law' (2016) 34 *Journal of Energy and Natural Resources Law* 407–415. See also Environmental Audit Committee, *EU and UK Environmental Policy* (2015–2016, HC 537).

[5] R. G. Lee, 'Always Keep a Hold of Nurse: British Environmental Law and Exit from the European Union' (2017) 29 *Journal of Environmental Law* 155–164.

that the 'British way' to conservation was stronger than the EU one, and consequently, Brexit is nothing to fear as biodiversity will be better served following the exit from the EU.[6] According to Pontin, the 'British way' was stronger because premised on an ethics of voluntarism and good stewardship that has been replaced by a more coercive command and control style of regulation under EU law.[7] This argument, though, is made exclusively by reference to domestic terrestrial conservation law, notably more developed than marine conservation law under the Wildlife and Countryside Act 1981, as amended. In any case, the argument is problematic even for land-based conservation because voluntarism risks weakening land-based conservation, as observed by Lord Mustill a long time ago in the *Southern Water Authority*.[8]

More fundamentally, the defence of Brexit's implications for conservation law on those terms is debatable also because, as pertinently noted by Lee,[9] it is premised on a false dichotomy between domestic versus EU law, undermining the reality of multilevel governance which shapes conservation law and environmental law more generally. Relatedly, as Hilson notes, the 'traffic' between bodies of EU and domestic law is two way in that, as much as the EU has heavily influenced UK environmental law, the reverse is also true in specific environmental sectors such as climate change targets or the integrated pollution prevention and control industrial emission regime.[10] Indeed, as presented in Chapter 2, conservation law is the product of the fluid and dynamic entanglement between domestic, EU and international law, the latter continuing to play a central role in post-Brexit domestic conservation law as the UK remains a party to key international conventions such as the Convention on Biology Diversity and the Bern Convention.[11]

Moreover, evidently, EU law has not disappeared. Although the European Communities Act 1972 has been repealed,[12] a new category of UK law has been created under the name of 'retained EU law' by the EUWA, thereby creating a degree of legal continuity.[13] Retained EU law includes EU-derived domestic law[14] such as the Habitats Regulations, as amended; directly

6 B. Pontin, *The Environmental Case for Brexit: A Socio-Legal Perspective* (Bloomsbury, 2019).

7 Ibid.

8 *Southern Water Authority v Nature Conservancy Council* [1992] 1 WLR 775. Lord Mustill famously refers to the regime for the protection of SSSIs as 'toothless' (para 778).

9 M. Lee, 'Environmental Pasts and Futures: The European Union and the "British Way"', (2019) 31 *Journal of Environmental Law* 559–569.

10 C. Hilson, 'The Impact of Brexit on the Environment: Exploring the Dynamics of a Complex Relationship' (2018) 7 *Transnational Environmental Law* 89–113.

11 See for example United Kingdom Environmental Law Association, *The UK and International Environmental Law after Brexit* (UKELA, 2017). However, while EU law had strong enforcement mechanisms and individuals could enjoy rights conferred by EU law in domestic courts under the direct effect principle, this is not the case for international law.

12 Section 1 of the EUWA.

13 Section 6(7) of the EUWA provides the definition of EU retained law.

14 Section 2 of the EUWA.

applicable EU law[15] such as EU Regulations, so far as operative immediately before the Implementation Period (IP) completion day (that is the end of the transition period),[16] directly effective rights, etc.,[17] retained general principles of EU law[18] and EU courts judgements before IP completion day where a challenge succeeds on an EU point of law.[19] However, the Supreme Court is not bound by any retained EU case law[20] and in deciding whether to depart from it, it needs to apply the same test as that it would apply in deciding whether to depart from its own case law, that is where 'it appears right to do so'.[21]

Furthermore, the power to depart from retained EU case law has been extended to the Court of Appeal by Regulations amending the EUWA.[22] This confers on the Court of Appeal a broad power to revisit settled EU case law, potentially leading to more uncertainty regarding the interpretation of environmental law and the protection it can offer. However, while the Supreme Court has an unqualified power to depart from the case law, the Court of Appeal's power to depart is more limited and cannot be used in circumstances in which there is post-transition case law modifying or applying that retained EU case law and which is binding on the Court of Appeal.[23] The extent to which these powers are going to be exercised in the environmental field remains to be seen. The degree of uncertainty is even higher for the role of decisions of the European Courts on or after IP completion day as any court or tribunal is not bound by them, but it can have regard to them.[24]

To a certain extent, retained EU law can be conceptualised as frozen EU law at IP completion day, but this view does not give justice to the changes that can be introduced by Statutory Instruments amending EU-derived domestic law to correct the deficiencies of EU-derived domestic law arising

[15] Section 3 of the EUWA. [16] 11 pm UK time on the 31 December 2020.

[17] Section 4 of the EUWA 2018. This includes directly effective treaty articles but not all of them. For example, free movement of persons provisions were removed from retained EU law by the Freedom of Establishment and Free Movement of Services (EU Exit) Regulations 2019, SI 2019/1401. Section 4(2)(b) also includes rights, etc., that arise under an EU Directive and are of a kind recognised by the European Court or any court or tribunal in the United Kingdom in a case decided before IP completion day. This is interesting because, although Directives are not retained EU law, rights, etc., arising out of Directives are directly effective.

[18] Section 6(7) of the EUWA.

[19] Section 6(3) of the EUWA. See also *Lipton v BA City Flyer* [2021] EWCA Civ 454, para 69; *Pearce* v. *Secretary of State for Business Energy and Industrial Strategy* [2021] EWHC 326 (Admin), para 148.

[20] Section 4(a) of the EUWA. [21] Section 6(5) of the EUWA.

[22] EUWA (Relevant Court) Regulations. Powers to make Regulations amending the EUWA are conferred by Sections 6(5A)(a), (b) and (c) and (5B)(a)of the EUWA. Section 6 was amended by Section 26(1) of the European Union (Withdrawal Agreement) Act 2021.

[23] Regulation 4(2) of the EUWA (Relevant Court) Regulations.

[24] Ss 6(1) and (2) of the EUWA.

from withdrawal.[25] In the case of the Habitats Regulations, the Brexit amendments to the Habitats Regulations were introduced by the EU Exit Habitats Regulations and the retained EU law is the Habitats Regulations, as amended, not the Habitats Regulations in their original format. This has been confirmed in *Lipton* in which the law under discussion was an EU Regulation on compensation to air passengers for cancelation or delayed flights,[26] as amended by EU Exit Regulations.[27] It applies even if the facts arose before IP completion day; Green LJ stated that 'the Court cannot therefore assume that the old ways of looking at EU derived law still hold good. We must apply the new approach. There is much that is familiar but there are also significant differences.'[28]

New approaches and interpretations can be developed, but this can give rise to legal uncertainty and can undermine the impact of much environmental law. The issue of legal uncertainty was also recognised by Arnold LJ[29] in a judgement on what the Master of the Rolls described as a 'paradigm case in which it would be inappropriate for the Court of Appeal to exercise its new-found power to depart from retained EU law'.[30] The case in question was not an environmental case as it concerned alleged infringement of music copyrights. Nevertheless, Arnold LJ reasoning is useful, not only for a discussion on legal uncertainty but also because it was stated that the Court of Appeal should not depart from the CJEU's jurisprudence given that there had been no change in the international legislative framework. As mentioned, the UK is a party to international conservation conventions, such as the Biodiversity Convention, which have had an important role also in shaping EU law. Interpretation of retained EU law with international treaties would ensure consistency. This provides some hope of avoiding a too a radical departure by the Supreme Court or the Court of Appeal from the Habitats Regulations, as amended, should the same reasoning be applied to an environmental case.[31]

[25] Section 8 of the EUWA allows a Minister of the Crown to make provisions by Regulations to prevent, remedy or mitigate any failure of retained EU law to operate effectively or any other deficiency in retained EU law such as where retained EU law confers function to the EU entities which no longer have functions in that respect in relation to the UK, contains anything which has no practical application in relation to the UK or is redundant.

[26] Regulation (EC) No 261/2004 of the European Parliament and of the Council of 11 February 2004 establishing common rules on compensation and assistance to passengers in the event of denied boarding and of cancellation or long delay of flights, and repealing Regulation (EEC) No 295/91 (SI 2004/261).

[27] The Air Passenger Rights and Air Travel Organisers' Licencing (Amendment) (EU Exit) Regulations 2019 (SI 2019/278)

[28] Para 53.

[29] *TuneIn Inc* v. *Warner Music UK Limited and Sony Music Entertainment UK Limited* [2021] EWCA Civ 441, para 83 (*TuneIn*).

[30] Ibid, para 197.

[31] See also R. Honey QC, 'Environmental Law and Retained EU Case Law' (*Environmental law Blog Francis Taylor Building*, 2021), at www.ftbchambers.co.uk/blogs/environmental-law-and-retained-eu-case-law.

However, what if there are changes to domestic legislation[32] and what if the Habitats Regulations, as amended, change? These questions are relevant because although the Habitats Regulations, as amended, fall within the category of EU-derived domestic legislation under Section 2(1) of the EUWA, the principle of the supremacy of EU law does not apply to any enactment or rule of law passed or made on or after exit day,[33] giving the government freedom to make new laws that may override the Habitats Regulations, as amended. Although retained EU law is defined in Section 6(7) of the EUWA as that body of law that is added to or otherwise modified by or under this Act or by domestic law from time to time, arguably new environmental laws, such as the new Environment Act 2021, do not fall into the retained EU law category. In response to the second question, modifications to the Habitats Regulations, as amended, made by virtue of the powers conferred under the Environment Act 2021 may mean the Habitats Regulations, as amended, change significantly. The Environment Act 2021 contains two sections that permit amendments to the Habitats Regulations, as amended, namely Sections 112 and 113 which enable, respectively, amendments to general duties and to assessments of plans and projects. Section 112 provides powers to amend regulation 9 of the Habitats Regulations, which sets out general duties to comply with the Habitats and Birds Directive. Section 113 confers powers to the Secretary of State to amend Part 6 of the Habitats Regulations on the assessment of plans and projects. In relation to the powers of both Sections 112 and 113, regard must be given to the particular importance of furthering the conservation and enhancement of biodiversity and persons as the Secretary of State considers appropriate must be consulted and the level of environmental protection provided by the Habitats Regulations, as amended, must not be reduced.

How these powers will be used by the Secretary of State remains to be seen. In any case, there is great uncertainty surrounding the future of the EU-derived conservation law as much is up to the choices of the Supreme and Court of Appeal Courts in departing from EU retained law, to any court or tribunal which may have regard to EU case law after exit day as well as to Parliament in passing laws departing from EU environmental law standards. Besides, in September 2021, the government has launched a plan to review retained EU law so that it will be improved or removed if it does not benefit citizens or business remove the special status that EU retained law still enjoys and it plans to establish a new Commission through which the public will be able to identify additional opportunities to cut or reform red tape.[34]

[32] Another reason gave by Arnold LJ for not departing from EU retained law was that there had been no change in domestic legislation. See para 78 of *Tuneln*.

[33] Section 5 of the EUWA.

[34] Cabinet Office and the Rt Hon Lord Frost CMG, 'Government Launches Plans to Capitalise on New Brexit Freedoms' (2021), at: www.gov.uk/government/news/government-launches-plans-to-capitalise-on-new-brexit-freedoms.

Question marks over the role of retained EU law are not the only uncertainties Brexit has brought about. Key issues regard also changes to governance structure and regulatory institutions, as considered below. Although governance issues are subject to a separate discussion, it is important to stress that they are interconnected with what has been discussed so far as the changes in the governance architecture, such as the disappearance of the CJEU, go hand in hand with the newfound powers of domestic courts in respect of retained EU law. The CJEU has played a major role to ensure the environmental protections agreed by Member States have been delivered and has often championed in the conservation field an ecocentric and strong precautionary approach. Arguably, domestic courts have adopted a less stringent approach in deciding conservation cases. For example, one can compare the domestic decision in *Hart*[35] with the CJEU judgement in *People Over Wind*[36] with the former allowing and the latter prohibiting the consideration of mitigation measures at the screening stage for the purposes of deciding whether an appropriate assessment of a plan or project's implications for the protected site is required. Subsequent UK Courts judgements followed *People Over Wind*.[37]

8.3 Adapting the Governance Architecture: Main Challenges

Having strong institutions to ensure the achievement of environmental objectives and government accountability is essential. The possibility of a governance gap in the environmental field has been one of the main worries of Brexit. The enforcement roles of the European Commission and the CJEU have been central to secure compliance and for the development of conservation law, as well as other branches of environmental law. Over the years, the European Commission has brought many cases to the CJEU against a Member State for failure to comply with the provisions under the Habitats and Birds

35 *Hart DC* v. *Secretary of State for Communities & Local Government & Ors* [2008] EWHC 1204 (Admin). Sullivan J at para 76: 'I am satisfied that there is no legal requirement that a screening assessment under Regulation 48(1) must be carried out in the absence of any mitigation measures that form part of a plan or project. On the contrary, the competent authority is required to consider whether the project, as a whole, including such measures, if they are part of the project, is likely to have a significant effect on the SPA. If the competent authority does not agree with the proponent's view as to the likely efficacy of the proposed mitigation measures or is left in some doubt as to their efficacy, then it will require an appropriate assessment because it will not have been able to exclude the risk of a significant effect on the basis of objective information (see *Waddenzee* above).'

36 *People over Wind*, paras 35–36: 'full and precise analysis of the measures capable of avoiding or reducing any significant effects on the site concerned must be carried out not at the screening stage, but specifically at the stage of the appropriate assessment. Taking account of such measures at the screening stage would be liable to compromise the practical effect of the Habitats Directive in general, and the assessment stage in particular, as the latter stage would be deprived of its purpose and there would be a risk of circumvention of that stage, which constitutes, however, an essential safeguard provided for by the directive.'

37 See, *Gladman Developments Limited* v. *Secretary of State for Housing, Communities and Local Government and Medway Council* [2019] EWHC 2001 (Admin).

Directives, exercising a fundamental function as a watchdog under article 258 of the Treaty on the Functioning of the European Union (TFEU) and, as already mentioned, the European Courts have mostly offered a purposive and ecocentric interpretation of the Habitats and Birds Directive in infringement cases as well as in preliminary rulings under article 267 of the TFEU. After Brexit, the Commission has ceased to exercise its functions in respect to the UK and, although UK courts are bound by retained EU law, as explained above, they have powers to depart from it and no UK court can refer questions to the CJEU anymore.[38] In EU law, the accountability of Member States has also been secured through the reporting obligations Member States have to the European Commission, such as those under article 17 under the Habitats Directive. Commentators have reasoned extensively on the governance gap brought about by the loss of the roles of the European Commission and the CJEU, thus there is no need to repeat those arguments here.[39]

The extent to which this governance gap is filled by the provisions of the Environment Act 2021 is highly debatable. The Environment Act 2021, which applies to England, has the aim of putting 'environmental ambition and accountability at the very heart of government'[40] and introduces the Office for Environmental Protection (OEP) as the new body contributing to environmental protection and the improvement of the natural environment.[41] The OEP must act objectively and impartially, and must have regard to the need to act proportionately and transparently.[42] The OEP has a variety of functions, including monitoring and reporting on environmental improvements plans and targets,[43] monitoring the implementation of environmental law,[44] advising on changes to environmental law[45] and holding enforcement functions related to public bodies' failures to comply with environmental law[46]; thus, it seems natural to think that it would be an adequate substitute for the European Commission. However, this is far from reality as the picture is more complicated than this.

Regarding the OEP monitoring of environmental law,[47] the Environment Act 2021 does not set specific timing for monitoring, and it leaves the OEP discretion

[38] Section 6(1)(b) EUWA.

[39] See, for example, UKELA, Brexit and Environmental Law; M. Lee, 'Brexit and Environmental Protection in the United Kingdom: Governance, Accountability and Law Making' (2018) 36 *Journal of Energy and Natural Resources Law* 351–359; E. Fisher, 'Executive Environmental Law' (2020) 83 *Modern Law Review* 163–189; C. T. Reid, 'Mapping Post-Brexit Environmental Law' (2021) 21 *ERA Forum* 655–665.

[40] DEFRA, *Environmental Bill: Policy Paper* (DEFRA, 2018), at: www.gov.uk/government/publications/draft-environment-principles-and-governance-bill-2018/environment-bill-policy-paper.

[41] Section 23(1) of the Environment Act 2021.

[42] Section 23(2) of the Environment Act 2021.

[43] Section 28 of the Environment Act 2021.

[44] Section 29 of the Environment Act 2021.

[45] Section 30 of the Environment Act 2021.

[46] Section 31–41 of the Environment Act 2021.

[47] Section 29 of the Environment Act 2021.

on whether to report of any matter concerned with the implementation of environmental law. No obligations are placed on public authorities to provide information to the OEP under Section 42, and the detail that exists in relation to reporting obligations under EU law is lost.

As for the enforcement functions, the OEP can exercise its power against a public authority[48] rather than against the government as a whole, as was the case for the European Commission, hence its power will be exercised in a more fragmented way and there is a clear shift from collective accountability to individual accountability. The OEP has discretion in deciding whether to carry out an investigation following a complaint, preparing a report that may (not must) be published[49] and has powers to give information notices first and decision notices after to the public authority.[50] Notably, the OEP may carry out an investigation without having received a complaint if it has information that, in its view, indicate that the authority has failed to comply with environmental law and such failure would be a serious one. This is an important addition to ensure a level of proactivity on the part of the OEP.[51] Following a decision notice, the OEP may apply to the court for an environmental review but only if it is satisfied that the authority has failed to comply and that the failure is serious.[52] The power to bring in an environmental review only after giving information and decision notices attempts to resolve the matter in the pre-litigation stages, thus reducing the number of environmental cases. However, the OEP is also able to initiate a judicial review case without having given an information or decision notice in urgent cases of serious failure. An environmental review is defined as a 'review of alleged conduct of the authority that is described in the decision notice as constituting a failure to comply with environmental law',[53] and the court needs to apply judicial review principles in determining whether the authority has failed to comply with environmental law. This narrows the grounds of the review as only process questions rather than substantive ones on the nature of the decision can be considered, thereby failing to achieve equivalence with the European Commission's powers.[54] Besides, as noted by Lee,[55] the remedies English courts can set are more limited than the EU law obligation on national court to take 'necessary measure' to ensure compliance

[48] Section 31 of the Environment Act 2021. [49] Section 33(9) of the Environment Act 2021.
[50] Sections 33, 35 and 36 of the Environment Act 2021.
[51] Section 33(2) of the Environment Act 2021. [52] Section 38 of the Environment Act 2021.
[53] Section 38(2) of the Environment Act 2021.
[54] To avoid romanticising the role of the European Commission, it should be recalled that the Commission's discretion on whether to pursue complaints has led to selective enforcement.
[55] M. Lee, 'The New Office for Environmental Protection: Scrutinising and Enforcing Environmental Law after Brexit' *SSRN Working Paper* (2019) at: https://ssrn.com/abstract=3312296.

with EU law.[56] Moreover, the remedy can be granted only if it will not likely cause substantial hardship, or substantially prejudice the rights of, any person other than the authority[57] or will not be detrimental to good administration.[58] However, in cases in which the court is satisfied that granting a remedy is necessary to prevent or mitigate serious damage to the natural environment or to human health and that there is an exceptional public interest reasons to grant it, these exceptions do not apply.[59] To sum up, in enforcement terms, the OEP is weaker than the European Commission, with its powers framed primarily in terms of judicial review and with additional constraints such as the 'seriousness' of failure and 'hardship'. Finally, the OEP's independence is questionable[60] as, although 'in exercising functions in respect of the OEP, the Secretary of State must have regard to the need to protect its independence',[61] non-executive members, including the Chair, of the OEP are appointed by the Secretary of State.[62] This is problematic from a transparency and democratic perspective.

Another governance aspect worthy of mention is the role of environment principles. Environmental principles occupy an important place in EU law, referred to in article 191(2) of the TFEU as the basis of Union policy on the environment and assuming relevant legal weight in environmental case law, as the *Waddenzee* case considering the meaning and application of the precautionary principle in relation to article 6(3) of the Habitats Directive exemplifies. They were effective in the UK through the European Communities Act 1972 so informing policy and regulatory decision-making.

Principles are presented in a rather different manner in the Environment Act 2021 and, without doubt, their role has been weakened compared to what was afforded under EU law. Before turning to the role of the principles in the Environment Act 2021, it is worth reflecting on the way in which EU law environmental principles continue to occupy a space on the domestic legislative landscape. They do so through retained EU law, especially retained case law that interprets environmental law in accordance with the principles. However, many environmental Directives refer to environmental principles in the preambles, but preambles are not retained in the transposing regulations. Besides, although some environmental Directives also expressly mention environmental principles in their text, such as the Waste Framework Directive referring to

[56] Under article 260 of the TFEU, the Member State that failed to fulfil an obligation under the Treaties shall be required to take the necessary measures to comply with the judgment of the Court. Under Section 38(8) of the Environment Act 2021, courts can grant remedies that could be granted on a judicial review other than damages.

[57] Section 38(9)(a) of the Environment Act 2021.

[58] Section 38(9)(b) of the Environment Act 2021.

[59] Section 38(10) of the Environment Act 2021.

[60] Select Committee on the Constitution, *Environment Bill* (2019–21, HL Paper 26).

[61] Schedule 1, para 17 of the Environment Act 2021.

[62] Schedule 1, para 2 of the Environment Act 2021.

the Polluter Pays Principle,[63] this is not the case for the Habitats Directive or Birds Directive, so environmental principles are not enshrined in post-Brexit conservation law in this way.

As for the Environment Act 2021, reference is made to a policy statement on environmental principles that the Secretary of State must prepare,[64] rather than to environmental principles themselves. Thus, the interpretation and application of the principles is not dependent on the Environment Act 2021, but conditional on the policy statement, failing to render the principles themselves statutory requirements. The policy statement is 'a statement explaining how the environmental principles should be interpreted and proportionately applied by Ministers of the Crown when making policy'.[65] This limits their scope in a number of respects: from the reference to proportionality, to the fact that they are to be interpreted and applied only by Ministers and only when making policy. The effect of the statement on environmental principles is also relatively weak as Section 19(1) states that a Minister of the Crown must, when making policy, have *due regard* to the policy statement on environmental principles. There is a further limitation introduced in Section 19(2) which states that nothing in subsection (1) requires a Minister to do anything (or refrain from doing anything) if doing it (or refraining from doing it) would have no significant environmental benefit or would be in any other way disproportionate to the environmental benefit, again reintroducing proportionality. Thus, principles under the Environment Act 2021 are merely policy standards, rather than guiding principles and do not appear to have any legal value.

The draft policy statement on environmental principles was published in March 2021,[66] and at the time of writing, feedback obtained during the consultation is under analysis. Although a full discussion of the draft policy statement is beyond the scope of this chapter,[67] it is worth mentioning the approach adopted in respect to one of the principles that has been central in conservation law, the precautionary principle. Firstly, the definition presented in draft statement of the precautionary principle is the narrow one borrowed from Principle 15 of the Rio Declaration 1992,[68] which placed a high threshold for

[63] Directive 2008/98/EC of the European Parliament and of the Council of 19 November 2008 on waste and repealing certain Directives, OJ 2008 No. L 312/3.

[64] Section 17(1) of the Environment Act 2021. [65] Section 17(2) of the Environment Act 2021.

[66] DEFRA. *Draft Environmental Principles Policy Statement* (DEFRA, 2021) at: https://consult.defra.gov.uk/environmental-principles/draft-policy-statement/supporting_documents/draftenvironmentalprinciplespolicystatement.pdf.

[67] For a complete analysis of the policy statement on environmental principles, see M. Lee, 'DEFRA's Draft Environmental Principles Policy Statement' *SSRN Working Paper* (2021) at: https://ssrn.com/abstract=3827270.

[68] Principle 15 of the 1992 Rio Declaration on Environment and Development, UN Doc. A/CONF.151/26/Rev.1 states that: 'Where there are threats of serious or irreversible damage, lack of full scientific certainty shall not be used as a reason for postponing cost-effective measures to prevent environmental degradation.'

assessing environmental damage ('serious or irreversible') and introduces the problematic concept of 'cost-effective measures'. Furthermore, there is no mention of the principle's role in the field of nature conservation, only focusing on risk regulation and public health, and it is not clear why extensive space is dedicated to the theme of technological innovation,[69] which may be a distraction from the aims of the precautionary principle, that is, managing risk in light of scientific uncertainty. Finally, as the OEP notes in its advice on the draft policy statement, the proportionality principle is confined to situations in which there is scientific uncertainty over both the likelihood *and* the severity of environmental damage, making its application very narrow.[70] Arguably, given that the Environment Act 2021 only discusses environmental principles in relation to environmental policy, rather than decisions on plans or projects, retained EU case law on article 6 of the Habitats Directive should continue to guide Courts' interpretations on the role of the precautionary principle for plans and projects affecting a European marine site. However, this is not guaranteed, given the Supreme Court and Court of Appeal's powers to depart and the Environment Act 2021 could become a factor to be taken into account if they decide to reinterpret the precautionary principle in the context of conservation law. Also, the Secretary of State powers under Sections 112 and 113 of the Environment Act 2021 may intervene.

To conclude, the governance architecture post-Brexit weakens enforcement and accountability mechanisms as well as the role of environmental principles, all central to the development of conservation law. The next section turns to a focused discussion of the changes brought about by the Brexit amendments to the Habitats Regulations.

8.4 Conservation Law Post-Brexit

Before Brexit, the Habitats Regulations 2017[71] were the latest transposition of the Habitats and Birds Directives, consolidating the previous version of the Habitats Regulations[72] and implementing aspects of the MCAA.[73] Due to Brexit, they have been, like all retained EU law, subject to EU Exit amendments. The power to make delegated legislation to translate EU law into retained EU law is to be found in Section 8 of the EUWA which gives Ministers extensive powers to make such regulations that they consider appropriate to prevent remedy or mitigate any failure of retained EU law to

[69] The draft policy statement states that the precautionary principle should not be invoked to hinder innovation and new technologies should not be held to a higher standard of safety than existing ones where the level of risk is comparable.

[70] OEP, *Advice on the Draft Environmental Principles Policy Statement* (OEP, 2021), at: www.theoep.org.uk/report/advice-draft-environmental-principles-policy-statement.

[71] Habitats Regulations; Offshore Habitats Regulations.

[72] The Conservation of Habitats and Species Regulations 2010 (SI 2010/490).

[73] Explanatory note to the Habitats Regulations.

operate effectively or any other deficiency in retained EU law arising from withdrawal of the UK from the EU. Section 8(2) clarifies the meaning of deficiencies, setting out a closed list including anything that has no practical application in relation to the UK or is redundant, that which confers functions to EU entities which no longer have functions, that which contains EU references which are no longer appropriate, etc. For example, transferring the European Commission's functions to domestic bodies and removing redundant terminology would fall in the category of remedying deficiencies under Section 8(2). Thus, generally, EU Exit amendments to retained EU law are of a technical and procedural nature, rather than material. This means that in principle the concern over limited Parliamentary scrutiny associated with delegated legislation is not so serious because the conversion of EU law into retained EU law is primarily a technical/mechanical exercise, leaving the making of substantive changes to certain areas covered by EU law to primarily legislation in the form of Government's Brexit Bills/Acts, such as the Fisheries Act 2020. However, under Section 8(3), broad residual powers are conferred to the Ministers to make regulations as deficiency in retained EU law also includes anything which is of a similar kind to any deficiency in the list under Section 8(2), or a deficiency in retained EU law of a kind described, or provided for, in regulations made by a Minister of the Crown. These powers are time-limited too, to two years.

To what extent are changes brought to the Habitats Regulations by the EU Exit amendments[74] merely technical? The government claims that they are, indeed, merely technical. The explanatory memorandum to Conservation of Habitats and Species (Amendment) (EU Exit) Regulations states that the changes are made to ensure the Habitats Regulations, as amended, 'continue to work (are operable)' upon the UK's exit from the EU[75] and that 'the intention is to ensure habitat and species protection and standards as set out under the Nature Directives are implemented in the same way or an equivalent way when the UK exists the EU. There is no change to policy.'[76] The changes to the Habitats Regulations are to be found in Part 3 of the Conservation of Habitats and Species (Amendment) (EU Exit) Regulations 2019.[77] Many of the changes introduced are in effect terminological. For example, reference to the 'territory of the EU' becomes reference to the 'territory of the UK'; the 'Natura 2000' network becomes 'the national site network', which includes SACs and SPAs designated before and after the EU Exit; terms in the Habitats and Birds Directive relating to the EU are amended to be relevant to the UK, and references to the 'requirements of the Directive' are to be read to include the management objectives of the national site network.

[74] EU Exit Habitats Regulations.

[75] Explanatory Memorandum to the EU Exit Regulations, para 2(1). [76] Ibid, para 2(4).

[77] Part 4 of the EU Exit Regulations makes the changes to the Offshore Habitats Regulations, which mirror those in Part 3 for the Habitats Regulation, so they will not be discussed here.

In addition, functions previously assigned to the European Commission are brought in-house. For example, reporting requirements are no longer to the European Commission but to the Secretary of State, which is also under a duty to compile the reports from each appropriate authority in a combined report. The selection of SACs, which under the Habitats Directive involves the role of the European Commission, is transferred into the hands of the appropriate authority acting on the advice of the SNCBs. All these amendments are necessary and primarily technical.

However, things get complicated in relation to the site management aspects on two fronts. Firstly, by conferring new powers to the appropriate authority (the Secretary of State in England) that used to be in the hands of the European Commission, there is a risk that more weight may be given to political and economic, rather than ecological, considerations. For example, for priority species and habitats, under article 6(4) of the Habitats Directive, the European Commission can issue an opinion as to whether IROPI apply in relation to plans and projects adversely affecting priority habitats and species, where the overriding public interest does not relate to human health, public safety or is of beneficial consequences of primary importance to the environment. Now, it is the Secretary of State that issues such opinion and, although it needs to seek advice from SNCBs, consult widely and have regard to the national interest,[78] it may be that the national interest requires the Secretary of State to lean towards economic and social factors more than ecological ones. More worryingly, it may happen that the Secretary of State is the promoter of the plan or project in question, and therefore, there is a conflict of interest when also asked to issue an opinion on IROPI.

Secondly, there are changes in relation to the management of the national site network that are of a more substantial nature. As mentioned in Chapter 7, the appropriate authorities are required by the Brexit amendments to the regulations to manage and where necessary to adapt the national site network in cooperation with each other to meet the network management objectives. Adaptation of the network is a concept that is not present in the Habitats Directive. It goes beyond mere declassification of sites under article 9 of the Habitats Directive, which is only possible due to natural developments noted as a result of surveillance. The inclusion of such provision on the adaptation of the network in the Habitats Regulations, as amended, is not to be regarded negatively as it can be useful for conservation in the context of climate change, although this does detract from the government claim that it is a mere technical amendment. Moreover, the new regulation 16(A) introduces a new proportionality requirement. It states that the 'management objectives of the national site network are—(a) to maintain at, or where appropriate restore to, a favourable conservation status in their natural range (so far as it lies in the United

[78] Regulation 25 of the EU Exit Habitats Regulations, amending regulation 64 of the Habitats Regulations.

Kingdom's territory, and so far as is proportionate)'. The inclusion of these new provisions has led leading environmental NGOs to challenge the EU Exit Habitats Regulations on ultra vires grounds.[79] Here, again we see the role of the environmental NGOs as protectors of environmental law standards, not as subverting the law, as discussed in Chapter 6. The NGOs argued that the full extent of the new power to adapt the national site network where necessary was unclear and that the introduction of the proportionality reference risks lowering environmental protection.[80] Mrs Justice Lieven refused permission stating that the words 'where necessary adapt' were intended to reflect the powers to declassify found in article 9 and, similarly, 'so far as is proportionate' was not changing the meaning of the Directive. However, notably, the Court stated that the new wording should not be used in practice to water down the protection of SACs and SPAs.[81] Thus, although the new words of the EU Exit Habitats Regulations do not make the Regulations ultra vires, challenges could arise if they are interpreted in a way that lower standards of protection or change the effects of EU law. Again, it will need to be seen how these provisions are going to be used by the Secretary of State.

8.5 Conclusion

This chapter has provided a discussion of the way in which conservation law is adapting to regulatory changes brought about by Brexit. Certain key aspects of the changing face of environmental law and conservation law in particular have been explored and, although five years have passed since the EU Exit Referendum and several months have passed since the transition period, the picture reveals high levels of uncertainty. Uncertainty regarding the relationship between 'retained EU law' and new environmental law created post-Brexit, uncertainty surrounding the way in which the Supreme Court and Court of Appeal will interpret retained case law, uncertainty on the role of environmental principles and the way in which the OEP will operate and finally uncertainty on the way in which the Secretary of State will use

[79] *R (Client Earth and MCS) v. Secretary of State for Environment Food and Rural Affairs* [2019] EWHC 2682 (Admin).

[80] They also took issue with the addition of 'which is distinct', added by EU Exit Habitats Regulation 10 to amend Habitats Regulation 12 in relation to the provision 'duty to designate SAC'. However, given that this was already present in the Offshore Habitats Regulations and given that a regulation does not wrongly transpose a directive because it does not use exactly the same words, as also noted by Mrs Justice Lieven (para 10), it is not a strong objection in my view.

[81] 'If the Secretary of State were to use the power to adapt given in Regulation 16(a)(1) to go beyond the power in Article 9, then that would be very likely, in my view, to be ultra vires because of the saving and interpretation provisions in the EU Withdrawal Act, which effectively preserved the EU law position, including any improvement to the terms of the Habitats Directive and the case law at exit day' (para 8). A similar point was made in relation to the proportionality provision.

in practice the new provisions inserted by regulation 16(A) to the Habitats Regulations, as amended. Moreover, issues related to potential conflicts of interest have been highlighted both in relation to the OEP's membership and in relation to the role of the Sectary of State in offering opinions for IROPI where the public interest is social and economic and the site in question hosts priority habitats or species. It is unknown how these potential conflicts will be resolved, how effective legal challenges might be and more generally how effective environmental regulation will be and the strategies that environmental NGOs and other actors will adopt. Ultimately, it is unknown whether the post-Brexit world will make processes for commoning MPAs regulation more difficult to achieve, with detrimental impacts on environmental democracy and the representation of the more-than human in regulatory strategies.

The chapter has kept the discussion firmly on legal grounds, without venturing into the politics of Brexit. However, it is worth reflecting that the effects on marine conservation practice of the strongly advocated government goal of a green Brexit,[82] though still largely unknown, may not necessarily be positive. The example of byelaws proposed for offshore European Marine Sites in early 2021, discussed in Chapter 7, is a case in point. The haste in which the government wants to show 'green' outputs may not enable long-term ecological thinking for long-term ecological solutions. This is not to argue that byelaws should not be introduced for the protection of sites that were, de facto, paper parks, but that in wanting quick outputs to tick green boxes, we may fall into the trap of delivering suboptimal ecological regulations, which fall short of protecting the marine commons and do not contribute to commoning marine conservation.

[82] M. Gove, 'The Unfrozen Moment: Delivering a Green Brexit' (2017), at www.gov.uk/government/speeches/the-unfrozen-moment-delivering-a-green-brexit.

Concluding Remarks

Introduction

Marine conservation is a global policy priority, and MPAs have been singled out as one of the preferred legal instruments to achieve conservation goals. In England, the field of marine conservation law has grown substantially in recent decades, being heavily influenced by international and EU law and, more recently, by new primary domestic legislation in the form of the MCAA. Despite these legal advances and the pressing international policy concerns and targets, the field of English marine conservation law and regulation has not yet attracted sustained academic commentary.

This book has aimed to fill the academic gap by providing a critical assessment of the processes of marine conservation law and regulation in England in a context of political and ecological change and uncertainty. As changes are underway, some of the legal discussion is time-bounded, especially that related to Brexit, as environmental regulation is rapidly evolving. However, by supporting the legal analysis of MPAs law and regulation with theoretical insights from regulatory theory and environmental social sciences, especially geography and politics, the book hopes to have a long-time span. The interdisciplinary lenses through which MPAs law and regulation has been viewed also positioned the book squarely into the socio-legal field. Both the 'law in books' and the 'law in action'[1] have been explored through a close examination of the legal texts and their implementation, investigated via desk-based research, complemented by semi-structured interviews conducted with various actors in the field. The critical mapping of the legal field and selected aspects of the implementation of marine conservation law have been explored adopting a theme-based approach. Delving deep into each theme has painted a multicoloured and complex picture of MPAs law and regulation.

This is primarily because MPAs are not a straightforward legal tool. As explained in Chapter 1, MPAs can be conceptualised in different ways depending on the perspective and scale employed. MPAs can be understood as tools to

[1] R. Pound, 'Law in Books and Law in Action' (1910) 44 *American law Review* 12–36.

govern the exploitation of CPRs or as institutional sites. If understood as tools to govern the exploitation of CPRs, they can be perceived positively, if the perspective employed is a global one about the conservation of biodiversity as a common concern of humankind, or they may be interpreted negatively, if the perspective is the one of local sea-users whose livelihoods depend on the exploitation of the marine resources that are given such protection. Similarly, if MPAs are understood as institutional sites, they can be seen as sites that contribute to the commoning of decision-making by, for instance, encouraging public participation, but they may also be perceived as sites un-commoning decision-making by those actors whose voices and knowledges are left out.

These different representations of MPAs are all played out in the context of English MPAs and, as much as it would be satisfying to provide a black or white type of argument, so to offer an authoritative conclusion on the role of MPAs in English conservation law, unfortunately it is not possible to be Manichean. As the book has showed, although there are certain progressive aspects of English MPAs law, which, for example, support the development of MPAs as commoning sites or as new commons, this potential is not fully realised. Below, the findings of the book are summarised applying the categories of new commons/enclosures, commoning/un-commoning, developed in Chapter 1, to English MPAs law and its implementation.

English MPAs as New Commons or Enclosures?

Overall, English MPAs fit more within the new commons' category, rather than the enclosure category because, simply put, they are ecologically driven, as they are set up for the protection of selected biodiversity, understood as the common concern of humankind and because their establishment has, to date, not been translated into fortress conservation, giving sea-users certain rights over resources or providing avenues for plans and projects development, within certain legal limits, on the whole more stringent for European Marine Sites than MCZs. More specifically, in the context of fisheries, Chapter 4 showed that the risk-based approach employed by the IFCAs and their attempt to balance precaution and proportionality has meant that MPAs are not acting as enclosures, banishing all fishing activities and Chapter 2, in reviewing the legal framework, showed that development can occur in MPAs if certain criteria are met. The only MPAs that may resemble fortress conservation and thus enclosures are HPMAs, which were discussed in Chapter 7, but it is too early to provide a thorough assessment of HPMAs, considering none has been designated to date. Thus, English MPAs are far from being enclosures.

However, English MPAs' potential for being new commons is curtailed by different factors, ranging from ecological destabilisations, some of which are anthropogenically caused, to regulatory methodologies, used to map ecological and non-ecological variables, to practical limitations. In relation to ecological destabilisations, Chapter 7 demonstrated how climate change re-designs ecological boundaries, and the protection of the more-than human elements of the ecosystem requires an adaptive governance approach, as species shift and habitats change to adapt to different climatic and environmental conditions. Another example of ecological destabilisations was discussed in Chapter 4 in relation to the difficulty of including ephemeral features, such as *Sabellaria* reef in definitions of environmental risk in the matrix for managing fisheries in European Marine Sites. The appearance and disappearance of *Sabellaria* reef renders it difficult to be a feature counted in regulatory interventions. The end result is a simplification of complex social–ecological relations to fit standardised risk-based regulation responses. This was also visible in relation to the way IAs, discussed in Chapter 3, calculated or better failed to calculate additional management costs for MCZs features with 'maintain' objective, disregarding possible future environmental changes happening within the 20 years timeframe covered by the IAs. Such simplifications can negatively impact on the potential for MPAs to be new commons as certain ecological features may not receive protection.

In relation to regulatory methodologies, Chapter 3 demonstrated that IAs fail to put non-quantifiable social–ecological issues and collective concerns at the forefront. In operating, following a quantity over quality logic underpinned by cost-benefit analysis, IAs risk privileging high sector-specific economic costs and considerations over ecological public benefits or cultural benefits which defy quantification.

As regards to practical constraints, these include the lack of appropriate funding for managing and monitoring MPAs, as discussed in relation to IFCAs as well as to SNCBs monitoring abilities in Chapter 2, as well as the paucity of management measures and plans for MPAs. Ironically, the lack of management measures in many MPAs avoids turning MPAs into enclosures. However, simultaneously, this does not benefit ecosystems within MPAs, thereby not contributing to the growth of MPAs as new commons either.

Thus, although English law in the books does represent a new commons approach on MPAs, in practice this is not entirely achieved, because of the regulatory choices/methodologies chosen, and of practical issues and also because of the way in which the more-than human elements of complex social–ecological systems subvert territorialisation practices.

Besides, although English MPAs are not enclosures, sea-users may nevertheless perceive them as such. This can be due to various reasons. For example, as explained in Chapter 5 in relation to MCZs designation, the lack of knowledge regarding management measures linked to the need to rely on assumptions, as well as the way participatory processes were structured, led to fishers' mistrust of decision-making and MPAs regulation more generally. Not dissimilarly, the way in which HPMAs are going to be presented and discussed with sea-users communities may foster a perception of HPMAs as enclosures.

Thus, when assessing MPAs as regulatory tools, we should not only consider what they do but also the way in which they are perceived and the reasons why certain perceptions develop as they hold weight for regulatory success as well as for the perceived legitimacy of decision-making.

English MPAs as Institutional Sites for Commoning or Un-Commoning?

The extent to which English MPAs are institutional sites for commoning is dubious, as demonstrated in multiple ways in this book. On the one hand, MPAs law is technocratic in nature leaving much discretion to the regulators and making the opinion of the public only marginal to decision-making over plans and project, as highlighted in Chapter 2. However, some avenues for democratising decision-making are in place, especially for including the voices of multiple actors through various consultation requirement enshrined in legislation in relation to designation but also management measures, such as byelaws. However, consultation is not a strong form of participation as Arnstein's ladder reminds us.[2] Efforts at public participation beyond consultation are especially visible at the implementation stage to ensure so-called stakeholder participation, such as in the process of MCZs designations discussed in Chapter 5 or the creation of the Implementation Group for advising on the revised approach to the management of fisheries in European Marine Sites, discussed in Chapter 4.

However, these various efforts are more directed at ensuring that conservation interventions are proportionate rather than at facilitating the co-creation of conservation objectives. This is reflected in the way that participatory initiatives are set up. As demonstrated in Chapter 5, 'thin' rather than 'thick' proceduralisation was at play during the first stage of designation of MCZs and this produced specific 'environmental subjectivities', as Agrawal would say.[3] Chapter 6 provided us with more potential by considering two very different types of institutions that are participating in MPAs regulation, the IFCAs and environmental NGOs, the former being a regulatory statutory body, while the latter being at the margins of regulation. Independently of their legal status, both organisations show a tendency towards the commoning of conservation. The IFCAs attempt to realise this by hosting and taking seriously different representatives and voices in their decision-making, given the varied membership and the way in which some of its members, namely MMO appointees, are selected. Environmental NGOs, who hold an important role in MPAs regulation, even if they are not regulators in the strict sense of the term, bring forth the silent voice of the more-than human world and the collective interest in the environment, in so doing pushing for a vision of MPAs as new commons. Nevertheless, both these organisations face various challenges. If the IFCAs struggle in properly carrying out all their duties and using all their powers due to a shortage of funding, environmental NGOs seldom move beyond the vision of conservation that is at the basis of MPAs law, operating to uphold environmental legal standards, rather than to think critically about such standards and propose anti-hegemonic social–ecological solutions.

[2] Arnstein, 'A Ladder of Citizens Participation'. [3] Agrawal, Environmentality.

Finally, a major drawback for the realisation of MPAs as commoning sites is Brexit, given the gaps left in relation to the enforcement of environmental law and its consequences for democratic accountability. As discussed in Chapter 8, Brexit has meant the disappearance from the UK of the key independent watchdog of conservation law, that is the European Commission and of the Court of Justice of the EU, which, for the most part, has provided purposive and ecocentric interpretations of conservation law. Although it is too early to assess the conduct of the OEP, its set up and powers are of a very different kind to those of the European Commission, raising questions regarding its independence as well as about what it can achieve. The question of independence of regulatory bodies was only raised in relation to the main SNCB that is Natural England in Chapter 2. Aside from the institutional gaps and changes, Brexit has brought much uncertainty given that many details are still to be ironed out as it is unclear for example how retained EU law will be interpreted by the Supreme Court and the Court of Appeal in future conservation cases. Such uncertainty is also problematic from a rule of law perspective as it leaves marine actors in a liminal place, hindering their ability to comprehend how to participate in the commoning of conservation law. Thus, although participatory rights in marine conservation law exist and they are the prerequisite for commoning practices, implementation choices and the current Brexit regulatory earthquake arguably contribute to the un-commoning of MPAs regulation.

MPAs Regulation and the Relation between Nature and Society

As this summary of findings demonstrates, there is no decisive positive or negative assessment of the role of MPAs in English conservation law, as many and sometimes opposing factors contribute to MPAs regulation. Despite the impossibility of offering definitive conclusions, a fundamental obstacle to the success of English MPAs regulation relates to the way in which the relationship between nature and society is articulated in the law and in much of its implementation. Marine law and regulation in England, as most of domestic environmental regulation, is premised on an ontological separation between what is natural as opposed to what is social, or better socio-economic. This is rather ironic considering policy efforts to think in social–ecological terms[4] and legal concepts at international law level, such as the 'ecosystem approach' under the Biodiversity Convention,[5] expressing the indissoluble entanglements between human and non-human elements and actors inhabiting the marine environment.

It should be noted that there may be spaces where more holistic social–ecological governance perspectives and practices are taking place in English

[4] HM Government, 'A Green Future'.

[5] See the preamble of the Biodiversity Convention and Decision V/6 of COP 5 of the Convention on Biological, 'Ecosystem Approach', UNEP/CBD/COP/5/6.

MPAs, which have not been the subject of discussion here. This book has been primarily concerned with regulatory issues, mostly analysing the law and its implementation from a national perspective, but there are many other aspects that contribute to the MPAs governance. These factors range from the role of marine publics and sea-users' values on marine conservation to alternative marine conservation arrangements that stem from voluntary practices and are not necessarily recognised and/or validated by official regulatory schemes but do impact on MPAs governance. Obviously, governance covers a much broader terrain than law and regulation, and this book, starting from the law, has been able to travel only through some aspects of this broader terrain. Besides, what constitutes governance and governance practices is contested as different actors may have different views of what and how to govern for marine conservation. To study MPAs governance embracing a broader perspective would have required a different methodological choice altogether, given that many of these hidden values and informal governance arrangements can only be revealed through in-depth ethnographic research, rather than desk-based analysis and interviews. Perhaps, this is a task for a future project.

The point to be made here is that the way in which the relation of nature and society is conceptualised by regulatory and governance frameworks has serious impacts. Constructing nature as a distinct ontological category from the socio-economic category, as it happens in English MPAs law and regulation has negative consequences of an epistemological and methodological nature. Epistemologically, marine conservation law separates ecological knowledges, attributed to certain actors, from social–economic ones, attributed to others, thereby downplaying the potential for the production and recognition of social–ecological knowledge. Although steps are taken to ensure the inclusion of many voices into decision-making fora, such voices are kept distinct and pigeon-holed under particular 'stakes', as was clearly made visible in Chapter 5. Efforts at inclusion are laudable, but they fall short of fulfilling their commoning promises if inclusion is conceptualised and practiced as a balancing exercise between atomistic, narrowly defined and categorised perspectives.

Methodologically, MPAs regulation uses methods to identify and value environmental costs and benefits, which do not allow a socio-ecological assessment but re-produce distinctions between environmental and socio-economic variables and an ethics of trade-offs rather than one of deliberation. The administrative ordering of nature and society, which serves, as Scott argued,[6] to render the regulatory field legible, is a schematic and simplified representation of more complex social–ecological systems. Some of the regulatory methods used, such as IAs discussed in Chapter 3, are centres of calculation required by the broader regulatory apparatus and, thus, many of their weaknesses, like the reliance on cost-benefit analysis, are independent of the choices of MPAs

[6] J. Scott, Seeing Like a State.

regulators. Nevertheless, they contribute to perpetuate the dichotomy between the ecological and the socio-economic and in doing so they silence relational perspectives and values.

Ultimately, by framing conservation interventions as a trade-off between separate, pre-existing social and ecological categories, MPAs law and regulation fails to acknowledge completely how the more-than human challenges regulatory boundaries, and how socio-economic contexts impact the production of ecological knowledge by putting constraints on what it is achievable and what ends up counting as a 'serviceable truth'.[7] As Science and Technology scholars argue, ecological/scientific knowledge does not operate in a context free from the social and the reverse is true as well. In this respect, Jasanoff's concept of co-production is relevant to highlight the coupling and co-evolution of natural and social orders and the way in which they end up being known.[8] For Jasanoff, co-production 'calls attention to the social dimensions of cognitive commitments and understandings, while at the same time underscoring the epistemic and material correlations of social formations'.[9] More reflexivity on the part of MPAs regulation to recognise such co-production would be a welcome step. At the bottom of it, MPAs law and regulation should rethink its ontological premises, understanding socio-economic factors as immanent in a more than human world, rather than positioning the socio-economic as against a world of nature out there. As the anthropologist Ingold writes:

> the world cannot realistically be divided into compartments, with some blocks reserved for society, and others set aside for nature. True, edges and borders are everywhere. We may speak of the water's edge, the roadside, the garden border, the fence. But not one of these marks the edge of nature, or the border of society. No-one yet has made the crossing from nature to society, or vice versa, and no-one ever will. There is no such boundary to be crossed.[10]

MPAs law and its implementation must realise this in order to meet its goals of rationality, democracy and adaptation and to deliver a sound spatial regulatory approach to marine conservation.

[7] S. Jasanoff, 'Serviceable Truths: Science for Action in Law and Policy' (2015) 93 *Texas Law Review* 1723–1749.

[8] S. Jasanoff, 'The Idiom of Co-production' in Jasanoff (ed) States of Knowledge, pp. 1–12.

[9] Ibid, 3.

[10] T. Ingold, 'Epilogue: Towards a Politics of Dwelling' (2005) 3 *Conservation and Society* 501–508, pp. 507–508.

Bibliography

Abbott, C. and Lee, M., 'Economic Actors in EU Environmental Law' (2015) 34 *Yearbook of European Law* 26–59.

Abbott, C. and Lee, M., *Environmental Groups and Legal Expertise: Shaping the Brexit Process* (University College London Press, 2021).

Acheson, J. M., *Capturing the Commons: Devising Institutions to Manage the Maine Lobster Industry* (University Press of New England, 2004).

Ackerman, F. and Heinzerling, L., *Priceless: On Knowing the Price of Everything and the Value of Nothing* (The New Press, 2004).

Adams, W. B., *Against Extinction: The Story of Conservation* (Earthscan, 2004).

Adams, W. and Sandbrook, C., 'Conservation, Evidence and Policy' (2013) 47 *Oryx* 329–335.

Agardy, T., *Marine Protected Areas and Ocean Conservation* (Academic Press, 1997).

Agardy, T., 'Dangerous Targets? Unresolved Issues and Ideological Clashes around Marine Protected Areas' (2003) 13 *Aquatic Conservation: Marine and Freshwater Ecosystems* 353–367.

Agrawal, A., 'Sustainable Use of Common-Pool Resources: Context, Methods and Politics' (2003) 32 *Annual Review of Anthropology* 243–262.

Agrawal, A., *Environmentality: Technologies of Government and the Making of Subjects* (Duke University Press, 2005).

Alder, M. D. and Posner, E. R., *New Foundations of Cost-Benefit Analysis* (Harvard University Press, 2006).

Appleby, T. and Jones, P. J. S., 'The Marine and Coastal Access Act – A Hornets' Nest?' (2012) 36 *Marine Policy* 73–77.

Appleby, T. and Harrison, J., 'Taking the Pulse of Environmental and Fisheries Law: The Common Fisheries Policy, the Habitats Directive, and Brexit' (2019) 31 *Journal of Environmental Law* 443–464.

Arnstein, S. R., 'A Ladder of Citizen Participation' (1969) 35 *Journal of the American Planning Association* 216–224.

Artioli, Y. et al., 'Heterogeneity of Impacts of High CO_2 on the North Western European Shelf' (2014) 11 *Biogeosciences* 601–612.

Baag, S. and Mandal, S., 'Combined Effects of Ocean Warming and Acidification on Marine Fish and Shellfish: A Molecule to Ecosystem Perspective' (2022) 802 *Science of the Total Environment* 149807.

Baldwin, R., 'Is Better Regulation Smarter Regulation?' (2005) (Autumn) *Public Law* 485–511.

Baldwin, R., Cave, M. and Lodge, M., *Understanding Regulation: Theory, Strategy, and Practice* (Oxford University Press, 2011).

Barad, K., *Meeting the Universe Halfway: Quantum Physics and the Entanglement of Matter and Meaning* (Duke University Press, 2007).

Basso, K. H., *Wisdom Sits in Places: Landscape and Language among the Western Apache* (University of New Mexico, 1996).

Baumgartner, F. R. et al., *Lobbying and Policy Change: Who Wins, Who Loses and Why* (University of Chicago Press, 2009).

Bear, C., 'Assembling the Sea: Materiality, Movement and Regulatory Practices in the Cardigan Bay Scallop Fishery' (2012) 20 *Cultural Geographies* 21–41.

Bennett, J., *Vibrant Matter: A Political Ecology of Things* (Duke University Press, 2010).

Berge, E., 'Protected Areas and Traditional Commons: Values and Institutions' (2006) 60 *Norsk Geografisk Tidsskrift–Norwegian Journal of Geography* 65–76.

Berkes, E. (ed.), *Common Property Resources: Ecology and Community-Based Sustainable Development* (Belhaven Press, 1990).

Berkes, F., 'Evolution of Co-management: Role of Knowledge Generation, Bridging Organizations and Social Learning' (2009) 90 *Journal of Environmental Management* 1692–1702.

Berkes, F., 'Fishery Resource Use in a Subarctic Indian Community' (1997) 5 *Human Ecology* 289–307.

Berkes, F., *Sacred Ecology: Traditional Ecological Knowledge and Resource Management* (Taylor and Francis, 1999).

Bernauer, T. and Betzold, C., 'Civil Society in Global Environmental Governance' (2012) 21 *The Journal of Environment and Development* 62–66.

Berny, N. and Rootes, C., 'Environmental NGOs at a Crossroads?' (2018) 7 *Environmental Politics* 947–972.

Biermann, F., 'Common Concern of Humankind: The Emergence of a New Concept of Environmental Law' (1996) 34 *Archiv des Volkerrechts* 426–481.

Bindoff, N. L. et al., 'Changing Ocean, Marine Ecosystems, and Dependent Communities', in H. O. Pörtner et al. (eds.), *IPCC Special Report on the Ocean and Cryosphere in a Changing Climate* (IPPC, 2019), pp. 447–587.

Bird-David, N., '"Animism" Revisited: Personhood, Environment, and Relational Epistemology' (1999) 40 *Current Anthropology*, S67–S91.

Black, J. and Baldwin, R., 'Really Responsive Risk-Based Regulation' (2010) 32 *Law and Policy* 181–213.

Black, J. and Baldwin, R., 'When Risk-Based Regulation Aims Low: Approaches and Challenges' (2012) 6 *Regulation and Governance* 131–148.

Black, J., 'Decentring Regulation: Understanding the Role of Regulation and Self-Regulation in a "Post-Regulatory" World' (2001) 54 *Current Legal Problems* 103–146.

Black, J., 'Proceduralizing Regulation: Part I' (2000) 20 *Oxford Journal of Legal Studies* 597–614.

Black, J., 'Proceduralizing Regulation: Part II' (2001) 21 *Oxford Journal of Legal Studies* 33–58.

Black, J., 'Risk-Based Regulation: Choices, Practices and Lessons Being Learned', in OECD (ed.), *Risk and Regulatory Policy: Improving the Governance of Risk* (OECD, 2010), pp. 185–224.

Black, J., 'Tensions in the Regulatory State' (2007) (Spring) *Public Law* 58–73.

Black, J., 'The Emergence of Risk-Based Regulation and the New Public Risk Management in the United Kingdom' (2005) (Autumn) *Public Law* 512–549.

Bollier, D. and Helfrich, S. (eds.), *Patterns of Commoning* (The Commons Strategies Group, 2015).

Bollier, D., 'Commoning as a Transformative Social Paradigm' (2018) at: https://thenextsystem.org/node/187.

Borrini-Feyerabend, G. et al., Sharing Power. Learning-by-Doing in Co-management of Natural Resources throughout the World (IIED and IUCN/CEESP, and Cenesta, 2004).

Bourdieu, P., *The Logic of Practice* (Stanford University Press, 1990).

Bratton, M., 'Beyond the State: Civil Society and Associational Life in Africa' (1989) 41 *World Politics* 407–430.

Bresnihan, P., 'The More-than-Human Commons: From Commons to Commoning', in S. Kirwan, L. Dawney and J. Brigstocke (eds.), *Space, Power and the Commons: The Struggle for Alternative Futures* (Routledge, 2016), pp. 93–112.

Brockington, D., Fortress Conservation: The Preservation of the Mkomazi Game Reserve, Tanzania (African Issues, 2002).

Brunnée, J., 'Common Areas, Common Heritage, and Common Concern', in D. Bodansky, J. Brunnée and E. Hey (eds.), *Oxford Handbook of International Environmental Law* (Oxford University Press, 2008), pp. 550–573.

Bryman, A., *Social Research Methods*, 4th ed. (Oxford University Press, 2012).

Bull, J., 'Encountering Fish, Flows, and Waterscapes through Angling' (2011) 43 *Environment and Planning A* 2267–2284.

Caffentzis, G. and Federici, S., 'Commons against and beyond Capitalism' (2014) 49 *Community Development Journal* i92–i105.

Callon, M., 'Some Elements of a Sociology of Translation: Domestication of the Scallops and the Fishermen of St. Brieuc Bay', in J. Law (ed.), *Power, Action and Belief: A New Sociology of Knowledge* (Routledge, 1986), pp. 196–223.

Callon, M., 'Struggles and Negotiations to Define What Is Problematic and What Is Not: The Socio-Logics of Translation', in K. D. Knorr, R. Krohn and R. Whitley (eds.), *The Social Process of Scientific Investigation* (D. Reidel Publishing Company, 1980), pp. 197–219.

Carlsson, L. and Berkes, F., 'Co-management: Concepts and Methodological Implications' (2005) 75 *Journal of Environmental Management* 65–76.

Chaffin, B. C., Gosnell, H. and Cosens, B. A., 'A Decade of Adaptive Governance Scholarship: Synthesis and Future Directions' (2014) 19 *Ecology and Society* 56.

Chan, K. M. A, Gould, R. K. and Pascual, U., 'Editorial Overview: Relational Values: What Are They, and What's the Fuss About?' (2018) 35 *Current Opinion in Environmental Sustainability* A1–A7.

Chan, K. M. A. et al., 'Opinion: Why Protect Nature? Rethinking Values and the Environment' (2016) 113 *Proceedings of the National Academy of Sciences of the United States of America* 1462–1465.

Cheng, B. S. et al., 'Can Marine Reserves Restore Lost Ecosystem Functioning? A Global Synthesis' (2019) 100 *Ecology*.

Christie, P. et al., 'Towards Developing a Complete Understanding: A Social Science Research Agenda for Marine Protected Areas' (2003) 28 *Fisheries* 22–25.

Chuenpagdee, R. et al., 'Marine Protected Areas: Re-thinking Their Inception' (2013) 39 *Marine Policy* 234–240.

Clark, R. et al., 'Dialectics of Nature: The Emergence of Policy on the Management of Commercial Fisheries in English European Marine Sites' (2017) 78 *Marine Policy* 11–17.

Cliquet, A. et al., 'International and European Law on Protected Areas and Climate Change: Need for Adaptation or Implementation?' (2014) 54 *Environmental Management* 720–731.

Corson, C. and MacDonald, K. I., 'Enclosing the Global Commons: The Convention on Biological Diversity and Green Grabbing' (2012) 39 *The Journal of Peasant Studies* 263–283.

Corson, C., 'Shifting Environmental Governance in a Neoliberal World: US AID for Conservation' (2010) 42 *Antipode* 576–602.

Cosens, B. A. et al., 'Designing Law to Enable Adaptive Governance of Modern Wicked Problems' (2020) 73 *Vanderbilt Law Review* 1687–1732.

Cosens, B. A. et al., 'The Role of Law in Adaptive Governance' (2017) 22 *Ecology and Society* 30.

Craig, R. K. et al., 'Balancing Stability and Flexibility in Adaptive Governance: An Analysis of Tools Available in U.S. Environmental Law' (2017) 22 *Ecology and Society* 3.

Craig, R. K., '"Stationarity Is Dead" – Long Live Transformation: Five Principles for Climate Change Adaptation Law' (2010) 34 *Harvard Environmental Law Review* 9–75.

Craig, R. K., *Comparative Ocean Governance: Place-Based Protections in an Era of Climate Change* (Edward Elgar, 2012).

Cumming, G. S. et al., 'Understanding Protected Area Resilience: A Multi-scale, Social-Ecological Approach' (2015) 25 *Ecological Applications* 299–319.

Day, J. et al., *IUCN Guidelines for Applying the IUCN Protected Area Management Categories to Marine Protected Areas*, 2nd ed. (IUCN, 2019).

De Angelis, M. and Harvie, D., 'The Commons', in M. Parker, G. Cheney, V. Fournier and C. Land (eds.), *The Routledge Companion to Alternative Organizations* (Routledge, 2014), pp. 280–294.

De Angelis, M., 'The Production of Commons and the "Explosion" of the Middle Class' (2010) 42 *Antipode* 954–977.

Deighton-Smith, R., Erbacci, A. and Kauffmann, C., 'Promoting Inclusive Growth through Better Regulation: The Role of Regulatory Impact Assessment', OECD Regulatory Policy Working Papers, No. 3 (OECD, 2016).

Delaney, D., *Territory: A Short Introduction* (Blackwell Publishing, 2005).

Deleuze, G. and Guattari, F., *A Thousand Plateaus: Capitalism and Schizofrenia* (University of Minnesota Press, 1987, translated by B. Massumi).

Descola, P., *Beyond Nature and Culture* (University of Chicago Press, 2013, translated by J. Lloyd).

Dewey, J., *The Public and Its Problems* (Holt and Company, 1927).

Dietz, T., Ostrom, E., Stern, P. C., 'The Struggle to Govern the Commons' (2003) 302 *Science* 1907–1912.

Diver, C. S., 'Policy Paradigms in Administrative Law' (1981) 95 *Harvard Law Review* 393–434.

Dorf, M. C. and Sabel, C. F., 'A Constitution of Democratic Experimentalism' (1998) 98 *Columbia Law Review* 267–473.

Dressler, W. et al., 'From Hope to Crisis and Back Again? A Critical History of the Global CBNRM Narrative' (2010) 37 *Environmental Conservation* 5–15.

Dryzek, J. S., 'Global Civil Society: The Progress of Post-Westphalian Politics' (2012) 15 *Annual Review of Political Science* 101–119.

Dunkley, F. and Solandt, J. L., *Marine Unprotected Areas: A Case for a Just Transition to Ban Bottom Trawl and Dredge Fishing in Offshore Marine Protected Areas* (The Marine Conservation Society, 2021).

Dunlop, C. A. and Radaelli, C. M., 'The Politics and Economics of Regulatory Impact Assessment', in C. A. Dunlop and C. M. Radaelli (eds.), *The Handbook of Regulatory Impact Assessment* (Edward Elgar, 2016), pp. 3–20.

Eagle, J., *Democracy and Natural Resources: British and American Approaches to Public Participation in Fisheries Management* (British Council, 2004).

Ebbesson, J., 'The Rule of Law in Governance of Complex Socio-ecological Change' (2010) 20 *Global Environmental Change* 414–422.

Edwards, M. and Hulme, D. (eds.), *Non-governmental Organisations: Performance and Accountability. Beyond the Magic Bullet* (Earthscan, 1995).

Edwards, M., *Civil Society* (Polity Press, 2004).

Elden, S., 'Land, Terrain, Territory' (2010) 34 *Progress in Human Geography* 799–817.

Escobar, A., 'Whose Knowledge, Whose Nature? Biodiversity Conservation, and the Political Ecology of Social Movements' (1998) 5 *Journal of Political Ecology* 53–82.

Escobar, A., *Designs for the Pluriverse: Radical Interdependence, Autonomy, and the Making of the Worlds* (Duke University Press, 2018).

Fairhead, J., Leach, M. and Scoones, I., 'Green Grabbing: A New Appropriation of Nature?' (2012) 39 *The Journal of Peasant Studies* 237–261.

Farber, D. A., 'Uncertainty' (2011) 99 *The Georgetown Law Journal* 901–960.

Federici, S., *Re-enchanting the World: Feminisms and the Politics of the Commons* (PM Press, 2019).

Fisher, E. Scotford, E. and Barritt, E., 'The Legally Disruptive Nature of Climate Change' (2017) 80 *Modern Law Review* 173–201.

Fisher, E., 'Executive Environmental Law' (2020) 83 *Modern Law Review* 163–189.

Fletcher, S. et al., Marine Ecosystem Services – Natural England Commissioned Reports, Number 088 (Natural England and Other Parties, 2012).

Folke, C. et al., 'Adaptive Governance of Social-Ecological Systems' (2005) 30 *Annual Review of Environmental Resources* 441–473.

Fortmann, L., 'What We Need Is a Community Bambi: The Perils and Possibilities of Powerful Symbols', in J. P. Brosius, A. L. Tsing and C. Zerner (eds.), *Communities and Conservation: Histories and Politics of Community-Based Natural Resource Management* (AltaMira Press, 2005), pp. 195–205.

Foucault, M., *Security, Territory, Population-Lectures at the College the France 1977–1978*, M. Senellart (ed.) (Palgrave, 2007, translated by G. Burchell).

Gibson, K., Healy, S. and Cameroon, J., 'Commoning as a Postcapitalist Politics', in A. Amin and P. Howell (eds.) *Releasing the Commons: Rethinking the Futures of the Commons* (Routledge, 2006), pp. 192–212.

Gieryn, T. G., 'Boundary-Work and the Demarcation of Science from Non-science: Strains and Interests in Professional Ideologies of Scientists' (1993) 48 *American Sociological Review* 781–795.

Gissi, E. et al., 'A Review of the Combined Effects of Climate Change and Other Local Human Stressors on the Marine Environment' (2021) 755 *Science of the Total Environment* 142564.

Gomez-Baggethun, E. and Ruiz- Perez, M., 'Economic Valuation and the Commodification of Ecosystem Services' (2011) 35 *Progress in Physical Geography: Earth and Environment* 613–628.

Gunderson, L. and Light, S. S., 'Adaptive Management and Adaptive Governance in the Everglades Ecosystem' (2006) 39 *Policy Sciences* 323–334.

Gutierrez, N. L., Hilborn, R. and Defeo, O., 'Leadership, Social Capital and Incentives Promote Successful Fisheries' (2011) 470 *Nature* 386–389.

Guyader, O. et al., 'Small Scale Fisheries in Europe: A Comparative Analysis Based on a Selection of Case Studies' (2013) 140 *Fisheries Research* 1–13.

Habermas, J., *Between Facts and Norms: Contributions to a Discourse Theory of Law and Democracy* (MIT Press, 1996, translated by W. Rehg).

Halpern, B. S. and Warner, R. R., 'Marine Reserves Have Rapid and Lasting Effects' (2002) 5 *Ecology Letters* 361–366.

Hardin, G., 'The Tragedy of the Commons' (1968) 162 *Science* 1243–1248.

Hardt, M. and Negri, A., *Commonwealth* (Harvard University Press, 2009).

Harvey, W. S., 'Methodological Approaches for Interviewing Elites' (2010) 4 *Geography Compass* 193–205.

Hasselman, L., 'Adaptive Management; Adaptive Co-management; Adaptive Governance: What's the Difference?' (2017) 24 *Australasian Journal of Environmental Management* 31–46.

Heidegger, M., *Being and Time* (Blackwell, 1996, translated by J. Macquarrie and E. Robinson).

Hess, C., 'Mapping the New Commons', Paper presented at the 12th Biennial Conference of the International Association for the Study of the Commons, Cheltenham, UK (2008).

Hilson, C., 'The Impact of Brexit on the Environment: Exploring the Dynamics of a Complex Relationship' (2018) 7 *Transnational Environmental Law* 89–113.

Holder, J. B. and Flessas, T., 'Emerging Commons' (2008) 17 *Social and Legal Studies* 299–310.

Hornborg, A., 'Knowledge of Persons, Knowledge of Things: Animism, Fetishism, and Objectivism as Strategies for Knowing (or Not Knowing) the World' (2006) 71 *Ethnos* 21–32.

Hutter, B. M., 'The Attractions of Risk-Based Regulation: Accounting for the Emergence of Risk Ideas in Regulation' (2005) CARR Discussion Paper 33 at: https://citeseerx.ist.psu.edu/viewdoc/download?doi=10.1.1.125.7494&rep=rep1&type=pdf.

Igoe, J. and Brockington, D., 'Neoliberal Conservation: A Brief Introduction' (2007) 5 *Conservation and Society* 432–449.

Ingold, T. and Palsson, G. (eds.), *Biosocial Becomings: Integrating Social and Biological Anthropology* (Cambridge University Press, 2013).

Ingold, T., 'Epilogue: Towards a Politics of Dwelling' (2005) 3 *Conservation and Society* 501–508.

Ingold, T., *Being Alive: Essays on Movement, Knowledge and Description* (Routledge, 2011).

Ingold, T., *The Perception on the Environment* (Routledge, 2000).

IPCC, 'Summary for Policymakers', in H. O. Pörtner et al. (eds.), *IPCC Special Report on the Ocean and Cryosphere in a Changing Climate* (IPCC, 2019).

Jasanoff, S., 'Serviceable Truths: Science for Action in Law and Policy' (2015) 93 *Texas Law Review* 1723–1749.

Jasanoff, S. (ed.), *States of Knowledge: The Co-production of Science and the Social Order* (Routledge, 2004).

Jasanoff, S., 'NGOs and the Environment: From Knowledge to Action' (1997) 18 *Third World Quarterly* 579–594.

Jentoft, S. and McCay, B. J., 'User Participation in Fisheries Management: Lessons Drawn from International Experiences' (1995) 19 *Marine Policy* 227–246.

Jentoft, S., 'Fisheries Co-management as Empowerment' (2005) 29 *Marine Policy* 1–7.

Jentoft, S., 'Fisheries Co-management: Delegating Government Responsibility to Fishermen's Organizations' (1989) 13 *Marine Policy* 137–154.

Jentoft, S., McCay, B. J. and Wilson, D. C., 'Social Theory and Fisheries Co-management' (1998) 22 *Marine Policy* 423–436.

Jepson, P., 'Governance and Accountability of Environmental NGOs' (2005) 8 *Environmental Science and Policy* 515–524.

Jones, P. J. and Burgess, J., 'Building Partnership Capacity for the Collaborative Management of Marine Protected Areas in the UK: A Preliminary Analysis' (2005) 77 *Journal of Environmental Management* 227–243.

Jones, P. J. S., *Governing Marine Protected Areas: Resilience through Diversity* (Routledge, 2013).

Kysar, D. A., *Regulating from Nowhere: Environmental Law and the Search for Objectivity* (Yale University Press, 2010).

Lambert, D., Martins, L. and Ogborn, M., 'Currents, Visions and Voyages: Historical Geographies of the Sea' (2006) 32 *Journal of Historical Geography* 479–493.

Larsen, P. B. and Brokington, D. (eds.), *The Anthropology of Conservation NGOs: Rethinking the Boundaries* (Palgrave, 2018).

Latour, B., *Facing Gaia: Eight Lectures on the New Climatic Regime* (Polity Press, 2017, translated by C. Porter).

Latour, B., *Politics of Nature: How to Bring the Sciences into Democracy* (Harvard University Press, 2004, translated by C. Porter).

Latour, B., *Science in Action: How to Follow Scientists and Engineers through Society* (Harvard University Press, 1987).

Lazarus, R. J., 'Super Wicked Problems and Climate Change: Restraining the Present to Liberate the Future' (2009) 94 *Cornell Law Review* 1153–1234.

Leach, M., Mearnes, R. and Scones, I., 'Environmental Entitlements: Dynamics and Institutions in Community-Based Natural Resource Management' (1999) 27 *World Development* 225–247.

Lee, M. and Abbot, C., 'The Usual Suspects? Public Participation under the Aarhus Convention' (2003) 66 *Modern Law Review* 80–108.

Lee, M. et al., 'Public Participation and Climate Change Infrastructure' (2013) 25 *Journal of Environmental Law* 33–62.

Lee, M., 'Brexit and Environmental Protection in the United Kingdom: Governance, Accountability and Law Making' (2018) 36 *Journal of Energy and Natural Resources Law* 351–359.

Lee, M., 'DEFRA's Draft Environmental Principles Policy Statement' SSRN Working Paper' (2021) at: https://ssrn. com/abstract=3827270.

Lee, M., 'Environmental Pasts and Futures: The European Union and the "British Way"' (2019) 31 *Journal of Environmental Law* 559–569.

Lee, M., 'The New Office for Environmental Protection: Scrutinising and Enforcing Environmental Law after Brexit' SSRN Working Paper (2019) at: https://ssrn.com/abstract=3312296.

Lee, R. G., 'Always Keep a Hold of Nurse: British Environmental Law and Exit from the European Union' (2017) 29 *Journal of Environmental Law* 155–164.

Li, T. M., 'Engaging Simplifications: Community-Based Resource Management, Market Processes and State Agendas in Upland Southeast Asia' (2002) 30 *World Development* 265–283.

Linebaugh, P., *The Magna Carta Manifesto: Liberties and Commons for All* (University of California Press, 2008).

Little, L. R. et al., 'Complementarity of No-Take Marine Reserves and Individual Transferable Catch Quotas for Managing the Line Fishery of the Great Barrier Reef' (2011) 25 *Conservation Biology* 333–340.

Lowther, J. and Rodwell, L. D., 'IFCAs: Stakeholder Perception of Roles, and Legal Impact' (2013) 15 *Environmental Law Review* 11–26.

Manzo, L. C. and Devine-Wright, P. (eds.), *Place Attachment: Advances in Theory, Methods and Applications* (Routledge, 2014).

Marcus, G. E. and Saka, E., 'Assemblage' (2006) 23 *Theory, Culture and Society* 101–106.

Mascia, M. B., 'The Human Dimension of Coral Reef Marine Protected Areas: Recent Social Science Research and Its Policy Implications' (2003) 17 *Conservation Biology* 630–632.

Mascia, M. B., Claus, C. A. and Naidoo, R., 'Impacts of Marine Protected Areas on Fishing Communities' (2010) 24 *Conservation Biology* 1424–1429.

Mattei, U. and Nader, L., *Plunder: When the Rule of Law Is Illegal* (Blackwell, 2008).

Mattei, U., *Beni Comuni. Un Manifesto* (Laterza, 2011).

Mauss, M., 'A Category of the Human Mind: The Notion of Person; the Notion of Self', in M. Carrithers, S. Collins and S. Lukes (eds.), *The Category of the Person: Anthropology, Philosophy, History* (Cambridge University Press, 1985, translated by W. D. Halls), pp. 1–25.

McCay, B. and Jentoft, S., 'From the Bottom Up: Participatory Issues in Fisheries Management' (1996) 9 *Society and Natural Resources* 237–250.

McCay, B., 'Enclosing the Fisheries Commons' in D. H. Cole and E. Ostrom (eds.), *Property in Land and Other Resources* 2012 (Lincoln Institute of Land Policy, 2012), pp. 219–258.

McCay, B., 'Muddling through the Clam Beds: Cooperative Management of New Jersey's Hard Clam Spawner Sanctuaries' (1988) 7 *Journal of Shellfish Research* 327–340.

McCay, B. J. and Acheson, J. M. (eds.), *The Question of the Commons: The Culture and Ecology of Communal Resources* (University of Arizona Press, 1987).

McCay, B. J. and Jones, P. J. S., 'Marine Protected Areas and the Governance of Marine Ecosystems and Fisheries' (2011) 25 *Conservation Biology* 1130–1133.

Mercer, C., 'NGOs, Civil Society and Democratization: A Critical Review of the Literature' (2002) 2 *Progress in Development Studies* 5–22.

Mol, A. P. J., 'The Environmental Nation State in Decline' (2016) 25 *Environmental Politics* 48–68.

Moore, J. W. (ed.), *Anthropocene or Capitalocene? Nature, History and the Crisis of Capitalism* (Kairos, 2016).

Moran, M., *The British Regulatory State: High Modernism and Hyper-Innovation* (Oxford University Press, 2003).

Morris, R. K. A. et al., 'Managing Natura 2000 in the Marine Environment – An Evaluation of the Effectiveness of "Management Schemes" in England' (2014) 87 *Ocean & Coastal Management* 40–51.

Mouffe, C., 'Deliberative Democracy or Agonistic Pluralism' (2000) 72 *Political Science Series* 1–17.

Mouffe, C., *On the Political* (Routledge, 2005).

Nancy, J. L., 'Of Being-in-Common', in Miami Theory Collective (ed.), *Community at Loose Ends* (University of Minnesota Press, 1991, translated by J. Creech), pp. 1–12.

Neumann, R. P., 'Nature-State-Territory: Toward a Critical Theorization of Conservation Enclosures', in R. Peet and M. Watts (eds.), *Liberation Ecologies*, 2nd ed. (Routledge, 2004), pp. 179–199.

Neumann, R. P., *Imposing Wilderness: Struggles over Livelihood and Nature Preservation in Africa* (University of California Press, 1998).

O'Leary, B. C. et al., 'Effective Coverage Targets for Ocean Protection' (2016) 9 *Conservation Letters* 398–404.

Ostrom, E., Gardner, R. and Walker, J., *Rules, Games and Common-Pool Resources* (The University of Michigan Press, 1994).

Ostrom, E., *Governing the Commons. The Evolution of Institutions for Collective Action.* (Cambridge University Press, 1990).

Oxman, B. H., 'The 1994 Agreement and the Convention' (1994) 88 *The American Journal of International Law* 687–696.

Peluso, N. L., 'Coercing Conservation: The Politics of State Resource Control' (1993) 3 *Global Environmental Change* 199–217.

Peters, K., 'Manipulating Material Hydro-Worlds: Rethinking Human and More-than-Human Relationality through Offshore Radio Piracy' (2012) 44 *Environment and Planning A* 1241–1254.

Pieraccini, M. and Cardwell, E., 'Divergent Perceptions of New Marine Protected Areas: Comparing Legal Consciousness in Scilly and Barra, UK' (2016) 119 *Ocean & Coastal Management* 21–29.

Pieraccini, M. and Cardwell, E., 'Impact Assessments for Nature Conservation: Effective and Reflexive?' (2016) (Jan) *Public Law* 93–110.

Pieraccini, M. and Cardwell, E., 'Towards Deliberative and Pragmatic Co-management: A Comparison between Inshore Fisheries Authorities in England and Scotland' (2016) 25 *Environmental Politics* 1–20.

Pieraccini, M., 'Democratic Legitimacy and New Commons: Examples from English Protected Areas' (2015) 9 *International Journal of the Commons* 552–572.

Pieraccini, M., 'Re-thinking Participation in Environmental Decision-Making: Epistemologies of Marine Conservation in South-East England' (2015) 27 *Journal of Environmental Law* 45–67.

Pieraccini, M., 'Towards Just Resilience: Representing and Including New Constituencies in Adaptive Governance and Law' (2019) 31 *Journal of Environmental Law* 213–234.

Pinkerton, E. (ed.), *Co-operative Management of Local Fisheries* (University of British Columbia Press, 1989).

Polanyi, K., *The Great Transformation: The Political and Economic Origins of Our Time* (Beacon Press, 1957).

Pontin, B., *The Environmental Case for Brexit: A Socio-Legal Perspective* (Bloomsbury, 2019).

Pörtner, H. O. et al., 'Ocean Systems', in C. B. Field et al. (eds.), *Climate Change 2014: Impacts, Adaptation, and Vulnerability. Part A: Global and Sectoral Aspects. Contribution of Working Group II to the Fifth Assessment Report of the Intergovernmental Panel on Climate Change* (Cambridge University Press, 2014), pp. 411–484.

Pound, R., 'Law in Books and Law in Action' (1910) 44 *American law Review* 12–36.

Pretty, J. and Ward, H., 'Social Capital and the Environment' (2001) 29 *World Development* 209–227.

Radaelli, C. M. and De Francesco, F., 'Regulatory Impact Assessment', in R. Baldwin, M. Cave and M. Lodge (eds.), *The Oxford Handbook of Regulation* (Oxford University Press 2010), pp. 279–301.

Reid, C. T., 'Brexit and the Future of UK Environmental Law' (2016) 34 *Journal of Energy and Natural Resources Law* 407–415.

Reid, C. T., 'Mapping Post-Brexit Environmental Law' (2021) 21 *ERA Forum* 655–665.

Revesz, R. L. and Livermore, M. A., *Retaking Rationale: How Cost-Benefit Analysis Can Better Protect the Environment and Our Health* (Oxford University Press, 2008).

Rhodes, R. A. W., 'The Hollowing out of the State: The Changing Nature of the Public Service in Britain' (1994) 65 *Political Quarterly* 138–151.

Rodotà, S., 'Postfazione. Beni comuni: Una strategia globale contro lo "human divide"', in M. R. Marella (ed.), *Oltre il pubblico e il privato. Per un diritto dei beni comuni* (Ombre Corte, 2012), pp. 311–331.

Rose, N. and Miller, P., 'Political Power beyond the State: Problematics of Government' (1992) 43 *The British Journal of Sociology* 173–205.

Rothstein, H. et al., 'The Risks of Risk-Based Regulation: Insights from the Environmental Policy Domain' (2007) 32 *Environment International* 1056–1065.

Ruhl, J. B., 'Climate Change Adaptation and the Structural Transformation of Environmental Law' (2010) 40 *Environmental Law* 363–435.

Rydin, Y. et al., 'Do Local Economic Interests Matter When Regulating Nationally Significant Infrastructure? The Case of Renewable Energy Infrastructure Projects' (2018) 33 *Local Economy: The Journal of the Local Economy Policy Unit* 269–286.

Sabel, C. F. and Zeitlin, J. (eds.), *Experimentalist Governance in the European Union: Towards a New Architecture* (Oxford University Press, 2010).

Sack, R., *Human Territoriality: Its Theory and History* (Cambridge University Press, 1986).

Sagoff, M., *The Economy of the Earth: Philosophy, Law, and the Environment*, 2nd ed. (Cambridge University Press, 2008).

Scott, C., 'Regulation in the Age of Governance: The Rise of the Post Regulatory State', in J. Jordana and D. Levi-Faure (eds.), *The Politics of Regulation: Institutions and Regulatory Reforms for the Age of Governance* (Edward Elgar, 2004), pp. 145–174.

Scott, J., *Seeing Like a State: How Certain Schemes to Improve the Human Condition Have Failed* (Yale University Press, 1998).

Shelton, D., 'Common Concern of Humanity' (2009) 39 *Environmental Policy and Law* 83–86.

Sidorkin, A. M., 'Ontology, Anthropology, and Epistemology of Relation' (2002) 173 *Counterpoints* 91–102.

Sienden, A., Kysar, D. A. and Driesen, D. M., 'Cost-Benefit Analysis: New Foundations on Shifting Sands' (2009) 3 *Regulation and Governance* 48–71.

Singer, R. and Jones, P. J. S., 'Lyme Bay Marine Protected Area: A Governance Analysis' (2021) 127 *Marine Policy* 103201.

Smith, K. E., 'Problematising Power Relations in "Elite" Interviews' (2006) 37 *Geoforum* 643–653.

Solandt, J. L. et al., 'Managing Marine Protected Areas in Europe: Moving from "Feature-Based" to "Whole-Site" Management of Sites', in J. Humphreys and R. Clark (eds.), *Marine Protected Areas: Science, Policy and Management* (Elsevier, 2019), pp. 157–182.

Solandt, J. L. et al., 'Revisiting UK Marine Protected Areas Governance: A Case Study of a Collaborative Approach to Managing an English MPA' (2020) 30 *Aquatic Conservation Marine and Freshwater Ecosystems* 1829–1835.

Solandt, J. L., 'A Stocktake of England's MPA Network – Taking a Global Perspective Approach' (2018) 19 *Biology* 34–41.

Soltau, F., 'Common Concern of Humankind', in K. R. Gray, R. Tarasofsky and C. Carlane (eds.), *The Oxford Handbook of International Climate Change Law* (Oxford University Press, 2016), pp. 203–212.

Spash, C. L., 'Bulldozing Biodiversity: The Economics of Offsets and Trading-in Nature' (2015) 192 *Biological Conservation* 541–551.

Spash, C. L., 'Deliberative Monetary Valuation and the Evidence for a New Value Theory' (2008) 84 *Land Economics* 469–488.

Steinberg, P. and Peters, K., 'Wet Ontologies, Fluid Spaces: Giving Depth through Volume through Oceanic Thinking' (2015) 33 *Environment and Planning D: Society and Space* 247–264.

Steinberg, P. E., 'Lines of Division, Lines of Connection: Stewardship in the World Ocean' (1999) 89 *Geographical Review* 254–264.

Steinberg, P. E., 'Of Other Seas: Metaphors and Materialities in Maritime Regions' (2013) 10 *Atlantic Studies* 156–169.

Steinberg, P. E., *The Social Construction of the Oceans* (Cambridge University Press, 2001).

Stone, C. D., 'Should Trees Have Standing? Towards Legal Rights for Natural Objects' (1972) 45 *Southern California Law Review* 450–501.

Strathern, M., *The Gender of the Gift: Problems with Women and Problems with Society in Melanesia* (University of California Press, 1988).

Sunstein, C. R., *The Cost-Benefit State: The Future of Regulatory Protection* (American Bar Association, 2002).

Sunstein, C. R., *The Cost-Benefit Revolution* (MIT Press, 2018).

Swyngedouw, E., 'Governance Innovation and the Citizen: The Janus Face of Governance-beyond-the-State' (2005) 42 *Urban Studies* 1991–2006.

Symes, D. and Phillipson, J., 'Inshore Fisheries Management in the UK: Sea Fisheries Committees and the Challenge of Marine Environmental Management' (1997) 21 *Marine Policy* 207–224.

Teubner, G., 'De Collissione Discursuum: Communicative Rationalities in Law, Morality, and Politics', in M. Rosenfeld and A. Arato (eds.), *Habermas on Law and Democracy: Critical Exchanges* (University of California Press, 1998), pp. 173–189.

Thorpe, A., Banvick, M. and Coulthard, S., 'Tracking the Debate around Marine Protected Areas: Key Issues and the BEG Framework' (2011) 47 *Environmental Management* 546–563.

Tuan, Y. F., *Topophilia: A Study of Environmental Perception, Attitudes, and Values* (Prentice Hall Inc., 1974).

United Kingdom Environmental Law Association, *The UK and International Environmental Law after Brexit* (UKELA, 2017).

van Putten, I. et al., 'A Framework for Incorporating Sense of Place into the Management of Marine Systems' (2018) 23 *Ecology and Society*.

Vandergeest, P. and Peluso, N. L., 'Territorialization and State Power in Thailand' (1995) 24 *Theory and Society* 385–426.

Vaughan, D., 'Fishing Effort Displacement and the Consequences of Implementing Marine Protected Area Management: An English Perspective' (2017) 84 *Marine Policy* 228–234.

Viveiros de Castro, E., 'Exchanging Perspectives: The Transformation of Objects into Subjects in Amerindian Ontologies' (2019) 25 *Common Knowledge* 21–42.

Weigel, J. Y. et al., 'Marine Protected Areas and Fisheries: Bridging the Divide' (2014) S2 *Aquatic Conservation Marine and Freshwater Ecosystems* 199–215.

West, P., Igoe, J. and Brockington, D., 'Parks and Peoples: The Social Impacts of Protected Areas' (2006) 35 *Annual Review of Anthropology* 251–277.

Whatmore, S., 'Humanism's Excess: Some Thoughts on the "Post-human/ist" Agenda' (2004) 36 *Environment and Planning A* 1360–1363.

Whatmore, S., 'Materialist Returns: Practising Cultural Geography in and for a More-than-Human World' (2006) 13 *Cultural Geographies* 600–609.

Whatmore, S., *Hybrid Geographies: Natures, Cultures, Spaces* (Sage, 2002).

Worm, B. et al., 'Impacts of Biodiversity Loss on Ocean Ecosystem Services' (2006) 314 *Science* 787–790.

Wynne, B., 'May the Sheep Safely Graze? A Reflexive View of the Expert-Lay Knowledge Divide', in S. Lash, B. Szerszynski and B. Wynne (eds.), *Risk, Environment and Modernity: Towards a New Ecology* (Sage, 1998), pp. 44–83.

Wynne, B., 'Uncertainty and Environmental Learning: Reconceiving Science and Policy in the Preventative Paradigm' (1992) 2 *Global Environmental Change* 111–127.

Index

Printed in the United Kingdom by TJ Clays Ltd.